Principles and Practices of Democracy in the Education of Social Studies Teachers

Civic Learning in Teacher Education

Edited by

John J. Patrick

and

Robert S. Leming

Volume 1

ERIC™
Educational Resources Information Center

The ERIC Clearinghouse for Social Studies/Social Science Education and
the Adjunct ERIC Clearinghouse for International Civic Education in
Association with Civitas:
An International Civic Education Exchange Program

Ordering Information

This publication is available from:
ERIC Clearinghouse for Social Studies/Social Science Education
Indiana University
2805 East Tenth Street, Suite 120
Bloomington, Indiana, U.S.A. 47408-2698
Toll-free Telephone: (800) 266-3815
Telephone: (812) 855-3838
Fax: (812) 855-0455
Electronic Mail: <ericso@indiana.edu>
World Wide Web: <http://www.indiana.edu/~ssdc/eric_chess.htm>

ISBN 0-941339-27-0

This publication was developed and published in 2001 at the ERIC Clearinghouse for Social Studies/Social Science Education (ERIC/ChESS) and its Adjunct ERIC Clearinghouse for International Civic Education at the Social Studies Development Center (SSDC) of Indiana University. This project has been funded at least in part with Federal funds from the U.S. Department of Education under contract number ED-99-CO-0016. The content of this publication does not necessarily reflect the views or policies of the U.S. Department of Education nor does mention of trade names, commercial products, or organizations imply endorsement by the U.S. Government.

Support was also provided for the printing and distribution of this publication with a subgrant to the SSDC from the Center for Civic Education (CCE) through Civitas: An International Civic Education Exchange Program, which is administered by the CCE in Calabasas, California, with funding from the Office of Educational Research and Improvement (OERI) of the U.S. Department of Education. The opinions expressed in this publication do not necessarily reflect the positions or policies of the Center for Civic Education or the U.S. Department of Education.

Civitas: An International Civic Education Exchange Program is a consortium of leading organizations in civic education in the United States and other nations. The Center for Civic Education, directed by Charles N. Quigley, coordinates and administers the Civitas program. The United States Department of Education supports the program, which has been conducted in cooperation with the United States Department of State and its affiliated offices throughout the world. Civitas enables civic educators from the United States of America and cooperating countries to learn from and help each other in improving civic education for democracy.

ERIC, Educational Resources Information Center,
is an information system within the U.S. Department of Education.

Contents

Preface

The contents of this volume were derived from a meeting sponsored by the Center for Civic Education in Calabasas, California and conducted by the Social Studies Development Center of Indiana University, Bloomington. This meeting, "Education in Democracy for Social Studies Teachers: An Institute for Teacher Educators," occurred at the University Place Conference Center in Indianapolis, Indiana from May 18-22, 2001.

The central theme of this meeting was education for democratic citizenship in the university-based education of prospective social studies teachers. We assume that improving education for democracy in programs of teacher education is a key to improving teaching and learning of democracy in elementary and secondary schools. If prospective teachers of the social studies would be effective educators for democracy, then they must know what it is, how to do it, and why it is good.

The speakers at our five-day "Institute for Teacher Educators" addressed the central theme of the meeting. They variously proposed core content and pedagogical practices for the civic foundations of teacher education programs. Papers presented by these speakers have been edited to become the eleven chapters of this book.

Spirited discussions followed each formal presentation of "The Institute." And each day's program was concluded by intensive focus-group discussions in which small groups of participants exchanged ideas about civic education in teacher education and offered recommendations about how to develop civics-centered teacher education courses and programs. A summary of recommendations and reactions to "The Institute" is presented in the concluding part of this book.

"The Institute" was graced by the presence of R. Freeman Butts, a distinguished scholar and advocate of education for citizenship in a democracy, who was the keynote speaker at this event. Professor Butts' ideas on civic education—expressed in such notable publications as *The Revival of Civic Learning, The Morality of Democratic Citizenship,* and *The Civic Mission in Educational Reform*—were catalysts of our work. Through his published works on civic education and his personal interactions with us, Professor Butts stimulated our conceptualization of "The Institute" and shaped the organization and execution of this meeting of prominent civic educators and teacher educators. So, this book is dedicated to him and his ideas on civic education.

We express gratitude to Gerardo Gonzales, Dean of the Indiana University School of Education, for his strong endorsement of our work to renew and improve civic education in the teacher education of prospective social studies teachers. He officially opened "The Institute" with an inspirational speech about the values of democracy and the importance of teaching them effectively to each generation of Americans. His remarks set the tone and terms for the successful meeting that ensued.

We gratefully acknowledge the contributions to "The Institute" of The Center for Civic Education and the Social Studies Development Center of Indiana University. The Center for Civic Education provided funding to support "The Institute," and the CCE cooperated with the Social Studies Development Center to plan, organize, and conduct the five-day program, May 18-22, 2001. In particular, we are grateful to Charles N. Quigley, Executive Director of the Center for Civic Education, for his support of "The Institute." Without his help, "The Institute" could not have happened. Finally, we acknowledge the resources provided for the development and publication of this book by Civitas: An International Civic Education Exchange Program and the ERIC Clearinghouse for Social Studies/Social Science Education at the Social Studies Development Center of Indiana University.

John J. Patrick and Robert S. Leming

Contributors

Marilynne Boyle-Baise is an Associate Professor in the School of Education of Indiana University, Bloomington.

Margaret Stimmann Branson is Associate Director of the Center for Civic Education in Calabasas, California.

R. Freeman Butts is the William F. Russell Professor Emeritus in the Foundations of Education, Teachers College of Columbia University, New York City. Professor Butts resides in Carmel, California.

Frederick D. Drake is an Associate Professor in the Department of History of Illinois State University, Normal.

Nancy Haas is an Associate Professor of Education at Arizona State University West.

Diana Hess is an Assistant Professor of Education at the University of Wisconsin, Madison.

Robert S. Leming is Director of the program on *We the People. . . The Citizen and the Constitution* at the Center for Civic Education in Calabasas, California.

Terrence C. Mason is an Associate Professor in the School of Education of Indiana University, Bloomington.

B. Edward McClellan is a Professor in the School of Education of Indiana University, Bloomington.

Lynn R. Nelson is an Associate Professor in the School of Education at Purdue University, West Lafayette, Indiana.

Walter C. Parker is a Professor in the College of Education at the University of Washington.

John J. Patrick is a Professor of Education in the School of Education of Indiana University, Bloomington, where he also is Director of the Social Studies Development Center and Director of the ERIC Clearinghouse for Social Studies/Social Science Education.

Murray Print is Director of the Centre for Research and Teaching in Civics in the Faculty of Education at the University of Sydney in New South Wales, Australia.

Stephen L. Schechter is a Professor in the Department of Political Science of Russell Sage College in Troy, New York, where he also is Director of the Council for Citizenship Education.

Diane Yendol Silva is an Assistant Professor of Education at the University of Florida.

Thomas S. Vontz was Director of the Indiana Program for Law-Related Education of the Social Studies Development Center at Indiana University, Bloomington. In August 2001, he became an Assistant Professor of Education at Rockhurst University in Kansas City, Missouri.

Donald Warren is a Professor in the School of Education of Indiana University, Bloomington.

Charles S. White is an Associate Professor in the School of Education of Boston University.

Introduction

John J. Patrick and Robert S. Leming

The seeds of the work that yielded this book were sown in the wake of the movements for democracy that overthrew the repressive regimes of the Soviet Union and its Central and Eastern European satellites. The demise of communist despotisms led to the rise of governments with democratic aspirations. They eagerly sought assistance from the world's oldest ongoing constitutional representative democracy, the United States of America. We were among the first wave of American civic educators to travel to the formerly communist countries.

As we worked with civic educators in Central and Eastern European countries to develop curricular frameworks and instructional materials, we examined various strategies by which to promote education for democracy. Prominent among the strategies was implementation of civic education for democracy in the pedagogical institutes and universities that educate prospective teachers. In pursuit of this strategy, our colleagues in Estonia, Latvia, Lithuania, and Poland, among other countries, asked us for exemplary syllabi and programs for the education of prospective teachers. They expected to find numerous models of education for democracy in American colleges and universities, which they could adapt for use in their own teacher education programs.

We responded with various examples of courses in social foundations of education and methods of teaching. We also cautioned our colleagues to think creatively, freshly, and independently about how to develop education for democracy in their pedagogical institutes and universities. And we were prompted to re-examine and re-think our ideas and practices about civic education in the preparation of social studies teachers.

We turned to colleagues in America to discuss the status of civic learning in the education of prospective social studies teachers. Our interactions revealed that many of them, like us, are very concerned about the place of civic education within teacher education and want to renew and reform it. Thus, we invited colleagues to meet with us for five-days (May 18-22, 2001) in Indianapolis to discuss "Education in Democracy for Social Studies Teachers." The discussions focused upon such topics as the rationale for civic learning in teacher education, content at the core of civic education, conceptualization of civic education, instructional strategies and methods for teaching about democracy and citizenship, and programmatic

1

examples of education for democratic citizenship in social studies teacher education.

This book is a product of our May 2001 meeting, "Education in Democracy for Social Studies Teachers: An Institute for Teacher Educators." Papers presented to participants in this meeting became the chapters of this book.

Chapter 1 by R. Freeman Butts addresses the reasons for civic learning in teacher education. He calls for the pervasive establishment of civic foundations in the preparation of prospective social studies teachers. He stresses renewal of the traditional civic mission of America's common schools and the preparation of teachers equipped to carry out this mission.

In Chapter 2, Margaret Stimmann Branson discusses the essential content of education for democracy in elementary and secondary schools and in the education of prospective teachers of democratic citizenship to children and adolescents. She specifies civic knowledge that is of most worth in a curriculum designed to educate students for citizenship in a constitutional representative democracy. A fundamental assumption of her work is that all content is not of equal worth, and that a primary responsibility of civic educators is to select and justify content at the core of the curriculum in elementary and secondary schools and in programs of teacher education.

In Chapter 3, John J. Patrick and Thomas S. Vontz present a four-component conceptualization of education for citizenship in a democracy. The four components pertain to civic knowledge, cognitive civic skills, participatory civic skills, and civic dispositions. Patrick and Vontz demonstrate how the four-component model can be used to develop a core curriculum for elementary and secondary schools and programs of university-based teacher education.

Chapter 4 by Terrence C. Mason and Diane Yendol Silva presents examples of civics-centered teacher education programs at two major public universities. They argue for civic education that goes beyond the methods of teaching courses and extends to all parts of social studies teacher education programs.

Diana Hess in Chapter 5 provides an example of a civics-centered pedagogical practice, the method of teaching about controversial public issues. She demonstrates how this method of instruction can be used in a university course on methods of teaching the social studies.

In Chapter 6, Walter C. Parker offers an example of how to teach prospective teachers to lead discussions about primary texts that treat civics-related topics or issues. He demonstrates how core content and processes can be conjoined to teach civic knowledge, skills, and dispositions.

The importance of history in education for democratic citizenship is discussed in Chapter 7 by Lynn R. Nelson and Frederick D. Drake. They argue for a history-centered civic education, which stresses context-based inquiry as an antidote to presentism in thinking about public issues. They also emphasize deliberation about primary documents as a method of teaching and learning civic knowledge through the study of history.

In Chapter 8, Nancy Haas demonstrates how to use the *We the People. . .* programs in a social studies teaching methods course. She explains why these exemplary instructional materials fit a civics-centered teacher education program.

Marilynne Boyle-Baise discusses in Chapter 9 how she teaches democratic citizenship to prospective teachers by involving them in a multicultural service learning program. She places her approach to multicultural service learning for democratic citizenship within a four-type conceptualization of different models of service learning. And she describes how her model of service learning is practiced within a course for prospective teachers.

An international perspective on civics-centered teacher education is provided in Chapters 10 and 11. Murray Print describes an innovative civics curriculum in Australia, which is being implemented in schools and used in the education of teachers. Stephen L. Schechter and Charles S. White present a proposal for civics-centered teacher education, which currently is being implemented in Russian Universities.

Following Chapter 11, we offer a conclusion that highlights recommendations and reactions in response to ideas and examples presented in the eleven chapters of this book. Participants in our meeting of May 18-22, 2001 deliberated daily in focus groups about the contents of papers presented to the plenary sessions. They recorded their reactions to the papers, and offered recommendations for improvement of civic education in university-based programs of social studies teacher education.

We hope that the contents of this book—derived from the May 18-22, 2001 meeting in Indianapolis, "Education in Democracy for Social Studies Teachers: An Institute for Teacher Educators"—will stimulate thought and deliberation among civic educators and teacher educators about how to improve the preparation of prospective social studies teachers. If so, our primary objective in organizing and conducting the May 2001 meeting and producing this book will be achieved.

1

Why Should Civic Learning Be at the Core of Social Studies Teacher Education in the United States?

R. Freeman Butts

The question John Patrick posed for me is "Why should civic learning be at the core of social studies teacher education in the United States?" The first thing that struck me about this title was the term "civic learning." I don't know why he chose that term, but I liked it. Why? Because it took me back to the first book I wrote on civic education in 1980, which was entitled *The Revival of Civic Learning*.[1]

My answer to John's question takes the form of four propositions that will sound very familiar to him and probably to all of you:

1. Preparing citizens to preserve and improve constitutional democracy has been the most important stated purpose of K12 education ever since there has been a United States of America.

2. While the civic learning that is required as preparation for democratic citizenship is a prime purpose of all institutional schooling in the United States, it is now *peculiarly* the function of *public* educational institutions to provide universal, free, compulsory, common schooling, which is accessible to all persons regardless of race, ethnicity, religion, gender, or socioeconomic status.

3. Above all other subject matter fields in the K-12 curriculum, the "social studies" (however they may be defined today) should be specifically designed to provide the civic knowledge, civic values, and civic skills of citizenship in our constitutional democracy.

4. Since the quality and training of teachers are the most important elements in achieving any educational goal in elementary and secondary schools, it is incumbent that the civic learning of prospective social studies teachers should be at the core of the preparation they undergo in their teacher education programs.

5

The problem is that too often these familiar propositions are not translated into specific content or practice, even by those who quote them and believe in them. And, they are often ignored by those who are determined to pursue other educational practices more suited to their own private or group purposes, whether it be individual and personal development, economic and vocational competence, intellectual achievement, family values and parental choice, moral or character building, or other ethnic, racial, cultural pluralisms. All of these civic and noncivic educational purposes and practices are subject to the prevailing political and constitutional agendas of influential groups in American society at any given time, and especially through the federal, state, and local levels of government.

I'd like to emphasize the political context of our theme. In his Inaugural Address on January 20, President George W. Bush made several points that any one of us might have given as a reason for addressing the theme of civic learning. President Bush said:

> We are bound by ideals that move us beyond our backgrounds, lift us above our interests and teach us what it means to be citizens. Every child must be taught these principles. Every citizen must uphold them. And every immigrant, by embracing these ideals, makes our country more, not less American. . . . I ask you to be citizens. Citizens, not spectators. Citizens, not subjects. Responsible citizens, building communities of service and a nation of character.[2]

Here are some of the phrases President Bush used in defining our "grand and enduring ideals": he urged us to renew our commitments to freedom and democracy, justice and opportunity, our union, our common good, civic duty, personal responsibility, and "civility, courage, compassion, and character." And who is a chief guardian of these values? "*Government has great responsibilities* for public safety and public health, for civil rights and *common schools*," said President Bush. Note especially the responsibility of government for "common schools."

President Bush's emphasis on citizenship at his inauguration surely must have appealed to many of us who are now gathered here to discuss why and how education for civic learning should be a core study in the education of social studies teachers. But in our deliberations at this meeting and in coming months, we must constantly be alert to see what the Bush administration proposes concerning the kind of *education* and teacher education that will achieve the citizenship so well described in the President's soaring inaugural rhetoric.

So how did *education* for citizenship fare during the first months of the Bush administration? On Tuesday, January 23, his second working day as president, George W. Bush did as he had promised in his campaign. He presented to Congress his education program as the first legislative proposal of his new administration. I cannot do it justice here and now, but I can make a few points that bear directly on the topic of our meeting. On the positive side, the overriding emphasis on strengthening the federal role to aid underprivileged children to attain a better education and to "leave no child behind" certainly represents the civic values of equality of opportunity and justice desirable in a democratic society. In this respect, his proposal abruptly turned around the approach of the Reagan administration and the Newt Gingrich "Republican Revolution" of 1994 in Congress, both of which had tried to deflate the federal role in education and even abolish the United States Department of Education. This aspect of the President's proposal for a stronger federal role and support for education met with strong approval among Democrats as well as among many Republicans in Congress.

In other respects, the proposal for "federal accountability" emphasized that national academic standards of achievement in the various school subjects were to be measured by states, school districts, local schools, and parents, but not by national standards of testing set in Washington. Each state would be required to test students in each year from third through eighth grade in reading and mathematics and to make the results known according to race, gender, English language proficiency, disability, and socioeconomic status. If a school did not make enough progress in two years, parents could send their children to another public school. And if that school is still failing after the third year, disadvantaged parents could receive federal funds to send their children to private schools (including religious ones) or to receive special help. States would also be required to set "challenging standards in history and science." Notice that neither "social studies" nor "civics and government" as such were listed as required subjects in which challenging standards were to be tested; and the words "religious schools" or "vouchers" were not mentioned.

What did gain much attention in the proposal was the plan to offer federal funds to poor and minority parents so that they could send their children to private schools instead of to their failing public schools. Although moderate Democrats and moderate Republicans also presented legislative proposals that were similar to Bush's, they did not include a voucher plan for aid to private schools. For example, on behalf of the "New Democratic Coalition," Senators Joseph Lieberman and Evan Bayh introduced an educational reform program in addition to Bush's in which they argued for charter schools, magnet schools, and choice limited to public schools.

At this point, neither Bush nor the Democrats confronted the basic constitutional issues of the First and Fourteenth Amendments that are raised by vouchers for religious schools. That issue continued to be muted, as it had been through most of the 2000 campaign. But it is sure to come up if the provision for private schools is still included in the bill when Congress begins to debate it. And it certainly needs to be debated when consideration is given to the values, principles, and content that should be taught as part of the schools' programs to prepare democratic citizens, as well as in the education of teachers, especially teachers of the social studies.

During the second week of his new administration, President George W. Bush turned from education to the role of the federal government in promoting social services through the "faith- based initiatives" of churches, synagogues, mosques, and other charitable organizations. Although his approach to education through schools did not mention religious schools, religion was front and center in his proposals to increase federal funding through religious charitable agencies for the aid and the "education" they provide to persons troubled by drug abuse, criminal activity, teenage pregnancy, or a life of poverty. By executive order, President Bush established a White House Office of Faith-Based and Community Initiatives and ordered the Secretaries of five cabinet departments to establish their own centers for faith-based initiatives, including the Departments of Education, Justice, Labor, Health and Human Services, and Housing and Urban Development. He also appointed Stephen Goldsmith, a former mayor of Indianapolis, to be chairman of a new national advisory board and official adviser to the president on faith-based initiatives.[3]

In contrast to President Bush's educational proposals, this expansion of the federal government's role in funding religiously motivated social services brought to the fore criticism that the constitutional separation of church and state was at stake. One sign of this was a letter to President Bush signed by 19 national civil rights organizations who wrote: "Your faith-based proposals raise . . . serious First Amendment establishment-clause and policy concerns, such as the religious-liberty rights of the beneficiaries of government programs" and "excessive entanglement between religion and government."[4]

Several other issues raised during the first four months of the George W. Bush administration are likely to require your attention as you design social studies courses. Debates over the value of large-scale testing are increasing, not only about the gap between racial and ethnic groups in achievement tests in the various grades of schools, but in the use of aptitude tests for admission to college. And these debates are heightened by the surprising expansion and diversity of minority populations as revealed by data from the 2000 census.

On March 8 the Senate education committee voted unanimously to support Bush's education bill to test all students in grades three to eight annually in reading and mathematics, but postponed consideration of the controversial and divisive voucher proposal until debate on the floor. Senator Kennedy said it was a good bill but could be made better still.

On March 23, the House Republicans unveiled their version of the Bush bill but included the voucher proposal that the Senate had postponed. Some modifications in the state testing requirements were made: states were not explicitly required to use tests comparable from year to year.

On April 10, key senators negotiated with the White House to drop vouchers for private schools but students in failing schools could use federal funds to pay for private tutoring in summers or after school or on weekends, or to pay transportation costs to another public school.

By April 25, Senate Republicans did back away from vouchers for private schools, but they tried to hold on a bit by proposing that failing schools after five years could reconstitute themselves as charter schools or students could use federal dollars for private tutoring.

By May 10, both houses of Congress had approved Bush's budget plan on a near party- line vote, but they would allow low-income students to use federal funds for tutoring after school hours or in the summer. But such a plan raises all sorts of questions about who could teach what, who would provide tutors, and whether religious instruction of any kind would be prohibited in the tutoring?

I cannot of course predict what the future will bring, but I will simply cite here three landmark United States Supreme Court cases which might serve as foundations for inquiry into issues about the relationship between church and state. They provide examples of the way history and contemporary public issues affecting educational policy can be woven together in a core course on civic learning in social studies teacher education.[5]

I emphasize three principles derived from the three landmark Supreme Court cases as examples that could be included in the civic education of prospective social studies teachers:

(1) Education for citizenship in our constitutional democracy is best achieved by a state system of public schools based on the separation of church and state (*Everson v. Board of Education*, 1947).

(2) In our constitutional democracy, parents are free to send their children to private and religious schools, but the state may require the teaching of the principles of democratic government and citizenship in *all* schools whether private, religious, or public (*Pierce v. Society of Sisters*, 1925).

(3) Civic learning through a public educational system must be available to all children and adolescents equally and cannot be achieved in schools that are segregated or separated on the basis of race, ethnicity, or religion (*Brown v. Board of Education*, 1954).

My general point is that the study of court cases dealing with the role of education in a democratic society, including the issues leading up to the cases and their consequences for education, is a very useful technique to use in dealing with the principles of separation of powers, checks and balances, and federalism, those topics usually dealt with in civics and government courses but often viewed by students as remote or theoretical or simply dull. And as we look to the future, such civic learning may be still more important if new appointments to the Supreme Court under President George W. Bush may strengthen the conservative leanings of the Rehnquist Court and speed the reversal of the liberal successes achieved under the Warren and Burger Courts.

President George W. Bush concluded his inaugural address with a reference to the inauguration of Thomas Jefferson in 1801. Bush said: "Much time has passed since Jefferson arrived for his inauguration. The years and the changes accumulate. But the themes of this day he would know." There is indeed a similarity between President Jefferson's and President Bush's stress on citizenship in their inaugurals and on the need for bipartisan support. President Jefferson made it clear that with his fiercely fought election over, he expected the principles of the Constitution to prevail among both parties, Federalists and Republicans alike. In his First Inaugural Address, President Jefferson said:

> About to enter, fellow citizens, on the exercise of duties which comprehend every thing dear and valuable to you, it is proper you should understand what I deem the essential principles of our Government.... [They are] equal and exact justice to all men, of whatever state or persuasion, religious or political . . . freedom of religion, freedom of the press, and freedom of person under protection of the habeas corpus; and trial by juries impartially selected. These principles form the bright constellation which has gone before us and guided our steps through an age of revolution and reformation. The wisdom of our sages and blood of our heroes have been devoted to their attainment. They should be the creed of our political faith, the text of civic instruction.[6]

But there is a world of difference between the two Presidents' views of religion in civic life and education for citizenship. Note that President Jefferson spoke of "our political faith" not of religious character and certainly not of a "faith-based initiative" by the federal government. Remember that Jefferson had been an assemblyman and governor of the sovereign state of Virginia and was one of the first American statesman to propose that a system of secular public education was a basic necessity for the survival of a democratic republic. Just three years after writing the Declaration of Independence, Jefferson was convinced that the Virginia Constitution of 1776 had not gone nearly far enough to reform the aristocratic institutions and class distinctions inherited from British rule especially embedded in education and religion.

So, in 1779 he had introduced his *Bill for the More General Diffusion of Knowledge* which envisioned a system of public education that would become the crown jewel of democracy. And, in tune with his efforts to bring religious freedom to Virginia, Jefferson specifically recommended that the morality of democratic citizenship be the fundamental and common ground for public education rather than religious faith or practice. And the curriculum should be civics-centered rather than kinship- or religion-centered:

> Instead, therefore, of putting the Bible and Testament into the hands of children at an age when their judgments are not sufficiently matured for religious inquiries, their memories may be stored with the most useful facts from Grecian, Roman, European, and American history.[7]

He went on to pen some of the most memorable ideas in the history of American education:

> But of all the views of this law none is more important, none more legitimate, than that of rendering the people the safe, as they are the ultimate, guardians of their own liberty. . . . Every government degenerates when trusted to the rulers of the people alone. The people themselves are its only safe depositories.... An amendment for our constitution must here come in aid of public education.[8]

These proposals for a common public education were linked inseparably with his proposals for the separation of church and state. His original bill of 1779 proposing a Virginia Statute for Religious Freedom did not become law until James Madison roused the state by his vigorous campaign to approve it in 1786, defeating the efforts by Patrick Henry and the conservative Christian coalition of his day to gain tax funds for the support of religious teachers of all Protestant denominations. It states:

> [N]o man shall be compelled to frequent or support any religious worship, place, or ministry whatsoever, nor shall be enforced, restrained, molested, or burthened in his body or goods, nor shall otherwise suffer on account of his religious opinions or belief; but that all men shall be free to profess, and by argument to maintain, their opinion in matters of religion, and that the same shall in no wise diminish, enlarge, or affect their civil capacities.[9]

Thus was Madison nurtured by Jefferson and prepared to frame the first two clauses of the First Amendment of the U.S. Constitution whereby "Congress shall make no law respecting an establishment of religion, or prohibiting the free exercise thereof." Jefferson and Madison agreed that an assessment or tax for religious worship of any kind was the essence of "an establishment of religion," and that the government should not intervene in any way except to protect the freedom of religion.

Now note again that the constitutional issues involving the establishment clause of the First Amendment were relatively muted during the 2000 presidential campaign and remain so as of this writing, whereas it was in the forefront during the Reagan years (1981-89) with widespread public debates over the "original intent" of the founders. The landmark decision on this issue was *Everson v. Board of Education* (1947). The key principle was this:

> The "establishment of religion" clause of the First Amendment means at least this: Neither a state nor the Federal Government can set up a church. Neither can pass laws which aid one religion, aid all religions, or prefer one religion over another. . . . No tax in any amount, large or small, can be levied to support any religious activities or institutions, whatever they may be called, or whatever form they may adopt to teach or practice religion. . . . In the words of Jefferson, the clause against establishment of religion by law was intended to "erect a wall of separation against Church and State."[10]

I think this view won the historical argument about the meaning of the First Amendment in the 1980s; and that may be a reason why it has not been debated so vigorously in the elections of 1996 and 2000. But the conservative wing of the Supreme Court is still poised to argue that Jefferson's phrase was only a rhetorical metaphor and should be erased from constitutional and political discourse. In fact, the election of 2000 was not only about who dominates the Congress and the Presidency but also about who gets to nominate and approve the next justices of the Supreme Court. With the Republicans now in charge of both the Presidency and the Congress, a new majority on the Supreme Court may well overturn the Everson doctrine in order to permit larger public support for religious schools. Justices Rehnquist, Scalia, and White have already indicated they would do this. In their minority opinion in the *Wallace v. Jaffree* case of 1985 in which the majority outlawed school-sponsored prayers in the public schools, the dissenters argued that the "wall of separation of church and state is simply a metaphor based on bad history." I believe, on the contrary, that the great weight of historical scholarship supports the *Everson* doctrine.[11]

Now, 200 years after Jefferson's inauguration, we have had almost two decades of political controversy over the educational reform movement launched in 1983 by the Educational Excellence Commission appointed under the Reagan administration. During this past presidential election year, why have the words and actions of Jefferson about the crucial importance of a common civic education as the basis of good government been so little noted? They have been overshadowed by laments about the lagging economic competitiveness of our work force due to weaknesses in the teaching of science and math, and the necessity of strengthening the teaching of English to the bilingual children in deprived urban areas and to the growing numbers of immigrants and their children. And efforts for public school reform have been further complicated by growing fear of drugs, sex, gangs, violence, and crime affecting safety, order, and discipline in the public schools. But the constitutional issue of separation of church and state remains with us.

Another landmark Supreme Court decision that deserves study protected parents' right to send their children to private and religious schools if they so chose. An Oregon law of 1922 had required all normal children aged 8 to 16 to attend public schools only. It was instigated by the antagonism of a Protestant majority alarmed by a growing immigrant population of Roman Catholics attending their own parochial schools and by a widespread belief that public schools could better serve the common good. In recent years, this decision has been hailed as support for the growing pleas for greater emphasis on "family values" in the public school curriculum, and for the rights of parents to send their children to private and religious schools paid for by tax funds. But it is necessary to keep in mind the Supreme Court's justification for parental rights in education as defined in *Pierce v. Society of Sisters* (1925), the case disallowing the 1922 Oregon law. The Court said:

> We think it entirely plain that the Act of 1922 unreasonably interferes with the liberty of parents and guardians to direct the upbringing and education of children under their control. . . . The fundamental theory upon which all governments in this Union repose excludes any general power of the State to standardize its children by forcing them to accept instruction from public teachers only. The child is not the mere creature of the State; those who nurture him and direct his destiny have the right, coupled with the high duty, to recognize and prepare him for additional obligations.

Now what are those "additional obligations" for which parents have the "high duty" to prepare their children? The *Pierce* decision itself answers that question very clearly. The Court said that it is entirely within the competence of the state governments to exert the power "reasonably to regulate all schools, to inspect, supervise, and examine them, their teachers and pupils; to require . . . that certain studies plainly essential to good citizenship must be taught, and that nothing be taught which is manifestly inimical to the public welfare."[12]

I quote these words to remind parental-rights advocates that a state's requirement that *all* schools must teach civics and government was part of the original Supreme Court charter for parental rights in schooling, and that parents have the high duty to send their children to schools that teach good citizenship whatever other subjects they may teach. Under *Pierce*, parents have the right to choose the school to which they send their children, but an education for good citizenship must remain a top priority and requirement for all parties: government, schools, parents, and students. This principle too often is not recognized in the ongoing debates over charter schools, publicly funded vouchers for private and religious schools, and privatization efforts by profit-making organizations and corporations desiring to operate K-12 schools.

A third landmark Supreme Court decision was the outcome of the civil rights movement of the 1940s and 1950s seeking equality of educational opportunity, much as *Everson* and *Pierce* sought freedom of religion as well as civic responsibility. The constitutional breakthrough came in May 1954 when a unanimous Supreme Court reversed the *Plessy* doctrine of 1896, which had held that separate educational facilities were constitutional just so long as they were equal: the so-called "separate but equal" doctrine. In a decision, worked hard for and written by Chief Justice Earl Warren, *Brown v. Board of Education* held that segregated schools for black children in and of themselves denied black children the "equal protection of the laws" guaranteed to them by the Fourteenth Amendment and were thus unconstitutional:

> Today, education is perhaps the most important function of state and local governments. Compulsory attendance laws and the great expenditures for education both demonstrate our recognition of the importance of education to our democratic society. It is required in the performance of our basic public responsibilities. . . . It is the very foundation of good citizenship. . . . [T]he opportunity of an education...is a right which must be made available to all on equal terms. . . . We conclude that in the field of public education the doctrine of "separate but equal" has no place. Separate educational facilities are inherently unequal.[13]

This case added a powerful impetus to the desegregation of schools and the non-violent civil rights movements from the bus boycott in Montgomery in 1955 to the climactic events of Martin Luther King's march on Washington in 1963 and the march on Selma in 1965. Meanwhile, the principle that the federal government could actively promote educational equality for minority and poverty-stricken children was embedded in the Civil Rights Act of 1964 and in the Elementary and Secondary Education Act of 1965. These momentous movements illustrate beautifully how the interplay of the three branches of government was involved in the march toward greater democracy in the United States.

The succeeding retreats from the principles of affirmative action illustrate how the growth of conservative power in the judiciary as well as in the Congress and the presidency of the1980s and 1990s can be instrumental in weakening the role of government programs to improve the educational opportunities of minorities and dwellers in the low-income regions of states, counties, cities, and districts. It remains to be seen how far the George W. Bush Presidency and the present Republican Congress will go in limiting the role of government and increasing the role of market competition in American education.

In any event, I propose that we face the question: should these and other constitutional questions about American educational policy be emphasized

in the core preparation of all social studies teachers? Should they be emphasized in the preparation of social studies teachers in all schools, private as
well as public, religious as well as secular, not-for-profit as well as for prof-
it, and home schoolteachers and tutors?

There are questions lurking in the background of all of the movements
for educational reform and especially in the debates that are beginning to
churn around the question of certification of teachers as the nation tries to
improve the quality of teachers, their training, and their selection. I note
that the Carnegie Foundation for the Advancement of Teaching under the
presidency of Lee Shulman has announced the beginning of a five year initiative "to examine how teacher education classes are taught, how prospective teachers learn, and how their learning is evaluated." The research team
will examine at least a dozen teacher-preparation programs and try to
determine what are the most promising practices for teaching methods of
teaching (Blair 2001). When we arrive at some conclusions about social
studies methods courses, we might offer to collaborate with Lee and his
participating scholars in several schools of education around the country,
which include the universities of Delaware, Stanford, Northwestern, Michigan State, and the University of Wisconsin-Madison.

And we should be aware of another group that is holding a conference
in July under the joint auspices of the Center for Civic Education, the Pew
Partnership for Civic Change, and the McCormick Tribune Foundation.
The logistics are being arranged by the National Strategy Forum. Are some
of us invited? Its themes are strikingly like ours:

- The Context of Education for Democracy
- Civic Education as Education in the American Constitutional System
- Core Civic Knowledge of Civic Life, Politics, and Government
- Civic Education as the Foundation for Civic Practice
- Practicing Citizenship
- New Strategies for Citizenship

The three landmark Supreme Court decisions I have mentioned, the
issues they raise concerning the respective roles of liberty and equality in
American democracy, and their consequences for fundamental policy issues
in education illustrate some of the questions that we need to face more
directly than ever as the movements for vouchers, charter schools, home
schooling, and privatization gain ever greater momentum under President
George W. Bush. So far, I find no particular interest among the advocates
of those movements in assuring that schools run by parents, teachers, or
private interest groups with public funds will concentrate on providing a
lively and fruitful civic education for the public good, justice, equality, and

the other values of civic learning essential to our constitutional democracy. Whatever the fault of public schools, their main rationale and justification has been their foundational contribution to civic education for all students. I do not find such a rationale in the ideology of voucher or charter school advocates, let alone in the growing number of research studies focused on their value in raising the achievement levels of students. So, it becomes more necessary than ever that the civic learning of students in private and charter schools be evaluated in terms of the schools' acceptance of the *National Standards for Civics and Government* (1994) and their willingness to have their students measured by the National Assessment of Educational Progress (NAEP) tests of achievement in civics and government (Lutkus et al. 1998).

If, however, charter schools or private and religious schools or home schoolers object to such testing on the grounds that their very rationale is to be free of such outside regulatory measures and to develop a curriculum that suits the needs of the children whose parents choose their particular school, what then should be the reply of the state or local educational authorities that permit such freedom to nonpublic schools? What should be the reply of the social studies professionals? Indeed, what would your reply be? Would it be that education for citizenship is the obligation of all schools in America, public, private, or religious, and that certain studies plainly essential to good citizenship must be taught in all of them? Whatever the other merits of private or charter or home schools may be, merits that entitle them to be considered as a new type of "public schools" or as substitutes for public schools, must they be held to account for their teaching of good citizenship as a prime goal of their charters? If there is to be a national requirement that tests of achievement in English literacy and in mathematics are required for all students in all states that receive federal or state funds, as President Bush's proposal provides, should there also be requirements for state tests of achievement in civics and government? If, by any chance, any of you say yes to that proposition, how would you proceed to bring it about in the political context of coming years?

Whatever you do will be affected by the efforts of President George W. Bush and his supporters and those who support vouchers, charter schools, home schooling, and the privatization of public education, as they focus on improving the quality of teachers. Often, they would bypass your courses in education or dump schools of education in favor of more rigorous academic training and the "natural ability" of the prospective teacher.

There are still ominous signs for public education and the role of government in civic learning. In coming years, we must continue to thread our way through the minefields being set for public education and for teacher education by extremists on the right as well as by extremists on the left.

The religious right is reinforcing its national campaigns to elect conservative majorities on local school boards as well as in state legislatures and in Congress. Their goals are largely devoted to reducing the role of government in education or, conversely, increasing the role of religion in public education. And extremists on the pluralist, multiculturalist left sometimes sound as though they would welcome a divided if not a segregated society. In this respect, I think Stephen Macedo strikes a useful balance between the values of individual and group freedoms and the necessary shared values of a democratic political order with his effort to define a "civic liberalism" (Macedo 2000, 8-12).

I hope that the newly energized enterprises of civic learning for democratic citizenship on both the domestic and international fronts can succeed on their own terms and in support of one another. For, above all, the success of democracy in any country in the world rests in the long run upon the success of education for democratic citizenship in its schools, in its higher educational institutions, and in its education of teachers.[14] I hope that we will do our share to mobilize its constituencies in the social studies field throughout the United States of America and abroad in such a way that civic knowledge, civic values, constitutional principles, and civic participation are all nicely balanced as "civic foundations" in teacher education and designed to promote a healthier *democratic government* and *democratic citizenry* as well as a vibrant *democratic civil society*.[15]

Notes

1. Civic learning at the core of social studies teacher education involves the preparation of teachers to play their roles as professional decision makers in an educational system devoted to strengthening a democratic society. Civic learning in the education of social studies teachers should take seriously and explicitly the historic argument that the primary reason for establishing and maintaining universal education in the American Republic is to develop among all students, whether in public or private schools, the knowledge, sentiments, virtues, and skills of democratic citizenship. This surely includes a reasoned commitment to the fundamental values and principles of the Constitution and the Bill of Rights as they apply to education as well as an understanding of the issues and controversies that still confront educators today. Teacher education programs should enable all members of the teaching profession to develop a coherent intellectual and moral framework of the meaning of American democratic society.

2. For full text and comments on Bush's inaugural address, see *The New York Times*, Sunday, January 21, 2001. In defining further "What it means to be a citizen," the president spoke of the Four C's: "Today we affirm a new commitment to live out our nation's promise through civility, courage, compassion, and character." This evokes the first federal educational policy statement made by William J. Bennett as Secretary of Education under President Reagan in 1985 when he spoke of educational reform in terms of three C's: "Character, Content, and Choice." When I approached Bennett at a conference soon after he had spoken on the three C's, I suggested that he should add a 4th C, the "Constitution." He seemed to agree and that point is strongly reflected in his recent venture into online education where he promises to

take the learner into "the heart of our intellectual and civic heritage." Perhaps we should suggest to Bennett that we would be glad to aid him in developing his online courses on "our civic heritage."

3. Frank Bruni and Laurie Goodstein, "New Bush Office Seeks Closer Ties to Church Groups," *The New York Times*, January 29, 2001, p. 1. Goldsmith, a Republican who was chief domestic policy adviser in Bush's presidential campaign, was described as a "two-time mayor in Indianapolis who privatized everything from golf course construction to sewage treatment and showed an interest in revitalizing long-neglected inner-city neighborhoods." Also with Indiana University degrees are two members of Bush's cabinet: Roderick Paige, Secretary of Education, and Paul O'Neill, Secretary of the Treasury.

4. Mark Walsh, "Bush Eyes After-School Role for Faith Groups," *Education Week*, February 7, 2001. Outspoken religious right conservatives like Pat Robertson were criticizing the proposal in fear that it would lead the government to interfere in the work of faith-based charities and limit the religious component of their activity. See Laurie Goodstein, "For Religious Right, Bush's Charity Plan is Raising Concerns," *The New York Times*, February 3, 2001. It should be noted, too, that Bush's Secretary of Education is Roderick Paige, who earned his masters and Ph.D. degrees at Indiana University's School of Health, Physical Education and Recreation and his Secretary of the Treasury Paul O'Neill earned his masters of public administration at IU.

5. I found to my delight that I agree with virtually all of the views of Toni Marie Massaro in her 1993 book stressing the importance of *Constitutional Literacy*, a book which I had not previously seen and which would be extremely useful in a social studies teacher education course. And I noticed an enticing article in *Education Week* about law students who are Marshall-Brennan fellows at American University teaching a high school civics class about the Supreme Court and the constitutional rights of students. The textbook they use is authored by James B. Raskin and is titled *We the Students: Supreme Court Cases For and About Students*. The publisher is Congressional Quarterly, Inc. It would also be a useful text in a civics-centered teacher education course.

6. Jefferson is quoted in Gordon C. Lee, ed. *Crusade Against Intolerance: Thomas Jefferson on Education* (New York: Teachers College, Columbia University, 1961), 53-54.

7. Ibid., 95.

8. Ibid., 97.

9. Ibid., 68.

10. *Everson v. Board of Education*, 330 US 1, (1947), 13.

11. See my original study, *The Tradition of Religion and Education in America* (1950) and more recently, *Religion, Education, and the First Amendment* (1986). The most exhaustive and reliable studies are by Leonard Levy, *The Establishment Clause: Religion and the First Amendment* (1986) and his *Original Intent and the Framers Constitution* (1968).

12. *Pierce v. Society of Sisters*, 268 U.S. 510 (1925).

13. *Brown v. Board of Education*, 347 U.S. 483 (1954).

14. As I say in my article in the *Journal of Teacher Education* (November/December, 1993): "I would not leave the [foundational] task solely to courses in the academic studies of general or liberal education or to case studies in the pedagogical methods or practice teaching periods of training. To understand and carry out the appropriate role of education in a democratic society, all teachers need (1) to know what the fundamental values and principles of a democratic society are, and they must (2) undertake sustained and specific study of those values, principles, and institutions in such way that they can then pursue their educative role in preserving and regenerating those democratic values and principles. The first point cannot be learned wholly in general education nor can the second point simply be left to the subject matter, pedagogical expertise, or practice of a particular school subject. Both goals should

be knit together in an integrated teaching and learning process that I am calling the civic foundations of teacher education. So, I urge the appropriate professional education associations to put that theme front and center in their efforts to improve the quality of teacher education.

15. I wish to thank John Patrick, Director of the Social Studies Development Center of Indiana University, and Robert Leming of the Center for Civic Education for inviting me to this occasion. I am surrounded here by many "old friends." No, let's say "long-time" friends. It gives me a chance to acknowledge publicly the enormous debt I owe to them for my being here and to other people who have done more than any others to get me involved and keep me involved in civic education during the twenty five years since I retired from Teachers College and came "out West" to California. Chuck Quigley, who is not here, deserves special recognition. He is dealing with civic education in Bosnia-Herzogovina, but he roped me into working with the Center for Civic Education in 1976 and has kept me at it ever since. Others are here. About 20 years ago, Margaret Branson had the nerve and persuasive powers to convince a California curriculum committee to incorporate some of the ideas of my *Revival of Civic Learning* into the state History-Social Science Framework of 1981, and she has been at it ever since, including helping with suggestions for this paper. I cherish our long association. Don Warren and I worked together long before I even knew the others. He called me up in 1974, the year I was retiring, and invited me to be the first speaker in an annual lecture series he was planning for the meetings of the American Educational Studies Association, of which he was then president. And after I had finished my talk, I was astonished when he announced that he had convinced his AESA colleagues to name their annual series of lectures for me. So those are some of the reasons I am very happy to be able to come back one more time to the heartland where I grew up in Springfield, Illinois and where Abraham Lincoln made his home after he left Indiana. And I'm proud to be an alumnus of Indiana University as well as of the University of Wisconsin.

References

Blair, Julie. "Foundation to Study Preparation of Teachers." *Education Week*, March 21, 2001.

Butts, R. Freeman. *The Civic Mission of Educational Reform: Perspectives for the Public and the Profession*. Stanford, CA: Hoover Institution Press, 1989.

Butts, R. Freeman. *The Morality of Democratic Citizenship*. Calabasas, CA: Center for Civic Education, 1988.

Butts, R. Freeman. *The Revival of Civic Learning*. Bloomington, IN: Phi Delta KappaEducational Foundation, 1980.

Center for Civic Education. *National Standards for Civics and Government*. Calabasas, CA: Center for Civic Education, 1994.

Lee, Gordon C., ed. *Crusade Against Intolerance: Thomas Jefferson on Education*. New York: Teachers College Press, 1961.

Levy, Leonard. *The Establishment Clause: Religion and the First Amendment*. New York: Macmillan, 1986.

Lutkins, Anthony, et. al. *NAEP 1998 Civic Report Card for the Nation*. Washington, DC: U.S. Department of Education, 1999.

Macedo, Stephen. *Diversity and Distrust: Civic Education in a Multicultural Democracy*. Cambridge, MA: Harvard University Press, 2000.

Massaro, Toni Marie. *Constitutional Literacy: A Core Curriculum for a Multicultural Nation*. Durham, NC: Duke University Press, 1993.

Raskin, James B. *We the Students: Supreme Court Cases For and Against Students*. Washington, DC: Congressional Quarterly Press, 2001.

2

Content at the Core of Education for Citizenship in a Democracy

Margaret Stimmann Branson

Among the questions at the forefront of today's debates about education are those in the following list.

- What knowledge is of most worth?
- What subjects should be studied by all students?
- Should the content and the rigor with which the subject is taught be modified according to the perceived intellectual abilities of students?
- What and how should schools teach about democracy?

Those questions are not new, however. Americans have been contending about them throughout their history. And rightly so! They are not trivial questions. They represent more than disputes among academics. The content of any core curriculum is of political significance. It represents the curriculum developers' views about what knowledge is necessary for participation in the national community of citizens. Conflicts over the content of a core curriculum are public issues about what a person must know to be prepared for citizenship in a democracy.

A brief review of some of the highlights of the more contentious historical encounters about the core curriculum and the purposes it should serve may help to put current controversies into perspective.

An early quarrel about the purposes of education was sparked by Benjamin Franklin when, in 1743, he put forth his original plan for the University of Pennsylvania. It was, in effect, a plan for a new kind of college which he believed was more appropriate for a new world and a democratic society. Franklin's associates who were devoted to the classical collegiate curriculum and to the traditional learned languages—Greek and Latin—were outraged. Franklin's main ideas, then considered very radical, have been summarized by the great historian, Edward P. Cheney (1940, 29) in this fashion:

He would have an education utilitarian rather than cultural, entirely in the English language, though following the best models in the language, devoting much attention to training in thought and expression. It should include mathematics, geography and history, logic, and natural and moral philosophy. It should be an education for citizenship, and should lead to mercantile and civic success and usefulness.

Franklin was obliged to compromise with his more traditional colleagues in a subsequent plan submitted in 1749. Even so, Franklin did not retract his own deep-seated conviction that "the great Aim and End of all learning" was "an inclination joined with an ability to serve mankind." Schools, Franklin said, should hold up examples of "true merit" for youth to emulate. They should educate moral, able, creative young people whose purpose it would be to "Do Good to Men" (Franklin 1987/1749, 323-324).

Two Contrapositions Emerge

As Americans have continued to debate the purposes of education, two contrapositions have emerged. One position supports education for utility and for curriculum differentiated based on the perceived abilities of students. The other position avers that a liberal education, which includes the transmission of the cultural heritage, is essential for all students.

Utilitarian proponents, embracing the ideas of the English philosopher, Herbert Spencer, have argued that the purpose of education was "to prepare for complete living." Classical education, he argued, had no inherent merit. It survived only "as the badge marking a certain social position." Every school subject, therefore, must be judged by whether it had "practical value" and whether it would be "useful in later life." In accord with his criteria, Spencer insisted that the knowledge of most worth was knowledge for self-preservation: gaining a livelihood, being a parent, carrying out one's civic duties, and producing and enjoying art (Spencer 1859, 7-8).

Spencer's book entitled *Education: Intellectual, Moral and Physical*, published in 1859, was probably the most widely read book on education in America. "It requires an effort of the imagination, now, to appreciate the dominion that Spencer exercised over American thought in the quarter of a century or so after the Civil War and, in some quarters, down to the eve of the First World War," according to Henry Steele Commager (1967, xviii).

The Case for Utilitarian Education. Spencer's utilitarian ideas appealed strongly to Progressive education reformers, as well as to Americans of a more practical bent who were inclined to question the value of "book learning." His ideas also are apparent in the influential report "Cardinal Principles of Secondary Education." Issued in 1918 by the National Education Association's Commission of the Reorganization of Secondary Education

(CRSE), it was to have a profound effect on curricular offerings of junior and senior high schools, particularly offerings in the social studies.

"Seven cardinal principles" were identified. They were (1) health, (2) command of fundamental processes, (3) worthy home membership, (4) vocation, (5) citizenship, (6) worthy use of leisure, and (7) ethical character. The curriculum was to be designed to help students to apply knowledge to their daily lives rather than to represent the frameworks of academic disciplines (NEA 1918). Disciplines such as history, geography, civics/government, or economics were not entitled to a place in the curriculum because of their own inherent worth. Selections relevant to the needs of learners were to be made from among the concepts, generalizations, and modes of inquiry germane to each discipline. Justification for teaching what was selected was to be based on its potential for contributing to the realization of one or more of the "seven cardinal principles."

Those who adhere to a utilitarian approach to education have couched their appeals more recently in terms of relevance and the need to address the concerns of particular school populations. Their voices were most strident during the 1960s and 1970s, but they can still be heard today.

The Case for Transmitting the Cultural Heritage. Opposing a utilitarian view of education are those contending that the main purpose of education is the diffusion of knowledge for general intelligence and for the transmission of the cultural heritage. Prominent among the early advocates of this position was Lester Frank Ward, the first president of the American Sociological Society. He challenged Herbert Spencer and his cohorts arguing that not only all social classes but all races were equally capable of learning. Against both popular and scholarly opinion of his time, Ward maintained that, "the lower classes of society are the equals of the upper classes." The difference between those at the top and those at the bottom was due not to differences in intellect but to differences in knowledge and education. The main purpose of education, therefore, should be to ensure that, "the heritage of the past shall be transmitted to all its members alike." Ward insisted that, "All children should have the right to the accumulated knowledge of the past: the information, intelligence and power that comes from studying humankind's inheritance of arts and sciences" (Ward 1906, 95-96).

Ward's fervent advocacy of the diffusion of knowledge for general intelligence and the transmission of "the heritage of the past" is being echoed by many present-day educators. Among the more vocal of them are E. D. Hirsch Jr., Alan Bloom, Diane Ravitch, Chester Finn, William Bennett, and Lynne Cheney. In addition, three prestigious commissions have advanced similar arguments. They are the Committee of Ten, which published its report in 1893, The Bradley Commission on History in the Schools, whose recommendations were made public in 1988, and the National Commission on the High School Senior Year, which just released its preliminary findings in January 2001.

The Committee of Ten was the nation's first blue ribbon commission. Its members included two university presidents, Charles W. Eliot of Harvard and Woodrow Wilson of Princeton, as well as three high school principals and three other college presidents. William Torrey Harris, United States Commissioner of Education, served as chairman.

The Committee of Ten agreed that high schools should be committed to academic excellence for all students in a democratic society. Continuous intellectual growth of all students should be fostered through the study of the major disciplines. The Committee objected to what it called "a very general custom in American High Schools to make up separate courses of study for pupils of supposed different destinations." It then went on to make what was to become a very controversial recommendation that, "every subject which is taught at all in secondary school should be taught in the same way and to the same extent to every pupil so long as he pursues it, no matter what the probable destination of the pupil may be, or at what point his education is to cease" (NEA 1893, 17).

The Committee of Ten's report was a ringing endorsement of the democratic idea that all students should receive a liberal education, not just those preparing for college. Although the Committee insisted that the study of the academic disciplines be rigorous, it also endorsed the use of active teaching/learning methods, and it frowned on rote memorization.

Erosion and Renewal of the Study of History

When The Bradley Commission on History in the Schools was created in 1987, it acknowledged its kinship with the Committee of Ten and embraced many of its ideas. Kenneth T. Jackson of Columbia University served as chairman of The Bradley Commission. Some of America's leading historians were counted as members. Among them were Gordon Craig of Stanford, Nathan Huggins of Harvard, Michael Kammen of Cornell, Leon Litwack of the University of California, Berkeley, and C. Vann Woodward of Yale.

In its report, The Bradley Commission (1988, 1) lamented the fact that, "While other social science disciplines and many new fields such as sex and health education, driver education, and computer education had expanded their roles in the curriculum, the number of required courses in history had declined. Currently (in 1987) fifteen percent of our students do not take any American history in high school, and at least fifty percent do not study either world history or Western civilization."

Erosion in the study of history is a matter that ought to be a serious concern to all Americans, The Bradley Commission contended. Like the Committee of Ten, it believed that, "History belongs in the school programs of all students, regardless of their academic standing and preparation, of their curricular track, or their plans for the future. It is vital for all citizens in a democracy, because it provides the only avenue we have to reach an understanding of ourselves and of our society, in relation to the human condition over time, and of how some things change and others continue" (1988, 5).

The National Commission on the High School Senior Year is still at work. It was formed in June 2000 with the United States Department of Education, the Carnegie Corporation, the Charles Steward Mott Foundation, and the Woodrow Wilson National Fellowship serving as partners. The Commission is headed by Paul Patton, Governor of Kentucky. Its 30 members include legislators, K-12 and collegiate educators, and representatives of parent groups. Roderick Paige, now U.S. Secretary of Education, also is a member, but his appointment was made while he was Superintendent of the Houston, Texas Independent School District.

In the preface to its recently released report (2001), this Commission acknowledges its indebtedness to the Committee of Ten and "the very high standards it set more than a century ago." It also expresses concern that, "national life and the economy are changing much faster than our schools." The Commission, therefore, hopes to find out "if changes could be made in how we structure the existing twelve years of schooling to increase the achievement for all students at the end of the senior year."

Education in History for the Demands of Citizenship. Increasing the achievement level of all students is imperative, the Commission insists, because, "if we go along as we have been, about half our people, perhaps two-thirds, will flourish. Well-educated, comfortable with ambiguity, and possessed of the confidence that accompanies self-knowledge, they will be well-suited to participate in an increasingly global and multicultural world and exercise the responsibilities of citizenship. The other one-third to one-half of our people are more likely to flounder. Poorly educated, worried about their place in a rapidly changing world, they may look on the complexities of an interdependent world as threatening and the demands of citizenship as a burden" (National Commission on the High School Senior Year 2001, 7).

Although the Commission has yet to make its specific recommendations for changes in K-12 schooling, it has clearly indicated what it thinks some of the outcomes of pre-collegiate education ought to be. In a statement reminiscent of the call of the Committee of Ten for a curriculum rich in content and one which fosters mental discipline, the Commission on the High School Senior Year has declared: "All will need a sense of history (both of the United States and the world), an understanding of government and democratic values, and an appreciation for how the arts and literature explain the human condition and expand its possibilities. And, because they will be asked to decide complicated public questions (often with incomplete and conflicting information), all will need to be thoughtful observers of current events and be at ease with ambiguity" (2001, 7).

Because those desired outcomes have strong implications for K-12 schooling in general and for history and civic education in particular, they merit a closer look. A central claim of the Commission is that **all** need a sense of history and an understanding of government and democratic values, because **all** will be asked to decide complicated public questions.

What does having a "sense of history" mean and why do **all** need it? Having a sense of history means much more than knowing the answers to multiple choice questions or having a nodding acquaintance with an assortment of names, dates, and events. A sense of history means grappling with the great questions that have engaged human beings and societies over time. It means appreciating the significant achievements and learning from the experiences of those who have preceded us. A sense of history means that we are able to transcend the here and now—the time, place, and culture constraints of our own existence—and to empathize with those whose life circumstances were and are different from ours. Further, a sense of history enables us to view our own lives and time from a broader perspective, so that we can make better judgments about what is truly significant and what is insignificant.

In a recent interview, James Oliver Horton, the Benjamin Banneker Professor of American Studies and History at George Washington University, was asked what he most wanted students to take away from an introductory United States history survey course. He spoke eloquently about a sense of history. Here is a portion of what Horton said:

> I want students to take away a sense of their place in American history and a realization that it is important to consider the issues of today's society in a historical context. And I want them to understand that individuals, working alone or in groups, have exerted significant influence over events in history and can in contemporary America. In this I hope to counter the cynical notion that I find in too many of my students, that nothing they do will make a difference. I find this attitude particularly troubling. If those who are among the most privileged, educated, and potentially powerful of Americans cannot influence their nation, the ideal of democracy needs serious reconsideration. (2001, 17)

The Importance of a Sense of Constitutional History. In addition to cultivating a broad sense of history, it is particularly important that all Americans have a sense of their constitutional history. They should understand how and why our country came into being, why the writing of our Constitution was a landmark event in the history of the world, how and why our Constitution has served as an impetus for social and political movements both at home and abroad, and how and why that Constitution has enabled us to govern ourselves successfully for more than two centuries. The importance of an understanding of the history, principles, and values of the American Constitution has been underscored from the time of the nation's founding to the present day. It was George Mason who, in writing the Virginia Bill of Rights in 1776, said, "No free government or the blessings of liberty can be preserved to any people but . . . by frequent recurrence to fundamental principles" (Article xv). Those "fundamental principles" are enunciated in our nation's founding documents, most explicitly in the Declaration of Independence and the United States Constitution. They have been reiterated and explicated, of course, in subsequent legislation, court decisions, and executive orders and addresses. Americans not only should understand those fundamental principles, they should recur to them in the course of making decisions as citizens.

Thomas Jefferson, who repeatedly stressed the importance of public education as a remedy for, and deterrent to, unconstitutional conduct, also emphasized the importance of citizens' acquaintance with the Constitution and the Bill of Rights. In a letter to Joseph Priestly, Jefferson wrote, "Written constitutions may be violated in moments of passion or delusion, yet they furnish a text to which those who are watching may again rally and recall the people; they fix too for the people the principles of their political creed" (Ford 1897/1802, 59-60).

More recently legal scholar Sanford Levinson has reiterated and extended Jefferson's position. Levinson (1992, 389) calls not only for broad popular education in the Constitution, he urges the participation of "every citizen" in an on-going conversation about constitutional meaning: "The United States Constitution can meaningfully structure our polity if and only if every public official—and ultimately every citizen—becomes a participant in the conversation about constitutional meaning, as opposed to the pernicious practice of identifying the Constitution with the decisions of the United States Supreme Court or even of courts and judges more generally."

Needed: An Understanding of Government and Democratic Values. The second part of the Commission on the Senior Year's injunction is that all "need an understanding of government and democratic values." What is an "understanding of government?" Certainly understanding government means more than just being familiar with the structure or the "anatomy" of a particular government. Understanding government means recognizing that government, no matter how it is organized, is the most powerful instrument for social control ever devised. Understanding government entails an appreciation of its impact on our own lives. It is government that can declare war or make peace, can foster justice or injustice, can enact fair or unfair laws, and can protect or violate human rights. Citizens, therefore, need the knowledge, the skills, and the will to monitor government and to influence its actions so that those actions conform to democratic values and comport with democratic processes.

The Case for Questions as Curriculum Organizers

Understanding government also means asking and seeking answers to probing questions about it—questions of the kind that thoughtful human beings have pondered at least since the time of Plato and Aristotle. Questions of that kind not only are used as the organizing principle in the *National Standards for Civics and Government* (Center for Civic Education 1994, 87-88). They were used in the framework for the 1998 National Assessment of Educational Progress in Civics (NAEP) and again for the recently revised General Education Diploma (GED) examination. Those five organizing questions are:

1. What are civic life, politics, and government?
2. What are the foundations of the American political system?
3. How does the government established by the Constitution embody the purposes, values, and principles of American democracy?
4. What is the relationship of the United States to other nations and to world affairs?
5. What are the roles of the citizen in American democracy?

From those heuristic, overarching questions the *National Standards for Civics and Government* poses subquestions such as these:

- What are the purposes of rules and laws, and how can you evaluate rules and laws?
- Why is it important to limit the power of government?
- Why do conflicts among fundamental values such as liberty and equality or individual rights and the common good arise, and how might those conflicts be resolved?
- What are the rights of citizens, and how should the scope and limits of those rights be determined?
- What are the personal and civic responsibilities of citizens in American constitutional democracy, and when and why might tensions arise between them?

When people ask and seek answers for themselves to those kinds of questions they come closer to understanding government, as opposed to just "knowing about" government. That understanding provides them with functional knowledge; it empowers them because their efficacy is enhanced. Further, learning how to ask probing, significant questions can become a lifelong habit that serves citizens well when they make judgments about public issues and proposed policies, or when they want to hold officials or institutions accountable. As Henry David Thoreau observed in his musings on education, questioning fosters thought and, "Thought breeds thought. It grows under your hands" (Brickman 1999/1860, 70).

Perhaps it is not surprising that some leading historians are proposing that the history curriculum be organized around a set of what are called "fundamental themes and questions." Theodore Rabb of Princeton University has proposed a set of ten questions which he calls "close to the classic questions of the field." They are classic because "they've been addressed by historians from Herodotus to Thucydides and from Gibbon to Burckhardt, yet they remain as salient today as they were when first they were asked." They are questions that "provoke thought that breeds thought." Here are Rabb's ten suggestions for organizing a history curriculum.

1. How and why do societies change?
2. When societies compete with one another, what makes for success or failure?
3. How does a society cohere, and how do some groups within it gain and retain authority over others?
4. At what point and why does political and/or social conflict erupt, and how is it resolved?
5. What are the causes and consequences of economic success?
6. Why does a distinct outlook or "culture" arise in a society, and why does it change?
7. How are religious beliefs related to political, social, intellectual, and economic developments?
8. Are individuals as important as underlying structures in bringing about change?
9. By what arguments or presentations of evidence does a historian most effectively explain the events of the past?
10. Are there general lessons to be learned from history? (Rabb 2000, 6)

There are good reasons for using questions as opposed to topics as the organizing principle for curriculum development in history and civics/government. In his classic, *Basic Principles of Curriculum and Instruction*, Ralph W. Tyler explained,

> Objectives stated in the form of topics and generalizations are unsatisfactory. If a history course is dealing with the Colonial Period, what is it the student is expected to get from it? Are there certain facts about the period he is to remember? Is he expected to identify trends in development that he can apply to other historic periods? (Tyler 1949, 45)

If curriculum developers and teachers fail to indicate the significance of an inquiry through the questions they pose, they afford students little guidance and less motivation. The advice Tyler imparted, therefore, is timeless.

> A smaller number of consistent highly important objectives need to be selected. . . . An educational program is not effective if so much is attempted that little is accomplished. It is essential therefore to select the number of objectives than can actually be attained in significant degree in the time available and that these be really important ones. (Tyler 1949, 47)

An International Framework for Education in Democracy. In addition to the proposals for organizing curriculum by the use of heuristic questions which have just been discussed, a new transnational model which employs questions is nearing publication. It is *An International Framework for Education in Democracy*, an attempt to develop a cross-cultural consensus on the central meanings and character of the ideas, values, and institutions of democracy. Its further purpose is to identify common elements of this knowledge that should be included in the curriculum of any nation wishing to promote an understanding of democratic citizenship and its practice. Development of the *International Framework* was begun in 1996 as part of "Civitas: An International Civic Education Exchange Program" funded through a grant from the United States Department of Education, Office of Educational Research and Improvement in cooperation with the United States Department of State. Successive drafts have been written by the Center for Civic Education and they have been commented upon by reviewers in every inhabited continent.

The *Framework* is being developed in the belief that there is a need among educators in democratic nations for a resource that attempts to survey the field of education for democratic citizenship and to set forth comprehensively its principal content. It is important to note that the *Framework* is intended as a starting point for discussion, rather than an attempt to pronounce a set of authoritative dogmas. Thus, like democracy itself, the *Framework* is to be viewed as perpetually unfinished, subject to continuing debate and emendation.

The intended audience for the *Framework* ranges from teachers and educational policy makers responsible for civic education programs to curriculum developers and teacher education and credentialing institutions responsible for training competent classroom teachers. The *Framework* can also be used as a resource by any group or individual interested in democracy. The *Framework* is not intended, however, as a student text.

Two versions of the first draft of the *Framework*—a Five-Part and Seven-Part version—were presented to reviewers, who were asked to give a preference. Since each format had its supporters, it was decided to publish both. The Five-Part version presents a logical development of ideas, while the Seven-Part version is more open ended, allowing parts to be added or deleted without violating some logical order. The present version is the Seven-Part format. There will, however, be a considerable overlap of material with the Five-Part format, which is yet to be developed.

The *Framework* begins with the most basic questions. What is democracy? What kinds of democracy may be possible? Who are the governing members of a democracy? It continues by asking, how can democracy be justified? What arguments have been leveled against democracy? What characteristics of society enhance and what characteristics inhibit or detract from the successful development of democracy?

The *Framework* then enquires how democracy emerges and develops from non-democratic settings and how, once established, it can survive and improve. Finally, the Framework raises questions about how democracy is changing our world today—and how contemporary social and economic processes are affecting the character of democracy.

The purpose of the *International Framework* is to provide a generic statement that any country wishing to educate citizens for democracy can use as a resource in developing curricular programs in civics and government. Accordingly the *Framework*:

- attempts to articulate the frame of reference for the creation of curricular programs—the ideas, concepts, principles, and values on which democracy rests—as a domain independent of other areas of inquiry;
- provides a basis for analysis, comparison, and evaluation as well as the fundamentals that underlie democracy;
- in order to provide a broad perspective useful in the examination of democracy, encompasses and integrates ideas from many disciplines, with particular attention to political science, history, and economics;
- provides the basis for arguments favorable to democracy, but it also acknowledges arguments against democracy;
- provides a comprehensive and sophisticated view of the field that curriculum developers and policy makers need to have in order to decide what elements of that field should be taught; and
- is organized under topical questions to highlight the importance of inquiry and debate to democracy that is suggestive of the teaching methodology consistent with democratic values.

The *International Framework for Democracy* is not intended to be a "final answer." Though prescriptive in character, it addresses democracy as problematic. Its objective is to promote robust debate and discussion. The *Framework* also is not intended to be a complete program; particular countries need to address issues and raise additional questions specific to themselves.

Core Curricula for Citizenship Education from England and
The Council of Europe

American educators will find the *International Framework for Democracy* to be a useful measure for comparing standards for teaching about democracy which have been developed in their own state or school district. Other useful measures for comparison are two recently published statements of core curriculum for citizenship education: *The National Curriculum for England* and the *Basic Concepts and Core Competencies for Democratic Citizenship* developed by the Council of Europe.

Citizenship Education in England. Education not only is in the forefront of public policy issues in the United States, it is a major concern in other countries as well. Prime Minister Tony Blair recently repeated what he said prior to the 1997 election, that his top priorities are "education, education, education." First and foremost among England's educational worries is literacy. One in five adults now is functionally illiterate, putting Britain's literacy levels near the bottom of the class among developed nations. An allied concern is civic education, which led to a revised National Curriculum published by the British Government in November 1999. For the first time in England, this included "Citizenship" as a statutory requirement for secondary schools and as non-statutory guidelines for primary schools. The "Citizenship" requirement is to come into force in August 2002.

The National Curriculum for England: Citizenship (1999, 1) highlights "the importance of citizenship" in these words:

> Citizenship gives pupils the knowledge, skills and understanding to play an effective role in society at local, national, and international levels. It helps them to become informed, thoughtful, and responsible citizens who are aware of their duties and rights. It promotes their spiritual, moral, social, and cultural development, making them more self-confident and responsible both in and beyond the classroom. It encourages pupils to play a helpful part in the life of their schools, neighborhoods, communities, and the wider world. It also teaches them about our economy and democratic institutions and values; encourages respect for different national, religious and ethnic identities; and develops pupils' ability to reflect on issues and take part in discussions.

Although schools may choose how to organize their school curriculum, they will have a statutory responsibility to teach "the programmes of study for citizenship at key stages 3 and 4." Programmes of study are defined in the Education Act of 1996 section 353b as "the matters, skills, and processes" that should be taught to pupils of different abilities and maturities during "key stages." Key stages 3 and 4 correspond roughly with grade levels at junior or senior high schools in the United States. The programmes of study list the topics or "knowledge and understanding" which students are expected to "acquire and apply." The skills of "enquiry and communication" and of "participation and responsible action" which pupils should develop also are specified.

An additional feature of the National Curriculum is the provision of short paragraphs which describe what "the majority of pupils should characteristically demonstrate by the end of each key stage, having been taught the relevant programme of study." The descriptions are designed to help teachers and parents judge the extent to which a student's attainment relates to the expectations that are set forth. American educators might find these key stage descriptions of interest, particularly in comparison with the "achievement levels" denoted in the National Assessment of Educational Progress in Civics (Lutkus et al. 1999, 19-21).

Attainment Target for Citizenship

Key Stage 3

Pupils have a broad knowledge and understanding of the topical events they study: the rights, responsibilities, and duties of citizens; the role of the voluntary sector; forms of government; provision of public services; and the criminal, and legal systems. They show how the public gets information and how opinion is formed and expressed, including through the media. They show understanding of how and why changes take place in society. Pupils take part in school and community-based activities, demonstrating personal and group responsibility in their attitudes to themselves and others.

Key Stage 4

Pupils have a comprehensive knowledge and understanding of the topical events they study: the rights, responsibilities, and duties of citizens; the role of the voluntary sector; forms of government; and the criminal and civil justice, legal, and economic systems. They obtain and use different kinds of information, including the media, to form and express an opinion. They evaluate the effectiveness of different ways of bringing about change at different levels of society. Pupils take part effectively in school and community-based activities, showing a willingness and commitment to evaluate such activities critically. They demonstrate personal and group responsibility in their attitudes to themselves and others. (*The National Curriculum for England* 1999)

The new National Curriculum for England also identifies eight key concepts which "underpin" all the required subjects, including history and citizenship. Those concepts are citizenship, sustainable development, values and perceptions, interdependence, social justice, conflict resolution, diversity, and human rights.

The Council of Europe and Citizenship Education. In 1997 the Council of Europe launched the Education for Democratic Citizenship project. A Project Group composed of education ministries representatives, specialists, international institutions, and NGOs active in the field of civic education was established and subsequently divided into three subgroups. Each subgroup was charged with a specific task. One group was to develop a framework of concepts for education for democratic citizenship and to identify the basic skills required for democratic practices in European societies. It is the work of that group which is of interest here. The other two subcommittees were concerned with the development of "citizenship sites" or locales other than schools in which adults could participate as citizens, and with training and support systems "to build a network of multipliers."

The final report on *Basic Concepts and Core Competencies for Education for Democratic Citizenship* was released in June 2000. It first notes the significant changes in the understanding of citizenship which have taken place in Europe, "We have thus passed from a conception of citizenship that placed the emphasis on feelings of belonging and where the corresponding education accompanied the transmission of this feeling by a very strong emphasis on obedience to the collective rules, to a more individualistic and more instrumentalist conception of citizenship, a citizenship that gives pride of place to the individual and his rights and relegates to the background the affirmation of collective and partial, in the geographic and cultural sense, identities embodied by States."

Although the several authors of the report express at the outset their reservations about the possibility and the value of drawing up a list of desired knowledge and behaviors, they recognize the need "to try to put a little order in such a vast field" as civic education. Accordingly, they offer two classifications of "competences" to serve as a "theoretical framework which can be used to define, orient, incite, and analyze activities."

The first classification comprises three broad categories: cognitive competences; affective competences and those connected with the choice of values; and those connected with action.

The cognitive competences are separated into "four families":

F-1: competences of a legal and political nature;

F-2: knowledge of the present world which implies both a historical and a cultural dimension;

F-3: competences of a procedural nature with particular attention to two capacities of particular relevance for democratic citizenship:

the ability to argue, which is related to debate, and the ability to reflect or the capacity to reexamine actions and arguments in light of principles and values;

F-4: knowledge of the principles and values of human rights and democratic citizenship. (EDCP 2000, 21-22)

A second and an alternate classification of core knowledge distinguishes four dimensions of citizenship, which are based on an analysis of life in society. They are the political and legal dimension, the social dimension, the economic dimension, and the cultural dimension.

- The **political and legal dimension** covers rights and duties with respect to the political system and law. It requires knowledge concerning the law and the political system, democratic attitudes, and the capacity to participate to exercise responsibilities at all levels of public life.
- The **social dimension** covers relations between individuals and requires knowledge of what these relations are based on and how they function in society. Social competences are paramount here. This dimension is connected to others, in particular the following one, through the weight of values such as solidarity.
- The **economic dimension** concerns the world of production and consumption of goods and services. It opens directly on labor and the way it is organized, on the fruits of labor, and their distribution. It requires economic competences, such as knowledge of how the economic world functions, including the world of work.
- The **cultural dimension** refers to collective representations and imaginations and to shared values. It implies, like the others and sometimes more than them, historical competence, recognition of a common heritage with its varied components, a mobile heritage, a heritage to exchange with others. (EDCJ 2000, 24)

Finally, just as the National Curriculum for England does, the Core Competencies of the Council of Europe identify the concepts which suffuse the proposed curriculum: freedom, equality, participation, responsibility, and solidarity. "Freedom as capacity for action, equality as access for all to basic goods and services in order to protect human dignity, participation as the need to contribute to the public interest, responsibility for oneself, others, and the future of the world, and solidarity between people transcending political, cultural, and social barriers. These are, and remain, the hard core of Education for Democratic Citizenship" (Council of Europe 2000, 16-17).

Conclusion

The content of the core curriculum is more than a matter about which academics contend. The core curriculum is an issue of political significance. In the course of their history, Americans have disagreed about the subjects which ought to be taught, but since the time of Benjamin Franklin they have agreed that education for citizenship is a primary, if not *the* primary purpose of schools. Unfortunately, schools have often given more lip service than real service to that purpose. There is growing awareness, however, of the need to improve education in civics, government, and history. If American constitutional democracy is to survive and to thrive, then its citizens must acquire the knowledge, develop the skills, and be imbued with the will to maintain and improve it.

References

American Council of Trustees and Alumni. *Losing America's Memory: Historical Illiteracy in the 21st Century*. Washington, DC: American Council of Trustees and Alumni, 2000.

Batstone, David, and Eduardo Mendieta. *The Good Citizen*. New York: Routledge, 1999.

Bradley Commission on History in Schools. *Building a History Curriculum: Guidelines for Teaching History in Schools*. Washington, DC: Educational Excellence Network, 1988.

Bahmueller, Charles F., and Charles N. Quigley, eds. *Civitas: A Framework for Civic Education*. Calabasas, CA: Center for Civic Education, 1991.

Brickman, Martin, ed. *Uncommon Learning: Thoreau on Education*. Boston: Houghton Mifflin, 1999.

Center for Civic Education. *An International Framework for Education in Democracy* (draft). Calabasas, CA: Center for Civic Education, 2001.

Center for Civic Education. *National Standards for Civics and Government*. Calabasas, CA: Center for Civic Education, 1994.

Cheney, Edward P. *History of the University of Pennsylvania, 1740-1940*. Philadelphia: University of Pennsylvania Press, 1940.

Commager, Henry Steele, ed. *Lester Ward and the Welfare State*. Indianapolis: Bobbs Merrill, 1967.

Council of Europe, Council for Cultural Cooperation, Project: Education for Democratic Citizenship. *Basic Concepts and Core Competencies for Education for Democratic Citizenship*. Strasbourg, France: Council of Europe, 2000.

Dahl, Robert A. *On Democracy*. New Haven, CT: Yale University Press, 1998.

Delli Carpini, Michael, and S. Keeter. *What Americans Know About Politics and Why It Matters*. New Haven, CT: Yale University Press, 1996.

EDCP (Education for Democratic Citizenship Project) *Basic Concepts and Core Competencies for Education for Democratic Citizenship*. Strasbourg: Council of Europe Publishing, 2000.

Ford, Paul Leicester, ed. "Letter from Thomas Jefferson to Joseph Priestly," (June 19, 1802). *The Writings of Thomas Jefferson*. New York: G.P. Putnams Sons, 1897.

Franklin, Benjamin. "Proposals Relating to the Education of Youth in Pennsylvania." In *Writings*. J. A. Lemay, ed. New York: Library of America, 1987.

Gutmann, Amy. *Democratic Education*. Revised Edition. Princeton, NJ: Princeton University Press, 1999.

Heineman, Robert A. *Political Science: An Introduction*. New York: McGraw Hill, 1996.

Horton, James O. Interviewed by Roy Rosenzweig. "Ideas, Notes, and News About History Education." *History Matters* 13 (February 2001): 17.

Janoski, Thomas. *Citizenship and Civil Society*. New York: Cambridge University Press, 1998.

Levinson, Sanford. "Constitutional Meta-Theory." *University of Colorado Law Review* 63 (1992): 389, 406.

Lutkus, Anthony D., et al. *NAEP 1998 Civics Report Card for the Nation*. Washington, DC: U.S. Department of Education, 1999.

March, James G., and Johan P. Olsen. *Democratic Governance*. New York: The Free Press, 1995.

Massaro, Toni Marie. *Constitutional Literacy: A Core Curriculum for a Multicultural Nation*. Durham: Duke University Press, 1993, 35.

McDonnell, Lorraine M., P. Michael Timpane, and Roger Benjamin, eds. *Rediscovering the Democratic Purposes of Education*. Lawrence: The University Press of Kansas, 2000.

NAEP Civics Consensus Project. *Civics Framework for the 1998 National Assessment of Educational Progress*. Washington, DC: National Assessment Governing Board, 1996.

National Center for Education Statistics. *Progress Through the Teacher Pipeline: 1992-93: College Graduates and Elementary/Secondary School Teaching as of 1997*. Washington, DC: U.S. Department of Education, 2000.

National Commission on Civic Renewal. *A Nation of Spectators: How Civic Disengagement Weakens America and What We Can Do About It*. College Park: Institute for Philosophy and Public Policy of the University of Maryland, 1998.

National Commission on the High School Senior Year. *The Lost Opportunity of the Senior Year: Finding a Better Way*. Washington, DC, 2001.

The Naional Curriculum for England: Citizenship. London: Jointly Published by the Department for Education and Employment and the Qualification and Curriculum Authority, 1999.

NEA (National Education Association). *Cardinal Principles of Secondary Education: A Report of the Commission on the Reorganization of Secondary Education*. Bulletin no. 35. Washington, DC: Bureau of Education, 1918.

NEA (National Education Association). *Report of the Committee on Secondary Social Studies, with the Reports of the Conferences Held by this Committee*, Document 205. Washington, DC: Bureau of Education, 1893.

Nie, Norman H., Jane Junn, and Kenneth Stehlik-Barry. *Education and Democratic Citizenship in America*. Chicago: The University of Chicago Press, 1996.

Niemi, Richard G., and Jane Junn. *Civic Education: What Makes Students Learn*. New Haven, CT: Yale University Press, 1998.

Norris, Pippa, ed. *Critical Citizens: Global Support for Democratic Governance*. New York: Oxford University Press, 1999.

Oldenquist, Andrew, ed. *Can Democracy Be Taught?* Bloomington, IN: Phi Delta Kappa Educational Association, 1996.

Patrick, John J. "Concepts at the Core of Education for Democratic Citizenship." In *Principles and Practices of Education for Democratic Citizenship: International Perspectives and Projects*, Charles F. Bahmueller and John J. Patrick, eds. Bloomington, IN: ERIC Clearinghouse for Social Studies/Social Science Education, 1999.

Rabb, Theodore. *Patterns and Themes for the History of Western Civilization*. Westlake, OH: National Council for History Education, 2000.

Ravitch, Diane. *Left Back: A Century of Failed School Reforms*. New York: Simon and Schuster, 2000, 26-29.

Schlesinger, Arthur M. Jr. *The Disuniting of America: Reflections on a Multicultural Society*. New York: W. W. Norton, 1998.

Schudson, Michael. *The Good Citizen: A History of American Civic Life*. Cambridge, MA: Harvard University Press, 1998.

Skocpol, Theda, and Morris P. Fiorina, eds. *Civic Engagement in American Democracy*. Washington, DC: Brookings Institution Press, 1999.

Spencer, Herbert. *Education: Intellectual, Moral, and Physical*. New York: Burt, 1859.

Tyler, Ralph. *Basic Principles of Curriculum Development*. Chicago: University of Chicago Press, 1949.

Ward, Lester Frank. *Applied Sociology: A Treatise on the Conscious Improvement of Society by Society*. Boston: Ginn, 1906.

3

Components of Education for Democratic Citizenship in the Preparation of Social Studies Teachers

John J. Patrick and Thomas S. Vontz

A particular type of civic education should be at the core of social studies teacher education in a constitutional democratic republic. If so, then teachers of the social studies will be equipped with the knowledge and skills they need to address effectively the enduring central goal of their profession, which has been, is, and likely will be the cultivation among students of competence for the office of citizen.[1]

A prerequisite to construction of exemplary civics-centered courses in teacher education is a compelling conceptualization of education for citizenship in a democracy. We need a generally acceptable model by which to define, construct, criticize, develop, and evaluate civic education in the education of social studies teachers. What are the justifiable components of a model of education for citizenship in a democracy by which we can construct worthwhile courses or curricula for the education of social studies teachers? How can the components of a generally acceptable model be used as criteria for the selection and implementation of content and processes, substance and methods, of social studies teacher education programs? Why are the model and its curricular applications warranted or reasonable?

This chapter responds to questions about what, how, and why in regard to a civics-centered education of social studies teachers. **First,** we present a four-component model or conceptualization of education for citizenship in a democracy. **Second,** we discuss how to implement the civic knowledge component of the model. **Third,** we show how to implement the two civic skills components of the model. **Fourth,** we address applications to curriculum and instruction of the civic dispositions component of the model.

Fifth, we conclude with a short list of recommendations and a brief commentary about civic education and democracy in the education of social studies teachers.

A Four-Component Model of Civic Education

In recent years, there has been general agreement among civic educators about the four fundamental categories or components of education for citizenship in a democracy, which are (1) civic knowledge, (2) cognitive civic skills, (3) participatory civic skills, and (4) civic dispositions. These four categories, for example, were the interrelated components of the framework for the 1998 National Assessment of Educational Progress (NAEP) in Civics. This framework will be used again to guide the next NAEP in civics (NAEP Civics Consensus Project 1996, 17-19). The generally accepted four components of civic education have been articulated with minor variations or differences in categorical denotations. But the similarities of alternative models are much greater than the differences. For example, the four-component model presented in Figure 3-1 is generally similar to the *Civics Framework for the 1998 National Assessment of Educational Progress* (NAEP Civics Consensus Project 1996) and to components of civic education in the *National Standards for Civics and Government* (Center for Civic Education 1994). The model in Figure 3-1, however, includes several distinct denotations within each of its four components or categories (Patrick 2000a, 5; Patrick 1999a, 34).[2]

We want to stress the interrelationships and interactions among the categories of our model. Although it is convenient for us to depict the components statically in a four-tiered illustration (Figure 3.1), we insist they be viewed and contemplated dynamically to emphasize continuous interactions of the categories in development and implementation of curriculum and instruction. As you view and respond to our discussion of the four-component model (Figure 3.1), use your imagination to transcend the linear depiction of categories to visualize and ponder the complex and continuous connections of the components in use.

As depicted in the first component of Figure 3.1, a basic objective of a civics-centered education for social studies teachers and their students is teaching and learning systematically and thoroughly a set of concepts by which democracy in today's world is defined, practiced, and evaluated. These concepts, listed in Figure 3.2, include representative democracy or republicanism; constitutionalism; rights to life, liberty, equality, and property; citizenship, civic identity, and responsibility for the common good; free and open society; and free and open economy. Acquisition of such concepts as a set, a framework of connected ideas, enables learners to know

---

Figure 3.1

COMPONENTS OF EDUCATION FOR CITIZENSHIP IN A DEMOCRACY

1. **KNOWLEDGE OF CITIZENSHIP AND GOVERNMENT IN A DEMOCRACY (CIVIC KNOWLEDGE)**
   a. Concepts/principles on the substance of democracy
   b. Issues about the meaning and implementation of core ideas
   c. Constitutions and institutions of representative democratic government
   d. Organization and functions of democratic institutions
   e. Practices of democratic citizenship and the roles of citizens
   f. Contexts of democracy: cultural, social, political, and economic
   g. History of democracy in particular states and throughout the world

2. **INTELLECTUAL SKILLS OF CITIZENSHIP IN A DEMOCRACY (COGNITIVE CIVIC SKILLS)**
   a. Identifying and describing phenomena (events and issues) of political/civic life
   b. Analyzing and explaining phenomena (events and issues) of political/civic life
   c. Evaluating, taking, and defending positions on public events and issues
   d. Thinking critically about conditions of political/civic life.
   e. Thinking constructively about how to improve political/civic life

3. **PARTICIPATORY SKILLS OF CITIZENSHIP IN A DEMOCRACY (PARTICIPATORY CIVIC SKILLS)**
   a. Interacting with other citizens to promote personal and common interests
   b. Monitoring public events and issues
   c. Deliberating and making decisions about public policy issues
   d. Influencing policy decisions on public issues
   e. Implementing policy decision on public issues
   f. Taking action to improve political/civic life

4. **DISPOSITIONS OF CITIZENSHIP IN A DEMOCRACY (CIVIC DISPOSITIONS)**
   a. Promoting the common good
   b. Affirming the common and equal humanity and dignity of each person
   c. Respecting, protecting, and using rights possessed equally by each person
   d. Participating responsibly in the political/civic life of the community
   e. Respecting, protecting, and practicing government by consent of the people
   f. Supporting and practicing civic virtues

---

what a democracy in today's world is, and what it is not; to distinguish democracy from other types of government; and to evaluate the extent to which their government and other governments of the world are or are not authentic constitutional representative democracies. However, teachers cannot teach democracy effectively unless they know it thoroughly. And they are not likely to acquire deep comprehension or conceptual understanding of core ideas about democracy unless they encounter them again and again through various facets of their teacher education program.

Basic knowledge of democracy, its principles and practices, must be applied effectively to civic and political life if it would be learned thoroughly and used effectively to serve the needs of citizens. Thus, a central facet of a civics-centered education for social studies teachers must be development of cognitive civic skills, which are included in the second component of Figure 3.1. Cognitive civic skills enable citizens to identify, describe, explain, and evaluate information and ideas in order to make sense of their political and civic experiences. Thus, they might respond to those experiences reasonably and effectively; and when faced with public issues, they might adroitly make and defend decisions about them.

The third component of Figure 3.1 treats participatory civic skills, which empower citizens to influence public policy decisions and to hold accountable their representatives in government. In combination with cognitive civic skills, participatory civic skills are tools of citizenship whereby individuals, whether acting alone or in groups, can participate effectively to promote personal and common interests in response to public issues, to secure their rights, and to promote the common good.

Teaching and learning civic skills, both cognitive and participatory, and their connections to civic knowledge must be a part of a civics-centered education for teachers of the social studies. Teachers are not likely to be effective developers of civic skills among their students in elementary and secondary schools unless they have developed these skills through lessons and activities within their teacher education program. Thus, students in civics-centered programs of teacher education should continually be challenged to use information and ideas, individually and collectively, to analyze and respond to public issues as reflective thinkers, deliberative decision makers, and responsible participators in political and civic life. They regularly should use and evaluate instructional materials and methods that exemplify how to teach civic skills for democratic citizenship.

The fourth and final component of education for citizenship in a democracy pertains to civic dispositions, which are traits of character necessary to the preservation and improvement of a constitutional representative democracy. If citizens would enjoy the privileges and rights of their polity, they must take responsibility for them by promoting the common good and participating constructively in the political and civic life of the community. Taking responsibility for the well being of government and civil society in which the rights and dignity of all persons are respected equally requires civic virtue in combination with the Tocquevillian idea of "self-interest rightly understood."[3] So, civic virtues such as self-discipline, civility, honesty, trust, courage, compassion, tolerance, temperance, and respect for the worth and dignity of all individuals are indispensable to the proper functioning of a democratic civil society and constitutional government. These characteristics must be nurtured through various social agencies, including the school, to sustain a healthy constitutional representative democracy.

Like civic skills, civic dispositions must be treated centrally in the education of social studies teachers. Otherwise, prospective teachers will not be prepared to nurture the democratic attitudes and traits of character in elementary and secondary school students, which are necessary for the maintenance and improvement of the best qualities of our political and civic life. So, students in civics-centered teacher education courses regularly should encounter instructional methods and materials designed to develop among learners the civic dispositions of democratic citizenship.

Effective education for citizenship in a democracy conjoins the four components in Figure 3.1, which interrelate civic knowledge, cognitive civic skills, participatory civic skills, and civic dispositions. Effective teaching and learning of civic knowledge, for example, requires that it be connected to civic skills and dispositions in various kinds of activities, which involve application of core concepts through exercise of civic skills and dispositions. Elevation of one component over the other—for example, civic knowledge over skills or vice-versa—is a pedagogical flaw that impedes civic learning (Bruer 1993, 15; Shanker 1997, 5). Thus, civics-centered teacher education programs should stress the blending and balancing of core content, processes, and skills in order to develop effective teachers of citizenship in a democracy.

The kind of civic education represented by our four-component model can yield citizens with deep understanding of the essential concepts and principles of democracy, strong commitment to them based on reason, high capacity for using them to analyze, appraise, and decide about the issues and problems of the political world, and the competence to act responsibly and effectively as engaged citizens to influence their civil society and government. But this desirable result will not be achieved unless the components of civic education are addressed adequately in well-designed programs for the preparation of social studies teachers (Butts 1989, 226-279; Niemi and Junn 1998, 158-159). Teachers cannot teach what they do not know and are unable to do. If they do not learn the principles and practices of democracy, and how to teach them, then they will not be prepared to educate their students for citizenship in a democracy. Let us, then, turn to the implementation of our four-component model (Figure 3.1) in programs of teacher education. How can it be done?

Implementation of the Model: Focus on Civic Knowledge

Implementation of the knowledge dimension of our model is founded on the assumption that all knowledge is **not** of equal worth. Rather, some ideas, information, and issues should be viewed by teachers and students as more important for particular purposes and thereby more worthy of emphasis in the school curriculum than other subject matter (Bruer 1993, 63-79; Cromer 1997, 177-184).

Students in civics-centered teacher education courses should learn that all knowledge is not equal in its value for constructive engagement in the political and civic life of a democracy. For example, concepts on the substance of democracy, listed in Figure 3.2, are prerequisites to the development and maintenance of an active and responsible community of self-governing citizens. Without this kind of common civic knowledge, which can be developed through common learning experiences in school, citizens are unable to act together to analyze public policy issues or problems, to make cogent decisions about them, or to participate intelligently to resolve them (Niemi and Junn 198, 19-20).

This list of core concepts in Figure 3.2 was developed from an extensive review of literature on the theory and practice of democracy.[4] A systematic discussion of each concept, its relationship to other concepts in this set, and the application of the set to civic education can be found in the first chapter of *Principles and Practices of Education for Democratic Citizenship: International Perspectives and Projects* (Patrick 1999b, 1-40). Each concept in this list and its connections to other basic ideas in democratic theory can also be found, among much broader treatments of democratic ideas, in such widely recognized standard works on civic education for democracy as *Civitas: A Framework for Civic Education* (Bahmueller and Quigley 1991), *National Standards for Civics and Government* (Center for Civic Education 1994), and *An International Framework for Education in Democracy* (Center for Civic Education 2001). So, the core concepts in Figure 3.2 can be presented justifiably as a generally acceptable and minimally essential set of ideas by which to construct the knowledge component of civic education in elementary and secondary schools as well as in civics-centered programs for the preparation of social studies teachers.[5]

Research on the learning of civic knowledge shows strong connections between conceptual understanding of core democratic principles, such as those in Figure 3.2, and "enlightened political engagement,"[6] which construct subsumes such attributes of democratic citizenship as political inter-est, sense of political efficacy, political tolerance, commitment to basic civil liberties, and civic competence (Delli Carpini and Keeter 1996, 19-20; Nie, Junn, and Stehlik-Barry 1996, 14-38; Niemi and Junn 1998, 9-10; Putnam 2000, 35-36). So knowledgeable citizens are better citizens of a democracy in regard to their possession and use of civic skills and civic dispositions, such as those in Figure 3.1.

A recent international assessment involving 14-year-old respondents in 28 countries found a strong correlation between civic knowledge and propen-sity to participate in civic and political life. The researchers concluded, "The more young people know about the functioning and the values of democ-racy, the more they expect to exercise this fundamental right [to political participation] of an adult citizen. This reinforces the importance of high quality and motivating civic education programs to foster knowledge of content and skills in teaching political communication" (Torney-Purta et al. 2001, 155). In particular, deep knowledge or conceptual understanding of core ideas in the theory and practice of democracy, such as those in Figure 3.2, is the foundation of competent and responsible citizenship in a democ-racy. According to Nie, Junn, and Stehlik-Barry (1996, 41), the kind of "ver-bal cognitive proficiency" that enables one to use core concepts to interpret information and act effectively in political and civic life "is the most rele-vant cognitive ability in relationship to democratic citizenship."

Concepts at the core of education for citizenship in a democracy (Fig-ure 3.2) might be used to structure the content and instructional activities of civics-centered teacher education courses. If so, then this set of ideas and the information and examples denoted by them could bring cohesion, coherence, and cogency to the content base of civics-centered teacher edu-cation courses. Thus, such common weaknesses of teaching methods cours-es as fragmentation of subject matter and subordination of content to process might be avoided.

Throughout a civics-centered teaching methods course, the concepts in Figure 3.2 could be the substantive focal points for planning, constructing, and demonstrating lessons. Various kinds of instructional materials and methods could be used consistently and coherently in terms of the core concepts on citizenship in a democracy. Further, connections easily could be made between the core concepts in Figure 3.2 and the curriculum frame-works, content standards, and courses of study commonly used in ele-mentary and secondary schools, such as history and civics courses of elementary and secondary schools. For example, the core concepts per-meate the instructional materials of *We the People. . . The Citizen and the Con-stitution*, a three-level civics program for elementary and secondary school students (Center for Civic Education 1997b).[7]

Figure 3.2

CONCEPTS AT THE CORE OF EDUCATION FOR CITIZENSHIP IN A DEMOCRACY (THE CIVIC KNOWLEDGE COMPONENT)

1. **REPRESENTATIVE DEMOCRACY (REPUBLICANISM)**
   a. Popular sovereignty (government by consent of the governed, the people)
   b. Representation and accountability in a government of, by, and for the people
   c. Free, fair, and competitive elections of representatives in government
   d. Comprehensive eligibility to participate freely to vote and campaign in elections
   e. Inclusive access to participate freely to promote personal and common interests
   f. Majority rule of the people for the common good

2. **CONSTITUTIONALISM**
   a. Rule of law in the government, society, and economy
   b. Limited and empowered government to secure rights of the people
   c. Separation and sharing of powers in government
   d. Independent judiciary with power of judicial or constitutional review

3. **RIGHTS (LIBERALISM)**
   a. Human rights/constitutional rights
   b. Political rights
   c. Personal or private rights
   d. Economic, social, cultural, and environmental rights
   e. Rights associated with negative and positive constitutionalism

4. **CITIZENSHIP**
   a. Membership in a people based on legal qualifications of citizenship
   b. Rights, responsibilities, and roles of citizenship
   c. Civic identity and other types of identity (e.g., ethnic, racial, religious)
   d. Rights of individual citizens and rights of groups of citizens

5. **CIVIL SOCIETY (FREE AND OPEN SOCIAL SYSTEM)**
   a. Voluntary membership in non-governmental organizations/civil associations
   b. Freedom of association, assembly, and social choice
   c. Pluralism/multiple and overlapping group memberships and identities
   d. Social regulation for the common good (rule of law, customs, traditions, virtues)

6. **MARKET ECONOMY (FREE AND OPEN ECONOMIC SYSTEM)**
   a. Freedom of exchange and economic choice
   b. Freedom to own and use property for personal gain
   c. Economic regulation for the common good (rule of law, customs, traditions, virtues)

7. **TYPES OF PUBLIC ISSUES**
   a. Majority rule and minority rights (limits on majorities and minorities/individuals)
   b. Liberty and equality (combining negative and positive constitutionalism)
   c. Liberty and order (limits on power and on liberty to achieve security for rights)
   d. Individual interests and the common good (limits of personal and public choice)
   e. Unity and diversity (conjoining civic identity with social/cultural identities)

The set of concepts listed in Figure 3.2 corresponds specifically to item 1-a in Figure 3.1, the four-component model on education for citizenship in a democracy. Further, the core concepts are variously applicable to each subsequent item of the civic knowledge category of the model (see items 1-b, 1-c, 1-d, 1-e, 1-f, and 1-g). For example, item 1-b pertains to public issues in history and current political and civic life about the meanings and applications of the core concepts. There may be, and certainly has been, general agreement, even consensus, about the fundamental worth of core concepts in Figure 3.2. The history of the United States, however, has been marked by public conflicts or issues about how to implement the core ideas in government, politics, and civil society.

These public issues in United States history can be focal points of teaching and learning in civics-centered teacher education courses. The core concepts and the issues associated with them can be found in every period of our national history and are deeply rooted in the founding of the Republic (Patrick 1995).[8] For example, civics-centered teacher education courses can involve students in analysis, evaluation, and decision making about constitutional and political issues embedded in primary documents, such as papers of the Federalists and Anti-Federalists of the founding era, or in Supreme Court opinions (for the Court and in dissent) in landmark cases throughout our national history. Thus, students preparing to become teachers might learn how to teach core concepts on democracy in connection with pivotal constitutional and political issues in United States history (Patrick and Long 1999).[9]

Toni Marie Massaro, the author of *Constitutional Literacy: A Core Curriculum for a Multicultural Nation*, persuasively advocates teaching and learning core ideas in constitutional history through analyses and evaluation of core constitutional conflicts or issues. She recommends a core curriculum consisting of the kind of civic knowledge exemplified in Figure 3.2 and the constitutional issues in history associated with political and governmental practices of the core ideas about democracy. Mastery of her proposed core curriculum, she maintains, will yield "constitutional literacy, which means not only recognition of constitutional terms, constitutional dilemmas, and historical assumptions on which the Constitution arguably rests but also the recognition of the paradox on which the document is based, its dynamism, and its multiple contested interpretations" (Massaro 1993, 153).

Massaro's proposal for the reform of civic education through teaching and learning core ideas and issues in constitutional history stresses the fundamental importance of a certain type of content: concepts on democracy and the critical controversies about them. So, she urges, we must teach "the conflicts" in conjunction with core civic knowledge (Massaro 1993, 128).

Only such a curriculum, she argues, "is likely to improve the quality of our public discourse and to prepare our students adequately for the complex demands of American citizenship in the twenty-first century" (Massaro 1993, 153). The kind of content-based curriculum reform advocated by Massaro is compatible with our four-component model (Figure 3.1) and the core concepts pertaining to the civic knowledge category of the model (Figure 3.2).

Another compatible example has been provided by R. Freeman Butts, which he labels "Twelve Tables of Civism for the Modern American Republic." His conception of the civic knowledge domain includes twelve core concepts: justice, freedom, equality, diversity, authority, privacy, participation, due process, truth, property, patriotism, and human rights (Butts 1989, 282). In line with curricular recommendations by Massaro and us, Butts emphasizes the analysis of public issues associated with his core ideas. For example, he urges examination of controversy about the latitude and limits of the individual's right to freedom. He also encourages investigation into "legitimate" and "corrupted" forms of the core concepts. Anarchy, for instance, is the "corrupted" form of freedom.

Butts, like us, would apply his conception of core content to the civic education of students in elementary and secondary schools and to the civic education of participants in teacher education programs. We agree with him that core content, some type of justifiable civic knowledge, must be at the center of teacher education for social studies teachers. However, no matter how well it is conceived and implemented, civic knowledge alone is not sufficient to education for citizenship in a democracy. The core knowledge component must be connected interactively with the civic skills and civic dispositions components. How might this be done in civics-centered teacher education?

Implementation of the Model: Focus on Civic Skills

The civic knowledge component of our model, though central to the education of citizens in a democracy, must be complemented by the development of civic skills and civic dispositions that enable and encourage participation.[10] Civics-centered courses in teacher education, therefore, should require aspiring teachers to develop a thorough understanding of each component of our model as well as their dynamic relationships to each other, to acquire the skills required to teach each component, and to expose students to exemplary methods and materials across the components of our model.

Effective participation in democracy requires the frequent utilization of civic skills. To participate effectively in civic and political life, for example, citizens must be able to identify important public problems, to describe them and explain their importance to others, to deliberate with others about possible solutions, and ultimately, to evaluate, take, and defend their own position to influence others. These experiences, according to political scientists Amy Gutmann and Dennis Thompson, should be important components in the education of citizens in a democracy:

> To prepare their students for citizenship, schools must go beyond teaching literacy and numeracy, though both are of course prerequisites for deliberating about public problems. Schools should aim to develop their students' capacities to understand different perspectives, communicate their understandings to other people, and engage in the give and take of moral argument with a view of making mutually acceptable decisions. These goals, which entail cultivating moral character and intellectual skills at the same time, are likely to require some significant changes in traditional civics education, which has neglected teaching this kind of moral reasoning about politics. (Gutmann and Thompson 1996, 339)

Without mastery of the civic skills and knowledge components, which are the tools of citizenship, citizens who desire to participate in civic and political life are highly disadvantaged (Delli Carpini and Keeter 1996, 60).

The effective teaching of civic skills assumes that teachers possess a well-developed understanding of all the components of our model (Figure 3.1) and the dynamic interplay among them. Civic skills are learned best in an environment that also encourages important civic dispositions and provides multiple opportunities to practice civic skills in concert with concepts and principles at the core of education for citizenship in a democracy (see Figure 3-2). Aspiring teachers need to develop, through civics-centered methods courses, the capacity for teaching across the components of the model.

It is difficult, if not impossible, for students to develop and refine important civic skills without providing them opportunities for practice under the guidance of a competent teacher. Even in the absence of a specific program or unit that emphasizes civic participation or thinking, the dynamics of the learning environment provide many opportunities for students to practice and refine civic skills. Teachers who closely monitor the thinking and interactions of students in cooperative learning situations, for example, will certainly find many opportunities to guide students to more sophisticated levels of participation and cognition that are consistent with education for citizenship in a democracy.

Civics-centered teacher education courses should help students develop a sophisticated understanding of important cognitive and participatory capacities and their relationship to the theory and practice of democratic citizenship. Students in pre-service teacher education courses, therefore, should be assigned readings and be allowed opportunities to analyze and discuss civic skills and their importance to democratic citizenship from sources such as the *Civics Framework for the 1998 National Assessment of Educational Progress* (NAEP Civics Consensus Project 1996) or *Civitas: A Framework for Civic Education* (Bahmueller and Quigley 1991).

Through civics-centered teacher education courses students should also be given opportunities to practice intellectual and participatory skills. However, we do not advocate the practice of civic skills, in civics-centered teacher education courses or in the schools, in isolation from the other components of our model; rather, students should practice and refine their civic skills using issues and concepts at the core of education for citizenship while at the same developing important civic dispositions. We assume, as do many democratic theorists, that the social and intellectual capital necessary for effective democratic citizenship is learned best through participation.[11] Students could be provided, or they might identify for themselves, an important public issue to describe, analyze, explain, and monitor. The methods instructor, like the effective civics teacher in the schools, should model effective teaching by guiding and evaluating the thinking and interactions of individuals and groups and highlighting for students the important civic skills they practice.

Civics-centered teacher education courses should expose students to exemplary methods and materials that emphasize the development of civic skills through in depth study of public issues.[12] Broadly speaking, issues-centered lessons or units pose social questions confronting citizens. In the process of examining questions about public issues reflectively and reaching decisions about them, there is an assessment of evidence, appraisal of competing values, and evaluation of possible outcomes.

We the People. . . Project Citizen is an exemplary program that might be used in teacher education courses. It focuses on public policy issues and the processes of democratic citizenship that enable and encourage participation in government and civil society.[13] The program requires students to become actively involved with governmental and civil society organizations to address a school or community issue while practicing critical thinking, dialogue, debate, negotiation, tolerance, decision making, and civic action (Tolo 1998, 2, 17).[14] The purpose of *Project Citizen*, then, is to motivate and empower adolescents to exercise the rights and accept the responsibilities of democratic citizenship through the intensive study of a school or community issue.

After selecting an important school or community issue, a class of students involved with *Project Citizen* is divided into research teams to gather information from multiple sources (e.g., libraries, newspapers, community members, community organizations, legislative offices, administrative agencies, and electronic sources). The class is again divided into cooperative teams for an in-depth focus on one of the stages of inquiry and engagement in the public policy making process (Center for Civic Education 1998, 24-25):

- *Explaining the problem.* This group is responsible for explaining the problem the class has chosen to study. The group also should explain why the problem is important and why a particular level of government or governmental agency should deal with it.
- *Evaluating alternative policies to deal with the problem.* This group is responsible for explaining alternative policies designed to solve the problem.
- *Developing a public policy the class will support.* This group is responsible for developing and justifying a specific public policy for which there is consensus in the class. The policy, however, must not violate federal or state constitutions or statutes.
- *Developing an action plan to get government to accept the class policy.* This group is responsible for developing an action plan showing how citizens can influence the appropriate government body or agency with authority to adopt the policy the class supports.

The efforts of each cooperative team are displayed in a four-part (one for each group) portfolio exhibit and documentation binder. The culminating activity for the program is a simulated legislative hearing, which provides students with an opportunity to demonstrate their knowledge by playing roles of expert witnesses; they testify before a panel of community members, who play roles of government officials. During the hearing, each of the four portfolio groups prepares and presents a statement on its section of the portfolio. After each opening statement, the panel of community members asks the students questions and judges the quality of each team's work according to specific rubrics provided to each judge. The format of the simulated hearing offers students an opportunity to demonstrate their knowledge and understanding of how public policy is formulated while providing teachers with an excellent means to assess student performance.

Project Citizen provides students with multiple opportunities to practice and refine their civic skills through the in-depth study of a highly relevant school or community issue. A recent quasi-experimental study of the effects of *Project Citizen* on the civic development of adolescent students in Indiana, Latvia, and Lithuania, conducted by the Social Studies Development Center and the Indiana Center for Evaluation of Indiana University, found that the program had a statistically significant effect on students' civic knowledge, propensity to participate (civic disposition), and self-perceived civic skills (Vontz, Metcalf, and Patrick 2000).

The National Issues Forums (NIF) is another example of an issue-centered activity that emphasizes the development of cognitive and participatory skills important for democratic citizenship.[15] NIF is an informal, non-partisan, national network of school, community, and civic organizations that brings citizens together to deliberate about important public issues. The NIF conducts and administers forums so that citizens may "work through complex public policy issues, and make judgments about the range of actions that they, as a public, can support" (Peng 2000, 74-75).

Many high school teachers elect to have their students practice deliberative democracy through NIF materials. A recent pilot study of high school students found that participation in a NIF program enhanced important civic skills, such as listening skills; discussion skills; skills in identifying and framing an issue for public deliberation; capacity for understanding and engaging complex public issues; participatory and intellectual skills associated with deliberation; capacity for identifying and respecting the rights of others; capacity for identifying the general, common, or public interest; and decision making skills (Peng 2000, 78-81).

If the NIF is to have the greatest impact on students' civic development, then students, directed by a competent teacher, should practice relevant civic skills in advance of their participation in a forum. Before participation in a NIF program, teachers may ask students to research and describe the issue, explain it to others, evaluate possible solutions, take and defend a reasoned position, interact with others to promote their interests, monitor new developments, and deliberate with their classmates. In addition, a teacher who is well-versed across the dimensions of our model (Figure 3.1) should help students relate the issue to important democratic principles and concepts and use participation in the forum as a way to promote civic dispositions, such as promoting the common good and respecting individual rights.

By emphasizing the cognitive and participatory processes of democracy, *Project Citizen* and the NIF are particularly well-suited to complement a well-structured, content-based civics curriculum. They provide students with opportunities to use knowledge acquired through formal instruction in conjunction with their practice of civic skills. Thus, they are outstanding examples of methods and materials that support the school's civic mission, and they should be used as exemplars in civics-centered teacher education courses. In addition, instructors should consider modeling the implementation of such programs by asking pre-service teachers to participate in a NIF program or in the in-depth study of a public issue through *Project Citizen*. Thus, they would develop civic skills of the kind they should teach to students in elementary and secondary schools.

Implementation of the Model: Focus on Civic Dispositions

The education of citizens in a democracy also must emphasize the cultivation of civic dispositions, which encourage responsible and humane participation in civic and political life; see the fourth component of our model (Figure 3.1). These "habits of the heart," as Alexis de Tocqueville called civic dispositions, are necessarily intertwined with the civic knowledge and civic skills components of democratic citizenship. Education for democratic citizenship requires the development of those traits of public and private character that compel citizens to exercise the rights and responsibilities of democratic citizenship and to promote the common good. Judge Learned Hand's famous quotation captures their importance in a democracy: "I often wonder whether we do not rest our hopes too much upon constitutions, upon laws, and upon courts. These are false hopes; believe me, these are false hopes. Liberty lies in the hearts of men and women, when it dies there, no constitution, no law, no court can save it" (Center for Civic Education 1997a, 66).

The exact dispositions and how many citizens must possess them are contested issues among democratic theorists. However, many theorists and political thinkers, from the founding era forward, have emphasized the importance of virtue among the citizenry in a constitutional representative democracy. Political scientist James Q. Wilson recently wrote (1985, 15): "In almost every area of important public concern, we are seeking to induce persons to act virtuously. In the long run, the public interest depends on private virtue."

Many scholars contend that participation in government and civil society equips citizens with the social capital and trust necessary for their participation in democratic politics and helps them to develop attitudes that motivate them to participate (Walzer 1992). According to Robert D. Putnam (1995, 664), social capital refers to those "features of social life—networks, norms, and trust—that enable participants to act together more effectively to pursue shared goals." Social capital consists of those civic skills and dispositions that enable the achievement through democratic government and civil society of desired and shared outcomes. Whereas social capital is developed through participation in civil society, a vibrant civil society depends on individuals who possess social capital; both are prerequisites of a workable democracy. Participation in government and civil society, then, is viewed as a strong socializing force in society and one of our primary vehicles to the development of the civic skills and civic dispositions components of our model (Figure 3.1).

Teachers who develop an understanding and appreciation of civic dispositions and their important relationship to the theory and practice of democracy are most likely to succeed in assisting their students to develop social capital and civic character. Even in the absence of a specific program, unit, or lesson, the dynamics of the classroom environment offer multiple opportunities for teachers to facilitate the development of civic dispositions. Competent teachers may help students develop important civic dispositions, for example, through positive examples in historical literature, role modeling, and the study of ethical problems in history. Further, teaching methods that encourage free expression of ideas in an open classroom environment have been related empirically to development of democratic dispositions, civic skills, and knowledge of democracy (Niemi and Junn 1999, 151-152). An international assessment of civic education and achievement revealed a strong relationship between the students' beliefs that they could speak freely about issues in their classroom and their development of knowledge, skills, and dispositions associated with democratic citizenship. "The extent to which students experience their classrooms as places to investigate issues and explore their opinions and those of their peers has been found to be an even more vital part of civic education" (Torney-Purta et al. 2001, 137).

Civics-centered teacher education courses should help students to identify those traits of character that are most consistent with a democratic polity and to develop them through warranted methods of teaching. Thus, students preparing to become teachers should analyze and discuss civic dispositions in such sources as the *Civics Framework for the 1998 National Assessment of Educational Progress* (NAEP Civics Consensus Project 1996) or *Civitas: A Framework for Civic Education* (Bahmueller and Quigley 1991). Such opportunities will not only deepen their understanding of civic dispositions, they will also enhance their ability to cultivate them in their elementary or secondary school students. Further, students in social studies teacher education programs should be required to develop lessons or units that aim, at least partially, to develop civic dispositions. Finally, they should both observe and practice methods of teaching and classroom management that are associated with development of democratic civic dispositions among students, such as maintaining an "open classroom climate" for discussions of political ideas and issues (Torney-Purta et al. 2001, 137-140).

Students in pre-service teacher education courses should also be exposed to methods and materials that emphasize the development of civic dispositions in conjunction with civic knowledge and civic skills. For example, *Reasoning With Democratic Values: Ethical Problems in United States History* by Alan Lockwood and David Harris (1985) emphasizes the values that undergird American democracy and the tensions between them. The Lockwood and Harris materials require students to examine and discuss openly and freely events involving public issues and ethical dilemmas in United States history (e.g., the Alien and Sedition Acts of 1798 or Japanese-American relocation during World War II) through a framework of democratic values (e.g., life, liberty, property, authority, justice), which may be in tension or conflict.

Pre-service teacher education students might be asked to analyze and evaluate public issues and policy decisions involving conflicts between values, such as national security and civil liberties. The instructor may model a lesson from the Lockwood and Harris material and discuss with students its effectiveness in developing civic dispositions and skills. Such activities not only teach important civic dispositions and skills, they are also likely to deepen students' knowledge of key events in United States history and the core concepts or principles of constitutional democracy connected to the events.

Character education is another category of methods and materials that has potential to develop important civic dispositions in students. For many advocates of character education, teaching "good character" necessarily involves cultivating in students those civic dispositions that are consistent with democratic governance in a constitutional representative democracy (e.g., promoting the general welfare, respecting the rights of others, participating responsibly and effectively in civic and political life).

Character education, as a stated goal or as an incidental outcome of instruction, has always been a part of teaching and learning (Schubert 1997, 17).[16] A wide variety of reform initiatives have been classified as "character education."[17] Despite the broad array of character education initiatives and methods, a few general principles seem descriptive of most programs. Generally, character education is the deliberate attempt to cultivate in students some set of virtues or dispositions.[18] By definition, virtues are desirable traits of character such as honesty, patience, courage, and humility. Virtues, then, transcend time and culture, although some cultures may emphasize some virtues more than others (Lickona 1998, 77). Virtues are good for the individual as well as the community—enabling people to live harmoniously within themselves and with others. Although thinking about and discussing virtues are important components of character education, virtues are not merely thoughts, but habits of behavior (Lickona 1998, 78).

Proponents of character education connect it to the school's civic mission (Eberly 1995).[19] In discussing the importance of focusing attention on character development in our Nation's schools, Paul D. Houston, executive director of the American Association of School Administrators, articulates a clear connection between character education and civic education:

> If you look back in history, you will find the core mission of public education in America was to create places of civic virtue for our children and for our society. As education undergoes the rigors of re-examination and the need for reinvention, it is crucial to remember that the key role of public schools is to preserve democracy. That sense of education as an instrument (a means to a good job) misses the point that the real goal of education is to produce a total person, one who has a sense of efficacy and a sense of responsibility to self, as well as others. (Houston 1998, 6)

According to many proponents, the dispositions and habits that form the core of many character education programs and activities are consistent with those that sustain and improve constitutional representative democracies.[20]

Schools and teachers interested in conjoining character education and civic education should use civic dispositions and democratic values to drive the conceptualization and implementation of character education programs and activities. R. Freeman Butts' "Twelve Tables of Civism for the Modern American Republic" include a detailed list of important democratic principles and values, which imply civic dispositions (Butts 1989, 280-309). As with the other components of our model, civic dispositions should be developed in concert with the other components of the model.

Aspiring social studies teachers should be given opportunities to examine, discuss, and evaluate the potential value of various conceptions of character education in fostering civic dispositions in concert with civic knowledge and skills. They might also be asked, as a class assignment, to design a unit or lessons that emphasize civic dispositions. By focusing on the dispositions of democratic citizenship and the values that undergird a democratic polity, character education can be an effective means to cultivating responsible democratic citizenship.

Conclusion: Commentary and Recommendations

The central theme of this chapter is a time-honored assertion: democratic civic education should be at the core of social studies teacher education in a constitutional democratic republic, such as the United States of America. This venerable assertion is based on three related assumptions. **First,** a democratic political order cannot be sustained unless a sufficient proportion of individuals within each succeeding generation learns the civic knowledge, skills, and dispositions needed by citizens to make the polity work. **Second,** sufficient numbers of persons in each succeeding generation of citizens are not likely to learn essential civic knowledge, skills, and dispositions unless they are taught them deliberately and effectively by well-educated teachers in primary and secondary schools. **Third,** social studies teachers in public and private schools are not likely to teach effectively the civic knowledge, skills, and dispositions needed by citizens to sustain and improve their democracy unless they are equipped to do so through civics-centered teacher education courses, which are connected to relevant university-based history and social science courses.

Since civics-centered teacher education is a categorical imperative in a constitutional representative democracy, we must be concerned about how to do it. Consider this short list of concluding recommendations, which is derived from the body of this chapter.

1. Construct some version of a four-component model of education for citizenship in a democracy, such as the one in Figure 3.1, and use it to guide the development, implementation, and evaluation of civics-centered courses and programs for the education of social studies teachers.

2. Construct a set of concepts and principles on the theory and practice of democracy, such as the list in Figure 3.2, and use it as the civic knowledge foundation for social studies teacher education courses.

3. Use interactively the four components of the model on education for citizenship in a democracy, or some similar model, so that each component is conjoined with every other one in the instructional methods and materials of social studies teacher education courses.

4. Use the four-component model in Figure 3.1, or some form of it, to guide the construction of connections between social studies teacher education courses and relevant courses for aspiring teachers in such academic disciplines as history, political science, economics, geography, sociology, and anthropology.

5. Use the four-component model in Figure 3.1, or something like it, to teach students in teacher education courses the necessity of "conscious social reproduction" to sustain liberty and order in a constitutional representative democracy, such as the government of the United States of America (Gutmann 1999, 39-41). "Conscious social reproduction" signifies Amy Gutmann's understanding of the process by which a free and open society, with a democratic and liberal political order, is maintained and improved. Gutmann claims, and we agree, that the open and free democratic society, if it would survive, must transmit its civic and political traditions from one generation to the next. "We are all committed to re-creating the society that we share" says Gutmann (1999, 39). Stephen Macedo concurs, "The project of creating citizens is one that every liberal democratic state must somehow undertake" (2000, ix). However, a central tradition and essential element of our free and open democratic society is the capacity of citizens to comprehend and think critically about the content and processes of the political socialization that they inevitably experience (Cremin 1977, 36-37).[21] "It follows," says Gutmann, "that a society in support of conscious social reproduction must educate all educable children to be capable of participating in collectively shaping their society" to sustain and improve it (1999, 39). If so, education for citizenship in a constitutional representative democracy is true to a core principle of its theory and practice—the individual's right to liberty within conditions of an open and orderly society (see Figure 3.2).

The five recommendations in our short list are directed to the conservation of a hallowed American educational tradition: the civic mission of schools (Patrick 2000b, 103-105). This mission entails a core curriculum available to all students and future citizens, which would enable them to learn, "the basic concepts and values underlying our democratic political community and constitutional order" (Butts, 1989, 308). However, if we would maintain and advance the civic mission of common schools in the United States, then we must revitalize it in programs of teacher education, which produce and nurture the teachers of our children. This must be, as R. Freeman Butts exclaims, "the first priority in the liberal and professional education" of social studies teachers. Let us resolve resoundingly to carry out this "first priority" for the good of our profession and our democracy.

Notes

1. Throughout its history the National Council for the Social Studies (NCSS) has proclaimed education for citizenship in a democracy to be the primary goal of social studies education; see, for example, *Curriculum Standards for Social Studies* (Washington, DC: National Council for the Social Studies, 1994), vii.

2. A previous formulation of the model depicted in Figure 3.1 was developed by John J. Patrick and published initially in 1999.

3. In his celebrated work, *Democracy in America*, Alexis de Tocqueville wrote about the need for voluntary civic and political participation through freely formed civil associations to maintain the general welfare of civil society and government. He referred to this kind of responsible civic behavior as "self-interest rightly understood" because through voluntary contributions of time and effort to the good of the community, the citizens helped one another to maintain conditions of public well-being needed for their fruitful pursuit of personal and private interests and fulfillment. Tocqueville wrote, "The principle of self-interest rightly understood is not a lofty one, but it is clear and sure. . . . Each American knows when to sacrifice some of his private interests to save the rest." See Volume II of *Democracy in America*, Phillips Bradley, editor (New York: Alfred A. Knopf, 1987, published originally in Paris, France in 1839), 122-123.

4. The core concepts in Figure 3.2 are derived from widely recognized standard works in political theory, such as Robert A. Dahl, *On Democracy* (New Haven, CT: Yale University Press, 1998); David Held, *Models of Democracy* (Stanford, CA: Stanford University Press, 1996); Samuel P. Huntington, *The Third Wave: Democratization in the Late Twentieth Century* (Norman: University of Oklahoma Press, 1991); Sanford Lakoff, *Democracy: History, Theory, Practice* (Boulder, CO: Westview Press, 1996); Paul Rahe, *Republics, Ancient and Modern* (Chapel Hill: University of North Carolina Press, 1992); Giovanni Sartori, *The Theory of Democracy Revisited* (Chatham, NJ: Chatham House Press, 1987); and Alain Touraine, *What Is Democracy?* (Boulder, CO: Westview Press, 1997). See also selected articles in Seymour Martin Lipset, ed., *The Encyclopedia of Democracy*, Four Volumes, (Washington, DC: Congressional Quarterly, Inc., 1995).

5. A previous formulation of this list of core concepts on citizenship in a democracy (Figure 3.2) was developed by John J. Patrick and published in 1999.

6. Nie, Junn, and Stehlik-Barry have constructed the concept of "enlightened political engagement" to denote characteristics of authentic democratic citizenship. Deep understanding of core principles of democracy is at the foundation of a citizen's capacity for "enlightened political engagement" (1996, 14-20).

7. An excellent curriculum for teaching elementary and secondary students about core concepts on democracy and issues connected to them is *We the People. . . the Citizen and the Constitution*, published by the Center for Civic Education. This civics curriculum includes three sets of materials: the first for students in grades 4 or 5, the second for students in grades 7 or 8, and the third for high school students in grades 11 or 12. These instructional materi-

als can also be used in civics-centered teacher education courses to prepare future social studies teachers.

8. During the founding era of United States history, there was a continuous and profound public debate about the meanings and applications of core ideas about political and civic life such as popular sovereignty, republicanism (representative democracy), federalism, constitutionalism, and liberalism (security for individual rights). The debate was a conflict within consensus, an argument about how best to implement generally accepted ideas on good government. This type of public debate on our constitutional and political order, anchored in core ideas of the founding era, has continued throughout United States history and marks the pivotal points of our national history. Core ideas of the founding era, the primary documents in which they are embedded, public debates about them, and how to teach the conflicts on these core ideas are all treated in John J. Patrick, *Founding the Republic: A Documentary History* (Westport, CT: Greenwood Press, 1995).

9. Constitutional issues, rooted in the founding era, are treated in relationship to themes in United States history in various publications. For example, Greenwood Press has developed a series of books for teachers on constitutional issues in U.S. history, which might be used in civics-centered methods of teaching courses. See books in this series, such as Frederick D. Drake and Lynn R. Nelson, *States' Rights and American Federalism: A Documentary History* (Westport, CT: Greenwood Press, 1999); Robert P. Green, Jr., *Equal Protection and the African American Constitutional Experience: A Documentary History* (Westport, CT: Greenwood Press, 2000); Sheila Suess Kennedy, *Free Expression in America: A Documentary History* (Westport, CT: Greenwood Press, 1999); and John J. Patrick and Gerald P. Long, *Constitutional Debates on Freedom of Religion: A Documentary History* (Westport, CT: Greenwood Press, 1999).

10. For an extended discussion of the relationship of civic skills to democratic theory and practice and their relationship to the other components of democratic citizenship in our model, see John J. Patrick, "Education for Constructive Engagement of Citizens in Democratic Civil Society and Government," in *Principles and Practices of Education for Democratic Citizenship: International Perspectives and Projects*, edited by Charles F. Bahmueller and John J. Patrick (Bloomington, IN: ERIC Clearinghouse for Social Studies/Social Science Education, 1999), 41-60.

11. Many democratic theorists have discussed the important relationship between participation in government and civil society and the development of intellectual and social capital necessary for effective participation. See, for example, Robert D. Putnam, "Bowling Alone: America's Declining Social Capital," *Journal of Democracy* 6 (January 1995): 65-78; and see Samuel P. Huntington, "Democracy for the Long-Haul," in *Consolidating the Third Wave Democracies: Themes and Perspectives*, edited by Larry Diamond, Marc F. Plattner, Yun-han Chu, and Hung-mao Tien (Baltimore: The Johns Hopkins University Press, 1997), 3-13.

12. Although advocates have traced the roots of issue-centered or problem-based civic education as far back as Socrates, in the United States the origin of the approach is most commonly associated with the Progressive era. Progressive-era leaders such as Henry Bourne, John Dewey, Arthur William Dunn, Jeremiah Jenks, William Heard Kilpatrick, Colonel Francis Parker, and David Snedden, to name a few, advocated some version of the in-depth study of social problems to develop in students the capacity for good citizenship. The seminal 1916 report of the National Education Association (NEA) Committee on the Social Studies reflects the prevailing attitudes of many Progressive-era leaders by featuring issue-centered civic education as a primary method of civics instruction. For a discussion of Progressive-era antecedents to issue-centered civic education see Thomas S. Vontz and William A. Nixon, "Issue-Centered Civic Education Among Early Adolescents in the United States and Abroad," in *Principles and Practices of Education for Democratic Citizenship*, edited by Charles F. Bahmueller and John J. Patrick (Bloomington, IN: ERIC Clearinghouse for Social Studies/Social Science Education, 1999), 141-161.

13. First implemented in California in 1992 and expanded into a national program in 1995, *Project Citizen* was developed and promoted by the Center for Civic Education and the National Conference of State Legislators. For an extended discussion of *Project Citizen* and its effect on the civic development of adolescent students in Indiana, Latvia, and Lithuania, see Thomas S. Vontz, Kim K. Metcalf, and John J. Patrick, *Project Citizen and the Civic Development of Adolescent Students in Indiana, Latvia, and Lithuania* (Bloomington, IN: ERIC Clearinghouse for Social Studies/Social Science Education, 2000).

14. *Project Citizen* is similar to a variety of other proposals that call for students to deliberate about public policy issues. For an excellent discussion of the benefits of student engagement in real public policy issues and a proposal to employ a different model of public policy analysis see Walter C. Parker, "Toward an Aristocracy of Everyone: Policy Study in the High School Curriculum." *Theory and Research in Social Education* 27 (Winter 1999): 9-44.

15. For an extended discussion of the NIF and its effect on civic development of students see Ira Peng, "Effects of Public Deliberation on High School Students: Bridging the Disconnection Between Young People and Public Life," in *Education for Civic Engagement in Democracy: Service Learning and Other Promising Practices*, edited by Sheilah Mann and John J. Patrick (Bloomington, IN: ERIC Clearinghouse for Social Studies/Social Science Education, 2000), 73-87.

16. Advocates of character education often trace its roots to classical philosophers such as Aristotle. Aristotle's conception of practical wisdom or *phronesis*—knowledge that guides one's conduct (as opposed to theoretical or technical knowledge)—is seen as an important antecedent to the character education movement. "In the case of conduct," Aristotle declared, "the end consists not in gaining theoretical knowledge but rather in putting our knowledge into practice." Practical wisdom, according to Aristotle, was the highest form of knowledge because it helped to shape the individual virtues that form character and helped to organize them in the best way possible given some experience. Thus, the practical knowledge or wisdom that formed and shaped a person's character was not the application of technical or theoretical knowledge; rather, it was the kind of knowledge that governed one's behavior and made possible a virtuous life. See Steven S. Tigner, "Character Education: Outline of a Seven-Point Program." *Journal of Education* 175 (Spring 1993): 13-22.

17. In the United States, character education, with varying degrees of emphasis, has been a part of teaching and learning from the founding of our republic to the present. During the 20th century, the current character education reform movement can be viewed as a revival of the character education movement of the 1920s. Character education flourished during the 1920s in response to the irresponsible behavior of youth, which is often cited as a justification for current efforts in character development. The character education reform movement of the 1920s steadily declined in the decades that followed. Increasing pluralism, logical positivism, relativism, secularism, individualism, and a series of Supreme Court decisions that made educators reluctant to teach values, contributed to the decline and eventual demise of the 1920s movement, which had enough momentum to sustain itself into the 1950s. Although claims about its direct influence on the demise of the 1920s movement are spurious, the release of large-scale study on character education conducted by Hugh Hartshorne and Mark May, conducted from 1928 to 1930, concluded that character education programs of the decade had little influence on student behavior. See B. Edward McClellan, *Schools and the Shaping of Character: Moral Education in America, 1607-Present* (Bloomington, IN: ERIC Clearinghouse for Social Studies/Social Science Education, 1992). See also Alan L. Lockwood, "Character Education: The Ten Percent Solution." *Social Education* 55 (April/May 1991): 246-248) and James S. Leming, "Whither Goes Character Education? Objectives, Pedagogy, and Research in Education Programs." in *Journal of Education* 175 (Spring 1993): 11-34.

18. Conflict resolution, issue-centered education, social and moral development, ethical decision making, violence prevention, service learning, values education/clarification, citi-

zenship education, multicultural education, safety education, resiliency education, life skills programs, and tolerance education all contain a character education component. In addition, the content, pedagogy, and scope of current character education initiatives vary greatly. Some initiatives emphasize traits of character that focus on the individual while others emphasize those traits that are connected to the community. Some character education initiatives emphasize "moral development," others "neutral" traits of character (e.g., honesty), while others emphasize those traits of character Americans share regardless of their ethnic, cultural, or religious backgrounds. Character education can be conducted as a lesson, as a unit, or as a class in social studies or other subjects of the curriculum. In addition, character education may be implemented across subjects as school-wide or district-wide initiatives. Role modeling, literature, direct instruction, biography, and participation in school governance have been used to cultivate good character.

19. For a discussion of the relationship of civic education and character education see Jacques S. Benninga, "Schools, Character Development, and Citizenship," in *The Construction of Children's Character. Ninety-Sixth Yearbook of the National Society for the Study of Education. Part 2*, edited by Alex Molnar (Chicago: National Society for the Study of Education, 1997), 17-30.

20. The degree to which civic dispositions generally, and which ones specifically, contribute to the maintenance and improvement of democracies is a contested issue among democratic theorists. For an overview of competing theories see William A. Galston, "Liberal Virtues and the Formation of Civic Character," in *Seedbeds of Virtue: Sources of Competence, Character, and Citizenship in American Society*, edited by Mary Ann Glendon and David Blankenhorn (Lanham, MD: Madison Books, 1995), 35-60.

21. Lawrence E. Cremin wrote insightfully about the inevitable paradox of political socialization in a free and open society in which transmission of democratic principles and traditions necessarily involves the individual's right to liberation as well as security in a stable community. He said, "On the one hand, schooling, like every other agency of deliberate nurture, socializes: it tends to convey the prevailing values and attitudes of the community or subcommunity that sponsors it. On the other hand, schooling, insofar as it exposes individuals to people and ideas not already encountered at home or in church, liberates and extends. As with the printed matter that is the essence of its instruction, schooling opens the mind to new options and new possibilities. Hence the outcomes of schooling are almost invariably contradictory. Schooling—like education in general—never liberates without at the same time limiting. It never frees without at the same time socializing. The question is not whether one or the other is occurring in isolation but what the balance is, and to what end, and in light of what alternatives." See Lawrence A. Cremin, *Traditions of American Education* (New York: Basic Books, 1977), 36-37.

References

Bahmueller, Charles F., and Charles N. Quigley, eds., *Civitas: A Framework for Civic Education.* Calabasas, CA: Center for Civic Education, 1991.

Bruer, John T. " The Mind's Journey From Novice to Expert." *American Educator* 17 (Summer 1993): 6-15 and 38-46.

Bruer, John T. *Schools for Thought: A Science of Learning in the Classroom.* Cambridge, MA: The MIT Press, 1993.

Butts, R. Freeman. *The Civic Mission in Educational Reform: Perspectives for the Public and the Profession.* Stanford, CA: Hoover Institution Press, 1989.

Center for Civic Education. *American Legacy: The United States Constitution and other Essential Documents of American Democracy.* Calabasas, CA: Center for Civic Education, 1997(a).

Center for Civic Education. *We the People. . . The Citizen and the Constitution.* Calabasas, CA: Center for Civic Education, 1997(b).

Center for Civic Education. *We the People. . . Project Citizen.* Calabasas, CA: Center for Civic Education, 1998.

Center for Civic Education. *An International Framework for Education in Democracy.* Calabasas, CA: Center for Civic Education, 2001.

Center for Civic Education. *National Standards for Civics and Government.* Calabasas, CA: Center for Civic Education, 1994.

Cremin, Lawrence A. *Traditions of American Education.* New York: Basic Books, 1977.

Cromer, Alan. *Connected Knowledge.* New York: Oxford University Press, 1997.

Delli Carpini, Michael X., and Scott Keeter. *What Americans Know about Politics and Why It Matters.* New Haven, CT: Yale University Press, 1996.

Eberly, Don E. "The Quest for America's Character." In *America's Character: Rediscovering Civic Virtue,* edited by Don E. Eberly. Lanham, MD: Madison Books, 1995, 3-24.

Foley, Michael W., and Bob Edwards. "Beyond Tocqueville: Civil Society and Social Capital in Comparative Perspective." *American Behavioral Scientist* 42 (September 1998): 11.

Gutmann, Amy. *Democratic Education.* Revised Edition. Princeton, NJ: Princeton University Press, 1999.

Gutmann, Amy, and Dennis Thompson. *Democracy and Disagreement.* Cambridge, MA: Harvard University Press, 1996.

Houston, Paul D. "The Centrality of Character Education." *School Administrator* 55 (May 1998): 6-8.

Lickona, Thomas. "Character Education: Seven Crucial Issues." *Action in Teacher Education* 20 (Winter 1998): 77-83.

Lockwood, Alan L., and David E. Harris. *Reasoning with Democratic Values: Ethical Problems in United States History. Volumes 1 and 2.* New York: Teachers College Press, 1985.

Macedo, Stephen. *Diversity and Distrust: Civic Education in a Multicultural Democracy.* Cambridge, MA: Harvard University Press, 2000.

Massaro, Toni Marie. *Constitutional Literacy: A Core Curriculum for a Multicultural Nation.* Durham, NC: Duke University Press, 1993.

NAEP Civics Consensus Project. *Civics Framework for the 1998 National Assessment of Educational Progress.* Washington, DC: National Assessment Governing Board, 1996.

Nie, Norman H., Jane Junn, and Kenneth Stehlik-Barry. *Education and Democratic Citizenship in America.* Chicago: The University of Chicago Press, 1996.

Niemi, Richard G., and Jane Junn. *Civic Education: What Makes Students Learn.* New Haven, CT: Yale University Press, 1998.

Parker, Walter C. "Toward an Aristocracy of Everyone: Policy Study in the High School Curriculum." *Theory and Research in Social Education* 27 (Winter 1999): 9-44.

Patrick, John J., and Gerald P. Long. *Constitutional Debates on Freedom of Religion: A Documentary History.* Westport, CT: Greenwood Press, 1999.

Patrick, John J. *Founding the Republic: A Documentary History.* Westport, CT: Greenwood Press, 1995.

Patrick, John J. "Concepts at the Core of Education for Democratic Citizenship." In *Principles and Practices of Education for Democratic Citizenship,* Charles F. Bahmueller and John J. Patrick, eds. Bloomington, IN: ERIC Clearinghouse for Social Studies/Social Science Education, 1999(a), 1-40.

Patrick, John J. "Education for Constructive Engagement of Citizens in Democratic Civil Society and Government." In *Principles and Practices of Education for Democratic Citizenship: International Perspectives and Projects,* Charles F. Bahmueller and John J. Patrick, eds. Bloomington, IN: ERIC Clearinghouse for Social Studies/Social Science Education, 1999(b), 41-60.

Patrick, John J. "Introduction to Education for Civic Engagement in Democracy." In *Education for Civic Engagement in Democracy: Service Learning and Other Promising Practices*, Sheilah Mann and John J. Patrick, eds. Bloomington, IN: ERIC Clearinghouse for Social Studies/Social Science Education, 2000(a), 1-8.

Patrick, John J. "Multicultural Education and the Civic Mission of Schools." In *Research Review for School Leaders*, William G. Wraga and Peter S. Hlebowitsh, eds. Mahwah, NJ: Lawrence Erlbaum Associates, Publishers, 2000(b), 103-134.

Peng, Ira. "Effects of Public Deliberation on High School Students: Bridging the Disconnection Between Young People and Public Life." In *Education for Civic Engagement in Democracy: Service Learning and Other Promising Practices*, Sheilah Mann and John J. Patrick, eds. Bloomington, IN: ERIC Clearinghouse for Social Studies/Social Science Education, 2000, 73-86.

Putnam, Robert D. "Bowling Alone: America's Declining Social Capital." *Journal of Democracy* 6 (January1995): 65-78.

Putnam, Robert D. *Bowling Alone: The Collapse and Revival of American Community*. New York: Simon & Schuster, 2000.

Schubert, William H. "Character Education from Four Perspectives on Curriculum." In *The Construction of Children's Character. Ninety-Sixth Yearbook of the National Society for the Study of Education, Part 2*. Alex Molnar, ed. Chicago, IL: National Society for the Study of Education, 1997, 17-30.

Shanker, Albert. "It's Content, Not Process, That Counts." *American Teacher* 81 (January 1997): 5.

Tolo, Kenneth W. *An Assessment of We the People. . . Project Citizen: Promoting Citizenship in Classrooms and Communities*. Austin: Lyndon B. Johnson School of Public Affairs at the University of Texas, 1998.

Torney-Purta, Judith, Rainer Lehmann, Hans Oswald, and Wolfram Schultz. *Citizenship and Education in Twenty-eight Countries: Civic Knowledge and Engagement at Age Fourteen*. Amsterdam: NEA (The International Association for the Evaluation of Educational Achievement), 2001.

Vontz, Thomas S., and William A. Nixon. "Issue-Centered Civic Education Among Early Adolescents in the United States and Abroad." In *Principles and Practices of Education for Democratic Citizenship*, Charles F. Bahmueller and John J. Patrick, eds. Bloomington, IN: ERIC Clearinghouse for Social Studies/Social Science Education, 1999, 141-161.

Vontz, Thomas S., Kim K. Metcalf, and John J. Patrick. *Project Citizen and the Civic Development of Adolescent Students in Indiana, Latvia, and Lithuania*. Bloomington, IN: ERIC Clearinghouse for Social Studies/Social Science Education, 2000.

Walzer, Michael. "The Civil Society Argument." In *Dimensions of Radical Democracy: Pluralism, Citizenship, and Community*. Chantal Mouffe, ed. London: Routledge, 1992, 89-107.

Wilson, James Q. "The Rediscovery of Character: Private Virtue and Public Policy." *The Public Interest* 81 (1985): 15-16.

4

Beyond the Methods Course: Civics as the Program Core in Elementary Teacher Education

Terrence C. Mason and Diane Yendol Silva

When we think of civic education we often recall a course in high school where we studied American political institutions, the beliefs and values that constitute the foundation of our system of government, and the origin of our democratic republic. But students' understanding of what it means to assume what Jefferson referred to as the "office of citizen" takes root long before this high school class. In both explicit and implicit ways, the curriculum of the elementary school provides a foundation for civic responsibility. For this reason, it is imperative that elementary school teachers be well prepared to guide their students toward an understanding of the roles and responsibilities that citizens of a democratic society must assume.

At a time when many teachers are being asked to focus their efforts on the "basic skills" of literacy and numeracy, teacher educators must not lose sight of the fact that a fundamental purpose of our educational system is to prepare individuals to exercise their rights and carry out their civic responsibilities in thoughtful ways. So how can we best prepare prospective elementary school teachers to instill in their students a commitment to the spirit of democracy in combination with the knowledge, skills, and dispositions needed to participate actively as citizens? In this chapter we will identify some of the key features of teacher education programs that seek to accomplish this goal and describe the elements of two programs that have been designed, at least in part, to promote civic values. First, let us turn to the unique features of the elementary school learner that provide the context for these early forms of civic education.

Teaching for Citizenship and the Elementary School Child

The question whether young learners, those of elementary-school age, possess the capacity to learn the abstract concepts that form the basis of the school curriculum has long been a source of debate in the field of education. From Jerome Bruner's assertion that "any idea or problem or body of knowledge can be presented in a form simple enough so that any particular learner can understand it in a recognizable form" (Bruner 1960, 33) to the "expanding environments" formulation of social studies curriculum (Hanna 1963) to Diane Ravitch's critique of that model to the advocates of "developmentally appropriate practice" (Bredekamp 1987) and their recent detractors (Cannella 1998; Zimiles 2000), educators have grappled with the issue of whether abstract ideas can be meaningfully understood by young students with limited experience who may not have reached intellectual maturity.

Research on children's acquisition of social studies concepts has also informed our understanding of how young children comprehend the content of the social studies curriculum and suggests that we must not underestimate young children's potential to grasp aspects of complex ideas (see for example, Berti and Bombi 1984; Connell 1969; Hess and Torney 1967; Barton 1997). At the same time we know that there are limits to children's capacity to reason (Piagetians would say they think "differently," but they still don't use the same reasoning as adults). For example, it is unlikely that children who have not yet reached Piaget's stage of formal operations would be able to exhibit "principled political tolerance" (Seiderman, Brody and Kuklinski 1991) unless they had been exposed to relevant teaching, *and* they had achieved a certain level of development with regard to moral reasoning (Kohlberg 1969). So we are left with the dilemma of providing meaningful educational experiences that are both sufficiently challenging and within the grasp of our learners.

While we will not insert ourselves here into the complexities of this debate, we take the position, based on our reading of the relevant research and theory, that children construct knowledge in the form of concepts through interaction with teachers, parents, peers, educational materials, the media, and other elements of the social, emotional, and intellectual environment. These interactions build upon basic human dispositions to understand one's world and gain competence for effective and responsible participation within it. Learners' prior experiences influence both how learning occurs and the kind of learning that takes place; knowledge is not simply transmitted from one person or text to another but is acted upon and transformed by the learner through his or her prior experience and knowledge (both affective and cognitive). Complex ideas, such as those that form the basis of the civics curriculum, are acquired gradually through a process of active experience and reflection through which simple, concrete ideas become progressively more abstract, differentiated, and complex. If we accept this essentially constructivist model of learning, then an understanding of such principles as *due process, pluralism,* or *popular sovereignty* that students are expected to gain in high school will be understood only to the extent that prior concepts, such as fairness, consent, respect, and responsibility, have been introduced and acquired earlier. Thus, the role of the elementary social studies curriculum should be grounded in experiences that emphasize these fundamental concepts and render them meaningful to young learners. These concepts, of course, are not only the building blocks of subsequent, more complex understandings, but constitute the "universal values" that form the basis of all education (Touraine 1998).

Challenges of Bringing Civics Content into the Teaching Methods Course

What can teacher educators do to increase the likelihood that the quality of social studies teaching will be enhanced by their efforts with prospective teachers? In this section, we will address how a conceptually based approach to teacher education that integrates civic education concepts can be a context for enhancing the elementary social studies curriculum and improving the prospective teacher's pedagogical content knowledge (PCK).

In its definition of the social studies, the National Council for the Social Studies emphasizes "the integrated study of the social sciences and humanities to promote civic competence" (NCSS 1993). We concur with Patrick and Vontz in this volume (see Chapter 3) that the foundation for civic competence lies in the development of knowledge, skills, and dispositions related to core concepts about the principles and practices of citizenship in a democracy.[1] In their four-component model for civic education (knowledge, intellectual skills, participatory skills, and dispositions), Patrick and Vontz identify a set of concepts that form the basis of successful civic participation by citizens in a democratic republic. These concepts fall into such categories as representative democracy (republicanism), constitutionalism, rights (liberalism), citizenship, civil society (free and open social system), market economy (free and open economic system), and types of public issues in a democracy, such as those arising from the inevitable tensions between majority rule and minority rights or liberty and equality. While a formal and deep understanding of these principles and issues may constitute the life work of a citizen in our society, we believe, as suggested earlier, that certain "pre-concepts" must be addressed during the elementary school years. As a means of illustrating the relationship between the more abstract concepts discussed by Patrick and Vontz and those that we feel should form the basis of an elementary civics curriculum, we will explore a few examples here in detail.

In Figure 4.1 we have identified some civic concepts, the "pre-concepts" that are associated with them, and ways that they can be integrated into the elementary and teacher education classroom. Taking "citizenship" as an example, elementary students must first understand that they have both rights and responsibilities within the social worlds they inhabit, including the school and classroom. These can be rendered concrete by working as a class to formulate a set of classroom rules through a democratic process of deliberation, compromise, and consensus. Such a process can focus on minority rights as well as majority rule and the need for effective and responsible participation. Teacher educators can create an appreciation for democratic values by engaging their students in decision making about issues and problems that may arise for students in the classroom. Eliciting students' participation in the formation of class policies (rules and procedures) can model for them the importance of seeking "the consent of the governed" as we enact our teaching practices. Similarly, self-efficacy and empathy can be seen as pre-concepts for democratic participation, as gaining a sense of empowerment or efficacy could form a foundation for social action and participation in public affairs. Developing empathy leads to the capacity to integrate multiple perspectives, tolerance, and appreciation of others.[2] The use of service learning with both prospective teachers and elementary students can also offer opportunities to gain empathy as well as consciousness of important social problems and strategies for resolving them.

As we seek to situate civics at the center of teacher education, how do we avoid slipping into the "modeling and exhortation" mode that has characterized many teacher education methods courses and programs? We suggest that the infusion of civics-based content throughout the program combined with an emphasis on the development of civics pedagogical content knowledge (civics PCK) may provide a means of resolving this dilemma. But what is meant by "civics PCK," how does it constitute a useful and viable framework for elementary teacher education, and what types of practices would be emphasized in such a program? To address these questions, let us turn to a discussion of civics PCK and its implications for teacher education curriculum.

Prospective teachers, like many citizens of the United States, possess weak conceptions of democracy that in turn limit their knowledge of how to teach elementary children about democratic citizenship. As a result, two types of teacher knowledge, content knowledge and pedagogical content knowledge, become tightly coupled as teacher educators explore ways to

Figure 4.1
Sample Civics Concepts in Elementary Education

Concept*	Elementary "Pre-Concepts"	Elementary Teaching Practices	Methods Used in Teacher Ed.
Citizenship	rights and responsibilities	students participate in the formulation of classroom rules	decision making about course procedures standards, evaluation criteria, etc.**
Constitutionalism	rules, fairness	students write a classroom constitution to formalize classroom rules, privileges	instructor negotiates content of syllabus; signed and "ratified" by the students
Civic Identity	group membership	classroom meetings to resolve problems, teacher and student concerns	students take responsibility for class activities, leading discussions preparing questions, etc.
Pluralism	similarities and differences, equality, tolerance, respect	inquiry projects on family and community history focusing on appreciation of diversity	service learning projects that focus on community needs, resolving social inequities
Civic Participation	self-efficacy, empathy	service learning projects	service learning for pre-service teachers***

*Taken from Patrick and Vontz (2001).

**As an example of this, Professor Patricia Avery of the University of Minnesota asks her education students to work in small groups to decide on a policy for dealing with work submitted late. She observes the group deliberations then holds a class discussion about the form and content of the groups' decision making process and its relation to democratic participation.

***See Boyle-Baise (2001, Chapter 8 of this volume).

develop prospective teachers. In the case of civic education, teacher education programs must begin by recognizing the importance of developing prospective teachers' understanding of the content-specific components of democracy (Patrick and Vontz, see Chapter 3). Prospective teachers can take courses in general education focusing on civic content knowledge. Teacher education programs can also offer opportunities for prospective teachers to learn the key concepts associated with citizenship. For example, in an effort to deepen prospective teacher understanding of civic values in Florida, the state's Law-Related Education Association partners with the University of Florida teacher education program to offer workshops where prospective teachers interact with state judges, other representatives of the legal profession, and community members involved in promoting education for democracy.

Although a conceptual understanding of democracy provides the underpinnings for becoming a civic educator, prospective teachers must also construct the pedagogical content knowledge necessary for citizenship education. Building on the work of Grossman (1990), Shulman (1986, 1987), and Magnusson et al. (1999), we define pedagogical content knowledge as the teacher's ability to transform content knowledge into pedagogy by constructing learning experiences that organize and represent the knowledge and processes of a content area in light of particular contexts and students. The construction of PCK is an intellectually demanding and complex activity that cannot be captured in a "teacher proof" curriculum. PCK requires the teacher to be a skilled decision maker who integrates and crafts the features of content, context, students, self, and pedagogy in unique ways. Developing teachers as decision makers who can cultivate pedagogical content knowledge around civic education is essential within teacher education programs committed to educating for citizenship in a democracy. As a result, teacher educators face two key questions. What types of PCK do prospective teachers need to teach civics? How do we develop a PCK of civic education?

The four components of civic education offered by Patrick and Vontz (see Chapter 3 of this volume)—*civic knowledge, intellectual skills, civic dispositions, and participatory skills*—offer insight into the question about "what types of PCK to develop." According to Patrick and Vontz, *civic knowledge* includes helping children understand the principles and practices of citizenship and government in a democracy. Through social studies methods courses, prospective teachers can become familiar with resources that support elementary students' development of civic knowledge. By focusing on the "pre-concepts" that underlie the knowledge and skills required of citizens, as we have suggested previously, we prepare elementary teachers to engage young learners in meaningful civic education. Curricula such as *We the People. . . The Citizen and the Constitution* (Center for Civic Education 1998) and Web-based resources that provide examples of primary documents related to civic concepts (e.g., The Library of Congress' American Memory Web site (http://www.lcweb2.loc.gov/ammem) can bring the content of civic education to elementary students. Additionally, primary resources coupled with opportunities for children to engage in "imaginative entry" (Levstik and Barton 2001) can provide children opportunities to assume the perspectives of citizens from another time or place. By familiarizing prospective teachers with resources that support the study of civics concepts, teacher education programs can offer a strong basis for elementary students' civics content development.

The *intellectual skills of citizenship* include helping children identify issues of civic life as well as analyzing, explaining, evaluating, and defending their own positions. Parker and Hess (2001) recommend discussions and seminars as vehicles for cultivating the intellectual skills of citizenship.[3] Prospective teachers can develop PCK in civics by watching, engaging in, analyzing, and conducting their own discussions and seminars around public issues. Wolk (1998) suggests that the inquiry project is another useful intellectual tool for helping elementary children define, explore, and experience civic questions. Similarly, Levstik and Barton (2001) describe disciplined reflective inquiry as a tool for developing children's intellectual skills. Additionally, social studies can be combined with language arts to promote descriptive, analytical, and persuasive writing as pedagogical strategies that promote these civic-minded intellectual skills (Gallavan 1997).

Civic dispositions are also central to citizenship education and these include helping children care about the common good of the community, the dignity of each person, the rights possessed equally by each person, and the importance of participating responsibly and effectively in political/civic life. To these ends, literature and social studies classes can partner to help prospective teachers identify and use children's literature that captures these civic dispositions and the character-related underpinnings. The Heartwood Foundation's Elementary Collection provides a model for using children's literature to teach civics-related concepts.

Participatory skills of citizenship in a democracy include promoting common interests, monitoring and deliberating about issues, implementing decisions, and working with others toward action. Programs like *We the People. . . Project Citizen*, a program developed and administered by the Center for Civic Education, and service learning activities can provide vehicles for upper-elementary children to develop the participatory skills of citizenship. Similarly, engaging prospective teachers in democratically organized teacher education classrooms offers them opportunities to experience democratic participation first-hand, and these experiences serve as a model for how they can structure their own classrooms as elementary school teachers.

Although these kinds of activities contribute to prospective teachers' development of civics PCK, they only scratch the surface. For example, social studies methods courses can only offer a sampling of the many ways to develop civic knowledge, dispositions, intellectual skills, and participatory skills. In fact, many practicing teachers suggest that PCK doesn't develop until prospective teachers begin making their own decisions as they are working with children in their own classrooms. If this is the case, then teacher educators must go beyond providing a sampling of civic education pedagogy to help prospective teachers begin identifying the conceptual underpinnings of PCK. Once prospective teachers are aware of the concepts that underlie PCK and are familiar with the attributes of powerful civics teaching, they can become active constructors of civics PCK. Teacher inquiry serves as a tool for prospective teachers to begin constructing their own PCK by raising questions about content in civics, pedagogical strategies, the school and classroom context, their students, available resources, and their own beliefs. As a result of asking these questions, prospective teachers can begin to study systematically their own practice. Through this process of inquiry, the teacher becomes a curricular decision-maker who constructs his or her own civics PCK.

If these ideas offer insight into what we teach prospective teachers, the second question that teacher educators must address is how do we develop a PCK of civic education? As noted, the development of prospective teacher PCK is highly complex, requiring teachers to become pedagogical and curriculum decision-makers. To develop teachers as decision-makers, we believe the development of PCK must go beyond modeling particular pedagogical techniques within a subject area. Developing prospective teacher civic PCK requires a multi-layered approach that builds civic knowledge, teaches powerful pedagogy, provides experience-based knowledge of the pedagogy, and helps prospective teachers make explicit connections among these components.

As we seek to promote the development of civics PCK in prospective teachers, we must also push teacher education beyond teaching *about* democracy to a more complex multilayered approach of teaching *about, for,* and *in* democracy. Toward this end several guiding principles may be useful here to help us identify the attributes that contribute to the development of civics PCK within teacher education programs. These include (1) linking professional education with general education, (2) setting programmatic goals and themes related to civic education, (3) integrating civics throughout the teacher education professional program curriculum, and

(4) making explicit connections between the core concepts in civics and the activities students engage in, as well as creating commitments to civic education principles and practices. To illustrate how these four attributes can be incorporated into a civics-based teacher education program, we will draw upon examples from two elementary teacher education programs: Indiana University's *Democracy, Diversity,* and *Social Justice* and the University of Florida's *Unified PROTEACH.* Before turning to these four attributes, we briefly describe each of these programs.

Democracy, Diversity, and Social Justice (DDSJ)

In an effort to reconceptualize its teacher education programs, the School of Education at Indiana University, Bloomington has developed an innovative undergraduate program for preparing elementary school teachers that focuses on the important role of teachers and schools in the creation of a just, inclusive, and democratic society. Not surprisingly given the program's title, a key curriculum focus is the development of forms of civic competence, particularly those that foster critical perspectives on the role of the school in society. In this program students study, experience, and discuss the values and underlying beliefs that are critical to the growth of a democratic public education system and a democratic society. Through courses that are interdisciplinary, team-taught, and in some cases field-based, DDSJ focuses on critical reflection, school/university/community partnerships, and inquiry. By focusing on the principles articulated in its program title, DDSJ shifts the focus of teacher education from a technical/rational model of teacher preparation to one of principled commitment to values that are connected to the purposes of education in a democracy. In doing so, DDSJ addresses some of the guiding principles for a civics-based teacher education that we have identified here.[4]

Unified Elementary PROTEACH Program

The University of Florida Unified Elementary PROTEACH Program is a large-scale teacher education program committed to providing the State of Florida with a strong pool of future teacher leaders committed to democracy and equity. This five-year program, resulting in a Masters Degree with preparation in both elementary and special education, targets developing elementary teachers who are prepared to teach *all* children. This commitment requires the program to prepare teachers who are capable of creating supportive classrooms for diverse student populations and working collaboratively with school personnel, families, and members of the community to develop alternative ways of educating *all* children, including those who have traditionally been labeled hard-to-teach and hard-to-man-age. PROTEACH seeks to develop reflective teachers who are committed to educational equity and student empowerment. Although the title of the program does not explicitly indicate a focus on democracy, the underpinnings of the program clearly do. Additionally, the program's commitment to nurturing leadership, educating all children, celebrating diversity, facilitating empowerment, creating community, and exploring issues of equity are central to developing civic competence in both prospective teachers and elementary children. Finally, the strength of the PROTEACH program lies in this emphasis on democratic education not just within a few targeted courses but rather in its programmatic infusion of teaching for democracy. Let us consider some specific ways that DDSJ and the Unified Elementary PROTEACH Program reflect the four attributes of a teacher education program focused on civics PCK.

Linking Professional Education and General Education

In order to link professional education with general education, core civics concepts should be emphasized in the liberal arts preparation prospective teachers receive during their undergraduate experience. Also, in creating a coherent experience, efforts should be made to connect the learning that occurs in general education courses, particularly those in the liberal arts and social sciences, with education courses so that students can see the relevance of the content in those courses to teaching. DDSJ recognizes the importance of these connections. For example, rather than mandating specific courses, DDSJ makes an effort to link general and professional education by asking students to select from a wide range of courses within areas (language arts, the arts, mathematics, science, social studies) that reflect students' interests. In an effort to prepare prospective teachers to become change agents within school settings, DDSJ students are encouraged to take courses that will enhance their understanding of social issues; cultural, ethnic, and social diversity; economic, political, and historical understanding; philosophical and aesthetic inquiry; and social action. Another feature of the program is the "inquiry base," a set of courses connected to a student selected inquiry project related to issues of schooling and society (e.g., gender, social class, culture, language, political and economic dimensions of civic life). Finally, the courses taken in the School of Education are designed to promote the "intellectual life" of students by linking the practical issues of teaching to the philosophical and moral dimensions of schooling and by making explicit the connections to the conceptual understanding promoted by many of the general education courses prospective teachers take.

Also central to DDSJ is the integration of general and professional education around themes of democracy, diversity, and social justice. These

themes provide a coherent education for prospective teachers that emphasizes the important civic function of teachers and schools. As a part of a
broader, university-wide initiative to integrate teacher education with the
Arts and Sciences (Indiana University's 21st Century Project), a specific
focus on civic education has been created. During the freshman and soph-
omore years, education students take topical seminars in history and political science that explore social science issues in depth by emphasizing
critical thinking, reading and writing, multiple perspectives, and social science inquiry, all of which are central to the civic skills, intellectual and participatory, referred to by Patrick and Vontz (see Chapter 3 of this volume).
The teaching of these skills and concepts will then be incorporated into the
content methods courses students take as a part of their professional program. Initially, this project will be introduced with secondary social studies majors, but will eventually it will be offered to elementary education
majors also.

Although linking early general education coursework to professional
education offers great possibility for enhancing prospective teacher content knowledge in the area of democratic education, the effort is problematic at the University of Florida since many prospective teachers take most
of their general education coursework prior to entering the teacher education program. In some cases, the students have taken this coursework at
other institutions or community colleges making a meaningful link between
general education and professional education early in their teacher preparation virtually impossible.

One way the PROTEACH program has tried to address this tension,
however, is to create partnerships with faculty in the Liberal Arts and Social
Sciences focused on co-constructing and delivering courses that provide a
strong knowledge base for the content-specific methods courses. To do this,
the program couples, for example, the social studies methods course with
a social science course. This course, in much the same way as Indiana University's topical seminars, helps prospective teachers understand multiple
perspectives and the interactions of these perspectives using historical and
geographical lenses with explicit attention to illuminating issues of democracy. One of the hallmarks of this effort is that the Liberal Arts coursework
is not only coupled with the social studies methods course but also a field
experience, which provides the possibility of developing prospective teachers' civics PCK as they work in classrooms with elementary children.

Programmatic Goals Related to Civic Education

If we are to advance the goals of civic education in our teacher education programs, we must move beyond addressing issues in civics solely in
our social studies methods courses. The concepts and principles that form

the basis for participation by citizens in their democracy should be integrated into the conceptual framework of teacher education programs as a whole. For example, if the principle of democratic participation is articulated as a fundamental goal of a teacher education program, then faculty should work toward using democratic classroom practices throughout the program. Also, issues of civic responsibility and social justice could be incorporated into courses and experiences that deal with science and technology and the ethical and equity questions that we face in these areas, such as the issue of equal access to information technology and the social costs of "virtual" vs. "real" experience.

The following statements that appear in the DDSJ program description literature illustrate how a strong civics focus is incorporated into the program goals:

> Democracy is the foundation for building a community that values and promotes equality and opportunity for all people. This is also the foundation for DDSJ and requires that all of us—faculty, public school teachers, and university students—join together to create intellectually stimulating relationships and conversations.

> We live in a diverse world. We have different backgrounds, experiences, abilities, cultures, languages, and ways of knowing. In DDSJ we don't see these differences as deficiencies or problems, but as essential contributions in a democratic society. We seek to understand how best to educate **all** students.

> Equality and social justice are themes that underlie the entire DDSJ curriculum. Education that makes a difference is education that is connected to action. Courses in DDSJ focus on how inequities in public schools and society impact teaching and learning. Our goal is to help alter and improve schools in ways that foster both educational and social change. Together, we focus on the moral nature of teaching and how to improve schools so that democracy and social justice are at the core of the curriculum.

By using such terms as democracy, equality, opportunity, community, and social change to describe the program as a whole and by organizing courses and educational experiences around these themes, the designers of the DDSJ program have sought to ensure that these important civic education concepts will form the foundation for the program. In a large-scale teacher education program such as Unified PROTEACH, program goals can unify faculty around a shared vision. For example, Unified PROTEACH uses program goals to clarify their shared commitment to democratic education. According to Ross, McCallum, and Lane (2001, 4), faculty at the University of Florida have developed the Unified Elementary PROTEACH Program by attending to the intellectual and professional development of teachers that a democratic society demands.

This program is based on two programmatic themes. The first theme, *Democratic Values*, drawn from the program description literature, rests on the shared belief that teachers within a democratic society must value equity in education and society. Prospective teachers must be able to work collaboratively with others to develop alternative ways of educating our diverse population, and they must accept responsibility for the learning of *all* children. To these ends, the Unified Elementary PROTEACH faculty members embrace a broad definition of diversity that includes ethnic and national heritage, special educational needs, gender, sexual orientation, social class, and religion.

The second theme, *knowledge of content and inclusive pedagogy*, drawn from the program description literature, is also central to the Unified Elementary PROTEACH mission because content is constantly expanding and teachers are increasingly asked to make decisions about what and how to teach. The program's aim is to help prospective teachers develop knowledge of subject area content, including but not limited to civics, democracy, and American history. Acquiring this content knowledge is central to identifying and organizing appropriate direction for inclusive elementary instruction that facilitates all students' learning. These two themes provide an example of how elementary teacher education programs can use programmatic goals and themes to provide a framework for prospective teacher development in civic education.

Integrating Civics Throughout the Professional Program

One of the persistent problems in education, particularly at the elementary level, is the overcrowded curriculum. Teachers are being asked to teach an increasingly broad range of subject matter and, as a result, often find difficulty doing justice to the content they address. As Wiggins (1985, 45) asserts:

> The inescapable dilemma at the heart of curriculum and instruction must, once and for all, be made clear: either teaching everything of importance reduces it to trivial, forgettable verbalisms or lists; or schooling is a *necessarily* inadequate apprenticeship, where "preparation" means something quite humble: learning to know and do a few things quite well and leaving out much of importance.

One solution to the overcrowded curriculum is finding ways to integrate content areas and thereby address more than one subject area at a time. To accomplish this without compromising the integrity of the subjects themselves is not a simple matter (Alleman and Brophy 1994; Mason 1996). If we follow Wiggins' lead, a particular kind of curriculum integration is needed at the elementary level. Curriculum integration for the elementary school should be organized around "big ideas" or concepts that can lend focus and coherence to the curriculum and avoid the tendency to combine subjects for the sake of convenience or efficiency. Concepts in civics, such as liberty, equality, democracy, constitutionalism, justice, rights, and responsibilities can serve as the organizing core for elementary students as they study history and geography, explore children's literature, engage in opportunities for authentic writing, or develop appreciation of various forms of artistic expression.

If integration is essential, teacher education must ensure that prospective teachers understand the core concepts in civics, see their relationship to other subject matter areas, and know how to integrate them in meaningful ways into pedagogical methods that constitute not only quality instruction in civics but also in language arts, history, geography, etc. Interdisciplinary methods courses that emphasize integrative concepts could offer opportunities for students to engage in forms of curriculum inquiry and development projects that could provide them with concrete experience in creating meaningful forms of integrated curriculum.

In addition to these more general ways that civic and democratic values are infused, more specific forms of content integration involving civics concepts occur in certain DDSJ courses. Let us consider some examples of integration. In a course entitled *Learning in Social Context*, students explore learning theories, student diversity, and the role of communication and language in the classroom. As they investigate these topics, they focus on essential questions that guide them toward understanding how children learn and the social factors that influence their learning. For example, in what ways does the school experience affect elementary students' developing conceptions of social justice? How do the school, the community, and society at large interact to form the educational context for the elementary school student? An emphasis on socio-cultural learning theories (Cazden 1988; Rogoff 1990) helps students view learning less as an individual process and more as a phenomenon that occurs in cooperation and interaction with others in multiple, diverse contexts. Issues of power and the role of language in classrooms are analyzed, and student exceptionality is considered within a systems orientation (Delpit 1988). Thus, democratic, inclusive frameworks for understanding how children learn form the basis for understanding how schooling is organized in our society.

Courses that focus specifically on curriculum and pedagogy are interdisciplinary in nature, thus they integrate multiple content areas with many civics-related concepts. A course devoted to teaching and learning in social studies, language arts (reading and writing), and visual arts emphasizes the role of literacy in a democratic society and how to foster appreciation for fairness, diversity, responsibility, individual and group rights, and the common good. The course includes activities that are intended to enhance undergraduates' understanding of the origins of our democratic institutions as well as prepare them to engage young learners in investigating civic issues and practices (e.g., *We the People. . . Project Citizen* 1998, and Levstik and Barton's *Doing History* 2001). As students learn how to use literature circles with elementary school children, they use examples from children's literature that focus on important civic ideals and concepts. In another integrated methods course addressing mathematics and science, students learn how to engage in culturally relevant forms of pedagogy in math, and how to guide young learners in inquiry-based science. A seminar on technology integration will address how to use new instructional technologies with all students and how to bridge the "digital divide" for those students who may not have equal access to these technologies. In these ways DDSJ provides integrated curriculum around its core values preparing elementary school teachers for a civics-oriented curriculum.

The PROTEACH program also seeks to provide integrated teacher education curriculum based on the program themes. These themes tie together each semester of coursework. For example, the children's literature faculty describes their course as providing prospective teachers with the opportunity to explore issues of freedom, justice, equity, and multiple perspectives within their Children's Literature course:

> We inquire into issues of freedom using books about slavery, reconstruction, civil rights, and modern yearnings for freedom. . . . A democracy is supposed to represent justice for **all** so the books we share in virtually all of the genres emphasize this focus.... In poetry we read poems of Laurence Dunbar and other great poets that deal with identity issues and quests for freedom, equity, and justice. In realistic fiction we emphasize books about minority populations and other cultures and books about kids who are different and don't fit in—where is the justice for them? The course also uses nonfiction books about child labor and other social justice issues.

This type of integration continues throughout the PROTEACH semesters. For example, during the senior year the language arts and social studies methods courses co-teach around the shared themes of democracy, diversity, and literacy (DDL). During that semester, prospective teachers inquire into their personal and professional selves by constructing a critical autobiography where they explore their own positions on the issues of democracy, equity, justice, diversity, etc. Additionally, during this semester, the focus is on creating a community of inquiry where prospective teachers raise questions within the DDL community about the purpose of public schools, who has been well-served by public schools and who has not, and why? These questions emerge naturally as students explore the core concepts of social studies and discuss various approaches to and purposes for writing in the integrated language arts class. In addition to integrating the content of democracy, this community is organized around pedagogy targeted at giving *all* members a voice in the community and the importance of creating a similar type of community in K-6 classrooms as well.

Making Explicit Connections and Developing Commitments to Democracy

For civics PCK to be successfully developed and implemented, prospective teachers must make explicit connections between the content, dispositions, intellectual skills, and participatory skills children need to develop as citizens and the curriculum and pedagogy they learn in teacher education. In the absence of these explicit connections, prospective teachers may fail to appreciate and understand the purposes of the kind of experiences they have in their teacher education classes and their implications for teaching at the elementary level. Thus, civics concepts need to be labeled and articulated as they are introduced, connected with the goals of education in a democracy, and linked to the kinds of teaching practices that they imply. Engaging in experiences and activities alone is not enough. Elaboration of the rationale for pedagogical choices and critical reflection on those choices must accompany active learning in a civics-based teacher education program. Finally, conceptual understanding must be accompanied by opportunities for action and the development of democratic commitments and values both within and beyond the classroom. Through the examples that follow here we can see how these ideas are put into practice in the DDSJ and PROTEACH programs.

Since DDSJ articulates its core values directly and incorporates democratic principles consciously into all its courses and experiences, the focus on civic education is by no means a "hidden curriculum." Understanding how teaching and learning of subject matter fits into our social, cultural, and political context constitutes the central purpose of the program and inquiry into this question forms the primary focus for student learning. Course syllabi, assignments, and readings are organized with these aims in mind and students' attention is continually directed toward the social implications of various pedagogical practices and curriculum theories and practices. An understanding of the teachers' role as an agent of social change is approached directly and teachers' work is defined in terms of how it promotes a better, more just society and how teachers can successfully prepare students to participate actively in that society.

Among the most important forms of PCK related to civic education is the knowledge and capacity to provide a democratic environment for learning. The DDSJ program provides students opportunities to acquire this ability in a variety of ways. First, classes are organized around participatory, democratic teaching structures. Multiple perspectives on issues are explored through discussion and deliberation in which students take active roles in framing topics and debates. Students select inquiry project topics according to their own interests and pursue in depth issues of personal concern related to the DDSJ themes. In this way they forge connections among civic-related concepts and teaching practices.

Through the use of student cohort groups that move the program together, a sense of community is created; on-going contact with program faculty also fosters cohesion among students and faculty that allows for more open discussion of issues and a setting where dissent and diversity are encouraged. The active participation of cooperating public school teachers and administrators in the program's operation seeks to eliminate the hierarchical relationships that sometimes characterize university/school partnerships. The program's principles are also infused into course readings, activities, and assignments, thus providing a consistent thematic focus based on democratic values and practices. During a two-semester teaching methods sequence, students examine approaches to teaching critically, and they develop teaching strategies and curriculum materials that focus on promoting equity and access for all students. A seminar entitled "Diversity and Social Justice" is offered in conjunction with integrated subject-matter methods courses focusing on the themes of equality and fairness, diversification and adaptation of curriculum and pedagogy, promoting student interaction, equitable assessment practices, and community/family connections. Opportunities for service learning and exploration of how to promote service learning activities with elementary students are also included during this course sequence. Finally, a focus on inquiry is intended to promote an orientation to knowledge that will encourage teachers to promote a spirit of criticism, deliberation, and an appreciation for diverse perspectives that DDSJ graduates will carry with them into their public school classrooms. These features of the DDSJ program coursework focus on specific dispositions toward teaching that promote democratic values and suggest ways to incorporate them into curriculum and pedagogy.

The PROTEACH program also provides prospective teachers with opportunities to make connections and develop commitment to democracy by coupling field experiences to coursework each semester. For example, during their first semester in the PROTEACH program, prospective teachers engage in a set of courses focused on understanding the child, family, community, and teaching self. These courses are paired with, Bright Futures, an early field experience (Bondy and Davis 2000; Clark and Bondy 2000). Bright Futures engages prospective teachers in learning about the lives of diverse learners and how to work with those who may be different from themselves. Over the last decade, Bright Futures has provided:

Support and dissonant learning opportunities for first semester prospective teachers. Prospective teachers need to experience such dissonance since their beliefs are often naive about children whose backgrounds and cultures are different from their own. (Bondy and Davis 2001, 26)

During this semester, PROTEACH students read to children in family day care homes, mentor a child in a public housing neighborhood, tutor a low achieving child or a child with a disability in reading, and work with ESOL students. According to Bondy, Schmitz, and Johnson (1993), Bright Futures stimulates self-discovery, questioning, caring, and commitment that are central to developing effective teachers of diverse learners and central skills for infusing democracy into teacher education.

Later in the program, prospective teachers enter the Democracy, Diversity, and Literacy (DDL) integrated teaching block and participate in nine credit hours of courses in language arts, social studies, and adaptations, which are organized around the PROTEACH shared themes. This block emphasizes blending coursework with the field experience by using inquiry as a tool for investigating one of the following areas: inquiry into students, inquiry into professional self, inquiry into context, inquiry into content, or inquiry into teaching (i.e., planning, pedagogy, assessment). As a result of this experience, prospective teachers co-investigate with their cooperating teachers a self-selected inquiry question that emerges in their teaching context using the lenses of democracy, diversity, and literacy. This project helps to make explicit both the prospective teachers' understanding of the program themes as well as their ability to apply and critically analyze a professional question. These inquiry projects force prospective teachers to begin grappling with the principles of democratic education as they work with children in their field placements.

Unresolved Issues, Cautions, and Conclusions

Throughout this chapter we have referred to the principles of civic education articulated by Patrick and Vontz (see Chapter 3) as the basis for a teacher education pedagogy that promotes education for citizenship in a democracy. There are, however, multiple approaches to civic education, and Patrick and Vontz offer but one, a perspective drawn from the democratic tradition of civic liberalism. Other models of civic education could form the foundation for teacher education programs. Among these are critical democracy (see Goodman 1992 for a discussion of how this approach can be applied to elementary education) and citizenship in a multicultural democracy (Banks 1997). Indiana University's DDSJ combines different perspectives on citizenship in a democracy, and the University of Florida's Unified PROTEACH incorporates some elements of them.

Another issue emerges as teacher educators conceptualize programs with a strong sense of purpose. For example, the problem of indoctrination arises when we consider the ideological perspective on civic education that programs take. When strong views are embedded into a program's philosophy, the potential exists for ideas to be conveyed to students without encouraging them to question the values that undergird those ideas. While some see this as problematic, others may not. Counts (1932), for example, argued that indoctrination toward maintaining the political and social status quo is promulgated by the traditional school curriculum, justifying the adoption of strong critical perspectives as a means of "making visible those social forces hidden by familiarity" (Westheimer and Kahne 1998). On the other hand, Franklin Bobbit proclaimed that "the school is not an agency of social change" (1937, 75, cited in Westheimer and Kahne 1998, 5). While this debate over the social role of schooling in our society continues, we believe that teacher education programs should articulate clearly their values and assumptions about the nature of citizenship in a democratic society and provide a context that encourages prospective teachers to deliberate over these ideological questions. In this way we can make "a democratic virtue out of our inevitable disagreement over educational problems" (Gutmann 1999, 11), and in doing so we teach our students a valuable lesson in civics.

In this chapter we have presented a program-based approach to the development of pedagogical content knowledge in civics. It is our contention that if teacher education programs assign responsibility to methods courses alone for preparing elementary (or any level) teachers to teach civics, prospective teachers will not gain adequate civics subject matter knowledge or the ability to transform that knowledge into meaningful teaching and learning for children. We do not, however, intend to suggest that there is no legitimate place for the methods course in teacher preparation. Rather, we advocate methods courses connected to program goals in civic education that are integrated with other coursework in general and professional education in particular. They explicitly link concepts in civics, methods for teaching them, and the skills required of citizens in a democracy. Thus, they can pull together the threads of content knowledge, teaching practices, civic responsibility, and action for prospective teachers. In doing so, the methods course can also serve to minimize gaps created by a pure "infusion" model, where everybody's responsibility for addressing civics content and pedagogy could become no one's responsibility. Through the two program examples described here, we have attempted to demonstrate how elementary teachers can be prepared to assume their professional responsibilities with the knowledge, skills, and commitments necessary to develop competent, active citizens for the future of our democratic republic.

Notes

1. We are grateful to John Patrick for his encouragement to offer our perspectives here in an effort to provide more attention to the importance of civic education in the elementary curriculum.

2. See Brophy (1999) for an example of how children's development of empathy enhances their understanding of the struggle of Native Americans in American history and contemporary society.

3. See Paley (1992) and Nicholls and Hazzard (1993) for excellent portrayals of elementary-aged children engaging in public deliberation over issues of curriculum and classroom practices.

4. For an extended discussion of the DDSJ program, see Beyer (2001). The program is currently undergoing some revision that may affect the structure of the program, but the principles and practices described here will continue to be a part of the teacher education program at Indiana University.

References

Alleman, Janet, and Jere Brophy. "Trade-offs Embedded in the Literary Approach to Elementary Social Studies." *Social Studies and the Young Learner* 6 (1994): 6-8.

Banks, James A. *Educating Citizens in a Multicultural Society*. New York: Teachers College Press, 1997.

Barton, Keith. "History—Can it be Elementary: An Overview of Elementary Students' Understanding of History. *Social Education* 61 (January 1997):13-16.

Berti, A., and A. Bombi. "The Child's Construction of Economics." In H. Tajfel, ed. *The Social Dimension*, Vol. 1. Cambridge: Cambridge University Press, 1984.

Beyer, Landon. "The Value of Critical Perspectives in Teacher Education." *Journal of Teacher Education* 52 (March/April 2001): 151-163.

Bondy, Elizabeth, and S. C. Davis. "Lessons from Ten Years of a Community-Based Field Experience." A paper presented at the annual meeting of the American Educational Research Association, Seattle, WA., April 13, 2001.

Bondy, Elizabeth, and S. C. Davis. "The Caring of Strangers: Insights from a Field Experience in a Culturally Unfamiliar Community." *Action in Teacher Education* 22 (Summer 2000): 54-66.

Bondy, Elizabeth, S. Schmitz, and M. Johnson. "The Impact of Coursework and Fieldwork on Preservice Teachers' Reported Beliefs about Teaching Poor and Minority Students." *Action in Teacher Education* 15 (Summer 1993): 55-69.

Bredekamp, Susan, ed. *Developmentally Appropriate Practice in Early Childhood Programs Serving Children from Birth through Age Eight*. Washington, DC: National Association for the Education of Young Children, 1987.

Brophy, Jere. "The Development of Knowledge and Empathy." *Social Education* 63 (January/February 1999): 39-45.

Bruner, Jerome. *The Process of Education*. Cambridge: Harvard University Press, 1960.

Cannella, Gaile. "Early Childhood Education: A Call for the Construction of Revolutionary Images." In *Curriculum: Toward New Identities*, William Pinar, ed., New York: Garland, 1998.

Cazden, Courtenay. *Classroom Discourse: The Language of Teaching and Learning*. Portsmouth, NH: Heinemann, 1988.

Center for Civic Education. *We the People. . . The Citizen and the Constitution*. Calabasas, CA: Center for Civic Education, 1998.

Center for Civic Education. *We the People. . . Project Citizen.* Calabasas, CA: Center for Civic Education, 1998.

Clark, M. A., and E. Bondy. "Building a Foundation for Effective Teaching of Poor and Minority Students: The Bright Futures Semester." *Educators for Urban Minorities* 1 (Spring 2000): 3-16.

Connell, R. W. *The Child's Construction of Politics.* Carlton: Melbourne University Press, 1971.

Counts, George. "Dare Progressive Education Be Progressive?" *Progressive Education* 9 (1932): 257-263.

Delpit, Lisa. "The Silenced Dialogue: Power and Pedagogy in Educating Other Peoples' Children." *Harvard Educational Review* 58 (August 1988): 280-298.

Gallavan, Nancy. "Achieving Civic Competence Through a DRAFT Writing Process." *Social Studies and the Young Learner* 10 (November/December 1997): 14-16.

Goodman, Jesse. *Elementary Schooling for Critical Democracy.* Albany, NY: SUNY Press, 1992.

Grossman, Pamela, L. *The Making of a Teacher: Teacher Knowledge and Teacher Education.* New York: Teachers College Press, 1990.

Gutmann, Amy. *Democratic Education.* Revised Edition. Princeton, NJ: Princeton University Press, 1999.

Hanna, Paul R. "Revising the Social Studies: What is Needed." *Social Education* 27 (April 1963): 190-196.

Hess, Robert, and Judith Torney. *The Development of Political Attitudes in Children.* Chicago: Aldine, 1967.

Kohlberg, Lawrence. "Stage and Sequence: The Cognitive-Developmental Approach to Socialization." In D. A. Goslin, ed., *Handbook of Socialization Theory and Research.* Chicago: Rand McNally, 1969.

Levstik, Linda S., and Keith Barton. *Doing History: Investigating with Children in Elementary and Middle School.* Mahwah, New Jersey: Lawrence Erlbaum Associates, Publishers, 2001.

Magnusson, S., J. Krajcik, and H. Borko. "Nature, Sources, and Development of Pedagogical Content Knowledge for Science Teaching." In *PCK and Science Education*, J. Gess-Newsome and N. G. Lederman, eds., 1999, 94-132.

Mason, Terrence C. "Integrated Curricula: Potential and Problems." *The Journal of Teacher Education* 47 (September/October 1996): 263-270.

National Council for the Social Studies. "A Vision of Powerful Teaching and Learning in the Social Studies: Building Social Understanding and Civic Efficacy." *Social Education* 57 (September 1993): 213-223.

Nicholls, John, and Susan Hazzard. *Education as Adventure: Lessons from the Second Grade.* New York: Teachers College Press, 1993.

Paley, Vivian. *You Can't Say You Can't Play.* Cambridge: Harvard University Press, 1992.

Parker, Walter, and Diana Hess. "Teaching With and For Discussion." *Teaching and Teacher Education* 17 (April 2001): 273-289.

Ravitch, Diane. "Tot Sociology or What Happened to History in the Grade Schools." *The American Scholar* 56 (Summer 1987): 343-353.

Rogoff, Barbara. *Apprenticeship in Thinking.* New York: Oxford University Press, 1990.

Ross, Dorene D., C. McCallum, and H. Lane. "Accomplishing Substantive Teacher Education Reform: Lessons from a Teacher Education Redevelopment Effort." Paper presented at the annual meeting of the American Educational Research Association, Seattle, Washington, April, 2001.

Shulman, Lee S. "Knowledge and Teaching: Foundations of the New Reform." *Harvard Educational Review* 57 (February 1987): 1-22.

Shulman, Lee S. "Those Who Understand: Knowledge Growth in Teaching." *Educational Researcher* 15 (February 1986): 4-14.

Sniderman, Paul M., Richard A. Brody, and James H. Kuklinski. *Reasoning and Choice: Explorations in Political Psychology*. New York: Cambridge University Press, 1991.

Touraine, Alain. *What is Democracy?* Boulder, CO: Westview Press, 1998.

Westheimer, Joel, and Joseph Kahne. "Education for Action: Preparing Youth for Democracy." In *Teaching for Social Justice*. William Ayers, Jean Ann Hunt, and Therese Quinn, eds. New York: The New Press, 1998.

Wiggins, Grant. "The Futility of Trying to Teach Everything of Importance." *Educational Leadership* 47 (November 1989): 44-59.

Wolk, Steven. *A Democratic Classroom*. Portsmouth, NH: Heinemann, 1998.

Zimiles, Herbert. "On Reassessing the Relevance of the Child Development Knowledge Base to Education." *Human Development* 43 (July 2000): 235-245.

5

Teaching to Public Controversy in a Democracy

Diana Hess

If social studies as a school subject is primarily designed to "help young people develop the ability to make informed and reasoned decisions for the public good as citizens of a culturally diverse, democratic society in an interdependent world" (NCSS 1994, 3), then it follows logically that controversial public issues should be foregrounded in social studies classes. Such issues are inherently present in a democracy and teaching young people how to identify, analyze, discuss, and make informed decisions about them is a necessary part of education for democracy. I define controversial public issues (CPI) as unresolved questions of public policy that spark significant disagreement. Such issues "present us with problems whose best solutions are open to disagreement" (Lockwood 1996, 28).

While there are a number of ways to include CPI in social studies classes, I advocate teaching young people how to participate effectively in discussions of issues because such public talk is itself a democratic act. Jane Mansbridge explains: "Democracy involves public discussion of common problems, not just silent counting of individual hands. And when people talk together, the discussion can sometimes lead the participants to see their own stake in the broader interests of the community" (1991, 122).

Recent research on how people become interested in public concerns (Doble Research Associates 1999; Kettering Foundation 1993) provides empirical evidence for the assertion that CPI discussions influence the formation and functioning of a healthy democracy. Specifically, the researchers find that citizens want to participate in public talk. When they do so, they enlarge, rather than narrow, the way they see and act on public concerns (Kettering Foundation 1993, 1). Conversations about CPI are linked to what people learn from other citizens and to the solution of important problems. The researchers concluded that the importance of CPI discussions to citizens and to a healthy democracy shows that "talk is not cheap to people, as the axiom goes; it is the valued currency of their public life" (Kettering Foundation 1993, 2).

This chapter focuses on teaching social studies teacher education students how to incorporate the discussion of CPI into their curriculum. I begin by explaining the rationale for the special place that such discussions should hold in a social studies curricula designed explicitly to support and improve democracy. Then I describe the need to include CPI discussion teaching in secondary social studies methods classes and two common misconceptions held by many social studies teacher education students that must be confronted if they are to have success teaching their own students to discuss CPI effectively. Next, I turn to eight components of the curriculum I use to teach teacher education social studies students about CPI discussions. I explain each component in some detail before concluding with challenges that I continue to confront in my own CPI teaching.

Rationales for CPI Discussions in Social Studies

There is a long history of educators promoting CPI discussions in social studies (NEA Commission 1916), and in recent years the enthusiasm has not waned (Hahn 1998; Evans and Saxe 1996). Most CPI advocates point to the democratic authenticity of such discussions as a primary reason to include them in the social studies curriculum. If healthy democracies have many people engaged in high quality talk about CPI, then including discussions on issues in the curriculum enables powerful connections to the "world beyond school." The social studies classroom, according to this line of reasoning, is a type of democracy laboratory (Gutmann 1987; Barber 1989) where what students learn should have "a connection to the larger social context in which students live" (Harris and Yocum 2000, Handout H51). In other words, CPI discussions should be included in the school curriculum because such issues abound in a democracy and effective democratic participants know how to talk about them in a productive and civil manner.

In terms of the student outcomes of CPI discussions, the *democracy* rationale focuses on competence in discussion as the primary rationale for participation in such discussions. That is, young people should be taught to discuss CPI because it will enhance their abilities to participate in a more democratic society. Another category of rationale for CPI discussions is that they may advance other student outcomes, such as the development of certain values or enhanced understanding of content. I call this rationale an instrumental rationale. The notion here is that students learn more from CPI discussions than the ability to participate in the discussions themselves. For example, CPI discussion may help students develop an understanding and commitment to democratic values, increase their willingness to engage in political life, and positively influence content understanding, critical thinking ability, and interpersonal skills (Gall and Gall 1990; Hahn 1996, 1998; Harris 1996; Wilen and White 1991).

The first claim in the instrumental rationale is that CPI discussions influence the development of democratic values, such as toleration of dissent and support for equality. This claim presumes the dynamics of effective CPI discussions to help students form and embrace values that support democracy (Lockwood and Harris 1985). Informed by the research of Lawrence Kohlberg (1981), the democratic values claim posits that the cognitive dissonance created by CPI discussions, as well as the likelihood that students will hear and be attracted to moral reasoning more sophisticated than their own, will combine to shape the development of democratic values.

CPI discussions are also recommended as a way to enhance students' desire to participate in the political world. Derived from research on political socialization (Hahn 1996, 1998), this claim suggests a connection between participation in discussion of CPI and an interest in political participation. Discussing CPI is seen as a way to help students feel more politically efficacious, an attitude correlated positively to people's willingness to engage in political affairs. Carole Hahn, in a recent international study of democratic citizenship education, expresses this point:

> It thus appears that when students report that they frequently discuss controversial issues in their classes, perceive that several sides of issues are presented and discussed, and feel comfortable expressing their views, they are more likely to develop attitudes that have the potential to foster later civic participation than are students without such experiences (1998, 233).

With regard to the influence of such discussions on what young people learn and say they will do, there exists strong and continuing support for the effectiveness of CPI discussions (Hahn 1996; Torney-Purta, Lehmann, Oswald, and Schultz, 2001). In particular, researchers have consistently found positive effects of democracy education that include an open climate for discussion and self-expression in the classroom. The recently released International Association for the Evaluation of Educational Achievement (IEA) study of 90,000 students in 28 countries shows that the United States is one of four countries (along with Columbia, Greece, and Norway) where students report an especially open climate for discussion (Torney-Purta, Lehmann, Oswald, and Schultz, 2001). Open classroom climate is a research-based construct that measures the "extent to which students experience their classrooms as places to investigate issues and explore their opinions and those of their peers" (Torney-Purta et al. 2001, 138). The IEA researchers report that open classroom climate for discussion is a significant predictor of civic knowledge, support for democratic values, participation in political discussion, and political engagement—measured by whether young people say they will vote when they are legally able to do so.

Participation in CPI discussions is often advocated as a means of helping students better understand important content, just as writing is recommended as a method to enhance understanding of content. David Harris explicated this claim when he wrote, "The effort to produce coherent language in response to a question of public policy puts knowledge in a meaningful context, making it more likely to be understood and remembered" (1996, 289). For example, in a CPI discussion about physician-assisted suicide, a teacher may hope that students will form a deeper understanding of social studies content, such as the meaning of liberty and authority in the U.S. Constitution. Underlying this hope is the idea that talking with others will shape (and indeed, improve) one's understanding when ideas are challenged, broadened, and refined by other discussants in the group.

Finally, CPI discussions are advocated because they are believed to improve both students' critical thinking and interpersonal skills. Nel Noddings connects controversy to critical thinking in this way: "We talk perennially about teaching critical thinking, but, too often, we settle for critical thinking as a bland (if powerful) set of techniques. We forget that critical thinking is induced by tackling critical issues—issues that matter deeply to us" (1993, 35). Noddings' point is that "tackling" (i.e., discussing) critical issues both requires and fosters critical thinking. In effective discussion, participants critically examine positions and the evidence that supports these positions. This process is an avenue to improving one's ability to think critically. In terms of interpersonal skills, an overall goal of CPI discussions is improving students' ability to engage in learning with others, including those with whom they disagree. For example, listening attentively and disagreeing respectfully are key relational skills that research indicates may be enhanced by participation in such discussions (Johnson and Johnson 1979).

The Need for CPI Discussion Teaching in Teacher Education. Two justifications for teaching CPI discussions to teacher education students stand out. One relates to pre-teachers' prior experience with high-quality discussions, particularly those on CPI. The second reason recognizes the difficulty of teaching students to discuss CPI.

Much has been written about the effects of the "apprenticeship of observation" on teacher education students' conceptions of what should happen in classrooms (Lortie 1975; Grossman 1990; Parker and Hess 2001). This "apprenticeship" consists of the many years teacher education students have observed—as students—the routines of teaching. I always ask my teacher education students to describe what they remember from their middle and high school social studies classes and often hear descriptions of impressive teachers and their teaching. I do not, however, often hear about CPI discussions, which convinces me that for most pre-service teachers, the apprenticeship of observation has failed to provide them with any models for what this kind of teaching looks like. Thus, the need to include CPI discussion teaching in teacher education is clear. If many students have not experienced this type of teaching themselves, it will not be on their radar screen unless we put it there.

A second reason to include CPI discussion teaching in social studies teacher education is that it is exceptionally difficult, although not impossible, to teach young people how to engage in high quality CPI discussions. Any teacher who has tried to do this can attest to the particular demands of this type of teaching and learning.

Confronting Misconceptions. Most teacher education students with whom I have worked begin their teacher education programs with a number of misconceptions about CPI and discussion that must be brought to the fore and gently counteracted. The most problematic of these is that discussion need not be taught at all. For some reason, students entering teacher education programs often downplay the difficulty of worthwhile discussion, believing that it happens naturally and spontaneously. They often hold a romantic ideal that a teacher can walk into a class, throw out a controversial topic for discussion (or better yet, have a student introduce the topic) and then watch a wonderful exchange of ideas unfold. Although this scenario rarely happens in schools (I have never seen it in more than 20 years of teaching), teacher education students often hold this as both a reality and an ideal. The potential result of this misconception, if not corrected, is incredible frustration on the teacher's part when their romantic idea of discussion does not happen during their student teaching.

A second misconception deals with the extent to which controversial public issues are inherently engaging to young people. My students often believe that controversy, in and of itself, will spark so much interest among their students that, as the teacher, they will not need to encourage students' engagement with what they are learning. Most notably, they misconstrue the necessity of well-thought-out and detailed lesson plans that appropriately scaffold the learning that needs to take place both before, during, and after a CPI discussion. Similar to the first misconception about the romantic ideal of discussion per se, teacher educators must challenge the idea that controversy is inherently engaging, or else teacher education students will be unable to create high quality CPI discussions with their own students. This, too, could lead to serious enough frustration that teacher education students would give up on discussions as part of their teaching repertoire. When preparing to teach CPI discussions to teacher education students, I keep these misconceptions in mind and plan activities and assignments that will surface and challenge them.

Components of CPI Discussion Teaching

The teacher education program in which I teach is a four-semester undergraduate program for students who want to teach in either middle or high schools. The students take two social studies methods courses, one during each of the two semesters they are student teaching. This structure provides students the opportunity to practice immediately what they are learning in the methods courses. While the syllabi for both courses emphasizes discussion, the unit on CPI discussions is in the first course—largely because I want students to have the benefit of practicing planning and facilitating CPI discussions in both semesters of their student teaching.

There are eight components to the curriculum I have created for CPI discussions in social studies methods, each of which I explain in this section.

1. Identify discussion participation skills to work on and develop a plan for doing so with a "critical friend" (Costa and Kallick 1993). Then, periodically assess their progress toward those goals.
2. Participate in a number of CPI discussions using a variety of discussion formats and models.
3. Build conceptual understanding of "discussion" and "controversial public issues."
4. Deliberate some "controversial pedagogical issues" of CPI discussions.
5. Develop CPI discussion curriculum to fit the context of their student teaching and, if possible, make use of existing, high quality CPI resources as part of this curriculum design process.
6. Incorporate a CPI discussion into the curriculum they have developed for their student teaching.
7. Reflect on the CPI discussion using the *Powerful and Authentic Social Studies Standards* for instruction (Harris and Yocum, 2000).
8. Revise the CPI discussion lesson and reflection into an artifact for inclusion in their electronic teaching portfolio.

Improving Discussion Skills. I begin the first social studies methods class by explaining the role that discussion will play in our class and how the course focus will include improvement of their discussion participation skills. This approach is designed to improve the quality of discussions we have in class and also provide them with a model for how to help their own students work on their discussion skills (see the Appendix at the end of this chapter). The specific skills that students identify to work on vary widely. For example, one student said she wanted to learn how to ask questions that challenged ideas and evidence without being insulting; another student said he was typically silent in discussions and wanted to become more comfortable participating verbally. By requiring that students work to improve their own participation skills, I am trying to reinforce James Dillon's basic discussion tenet that "far from coming naturally, discussion has to be learned" (1994, 105).

Participate in A Variety of CPI Discussions. After identifying a discussion skill to work on and developing a plan for doing so, we turn to learning and participating in a number of CPI discussions, using various formats and models (see Figure 5.1). I begin with a highly scaffolded, small group cooperative learning model entitled "Structured Academic Controversy." It was developed originally by Johnson and Johnson (1979) and modified by Walter Parker (Parker and Hess 2001) to more explicitly meet the goals of CPI discussions. Next, we use the "Public Issues Model" (Newmann 1970; Oliver and Shaver 1974) in a large group format and experiment with a scoring rubric developed by Harris for this type of discussion (1996). Other models are presented briefly as well, usually "National Issues Forum" and "Town Meetings" (see Hess 1998). While there are key distinctions among these discussion models (see Figure 5.1), they are all appropriate for deliberating CPI and have a track record of working well with middle and high school students.

By experiencing these discussions as participants, I hope my teacher education students will come to appreciate the power of CPI discussions so they are enthusiastic about trying them with their own students. Moreover, I have found the best way to learn the discussion models is to experience them. To that end, I ask my students to play two roles throughout the discussions—as participants seeking to experience fully the discussion and as teachers analyzing the component parts of the discussion model and noting its structure. After each discussion, we engage in two types of debriefing. First, we analyze how the discussion worked writ large, paying particular attention to what we did well as a group and what we need to work on in the future. Second, each student meets with a critical friend to give and receive feedback on his or her individual participation in the discussion. Following these steps, we then reconstruct the discussion model itself and identify its goals, component parts, strengths and weaknesses, and what steps a teacher would need to take to prepare students to participate in a discussion using that particular model.

Building Conceptual Understanding. More than discussion experiences, however, are necessary to help students develop a sophisticated under-

Figure 5.1
Selected CPI Discussion Models

Dimension for Comparison	Structured Academic Controversy	Public Issues Discussion	Town Meetings
What is the prupose of the discussion?	Greater student mastery of the subject, higher-quality decisions and solutions to problems, and enhanced perspective-taking abilities.	Engage in substantive conversation that enables each of them to make progress toward con-structing a thoughtful position on a question of public policy.	Develop an understand-ing of the multiple perspectives on historic and contemporary policy issues.
What is the structure of the discussion?	Cooperative learning groups of four students participate in six-step process. Pairs learn and present one side of an academic controversy. then present the other side before engaging in a consensus-seeking discussion.	Small or large group, begins with an issue, students discus factual, definitional, and ethical or value issues.	Large group, participants are assigned or select a role, research the likely position that a person in that role would have on the issue, prepare to represent that person's perspective.
What is the discussion about?	A matter of academic controversy - could be a public issue. Academic controversy exists when one student's ideas, information, conclusions, theories, and opinions are incompatible with those of another and the two seek to reach an agreement.	A public issue, defined as a matter of common concern about which there is (or was) disagreement on how to resolve it.	Discussion focuses on a variety of different kinds of evidence that are brought to bear on the larger issue. The emphasis is on the different perspectives that would be held by people in various roles.
What is the teacher's role in the discussion?	Selects the controversy, selects background and point/counterpoint materials, teaches discussion skills, monitors groups and works to keep them on task, formative and summative assessments.	Selects the issue, selects background material, instructs on various kinds of sub-issues, often facilitates the discussion, formative and summative assessment.	Selects the issue, often in conjunction with the students, works with students to develop the roles, structures the individual research of each student, facilitates the discussion skills, formative and summative assessment.

standing of discussion and CPI, the two fundamental concepts undergirding the unit. Beginning with the concept of discussion, I ask students to define what they think it means and then to apply their initial definitions to video excerpts of discussions with middle and high school students.

Invariably, my students have extremely high standards for what they think constitutes an effective discussion. In particular, they respond favorably to discussions where the teacher plays a minimal role and where there is evidence that the discussants are engaging in cross-talk that is not regulated or mediated by much teacher facilitation talk. They are also impressed by discussions in which virtually all of the students in a class participate verbally—viewing this as a sign of engagement and equality in the classroom. Finally, my students want to see evidence that students truly are listening to one another, as indicated by comments that either build on what a previous student has said or offer some kind of challenge or critique of a previous comment. All of these attributes of effective discussion make sense and resonate with what scholars say constitutes effective discussion (Dillon 1994; Nystrand, Gamoran, and Carbonara 1998), but I am typically struck by the degree to which they expect to find all of these attributes in middle and high school students' discussions. My students seem quick to judge a discussion inferior unless these standards are met to a very high degree, whereas I typically view these discussions in light of how difficult discussion is and am more easily satisfied with the quality of what we are viewing. This raises the interesting teaching dilemma for me of pegging standards at an appropriate level. I want my students, of course, to hold high standards for discussion, yet their standards are so high that they strike me as unrealistic and unattainable. This difference, I find, tends to diminish once students experience their use of discussions in their student teaching placements, a change I will discuss in some detail later in the chapter.

Just as discussion is a contested concept, so too is CPI. Recall, my personal definition: controversial public issues are unresolved questions of public policy that spark significant disagreement. Within that statement are a number of words that beg definition. What makes a question unresolved? What is a public policy versus a private one? How much disagreement, and among whom, is required to break the significance threshold? We talk about these questions—paying particular attention to developing criteria for issue selection (Hess 2000b). As a general rule, I want my students to define CPI broadly—in part because by doing so there are a multitude of issues that have the potential for being usefully included in the curriculum. Toward that end, I present students with a list of CPI that is broadly constructed along a number of dimensions and we work through the significant differences and similarities to develop a definition that crosses venue (local, state, national, international) and time (historical, contemporary, and future).

Examining the Controversial Pedagogical Issues of CPI Discussions.
In addition to participating in a variety of CPI discussions and working on
developing their conceptions of discussion and CPI, I also seek to surface
the controversial pedagogical issues that are part of this kind of teaching
and to provide opportunities for my students to deliberate about them. A
controversial pedagogical issue is a question requiring a decision about
teaching and learning that involves a choice between competing values.
Teachers are the ones who typically make these decisions. The inclusion
of the word "controversial" in the concept label signals that there is disagreement about how the questions should be answered. The degree of
controversy varies, and is dependent on the nature of the value conflict.
When issues provide a particularly clear and vexing conflict between different values, the level of controversy increases.

From my research on CPI discussions in secondary classes (Hess 2000),
I have induced a number of controversial pedagogical issues specific to
teaching students to participate more effectively in CPI discussions. The
issues are:

1. Is a particular matter under discussion a CPI or a question for which
   there is a clearly right answer that teachers want students to build
   and believe?
2. Who should make the decision about which issues will be discussed:
   the teacher, students, or the teacher and students together? A corollary issue focuses on selection criteria. Which criteria should be used
   to select from among the many CPI the ones that are most appropriate to include in the curriculum?
3. Of the many models of CPI discussions, which ones are most likely
   to help students achieve the desired educational goals?
4. What should be the contours of the teacher's role in organizing and
   facilitating CPI discussions? Should teachers disclose their personal views on the CPI under discussion? If so, in what way and at what
   point?
5. Should students be required to participate verbally in CPI discussions? A corollary issue is whether students' participation in CPI discussions should be formally assessed and graded?

Developing a CPI Discussion Curriculum. Because my students are
taking the methods courses at the same time they are student teaching,
the opportunity exists for them immediately to experiment with what they
have learned. One of the required methods assignments is to develop a
CPI discussion lesson plan that fits the school and course context in which
they are teaching and try it with their students. First, students must select
the CPI that their lesson will be about. Working through various issue
selection criteria, the students pick an issue that fits well into the existing

curriculum and is approved by their cooperating teacher. Next, they decide what kind of discussion model they want to use. Because different models will require different types of resources, this decision must be made before they begin the search for resources. It has been my experience that the most skilled teachers are able to locate and adapt existing high quality curricular resources. In light of that, we first search through the plethora of video and print materials developed by civic education organizations and also search the World Wide Web for high quality public policy sites with useful resources. Often the teacher education students will design lessons that also require their students to locate and evaluate sources for background on the issue and the various positions on how it should be resolved.

Before the lesson is due, the students bring in a draft and meet with one another in small groups to give and receive feedback on the design of the lesson and the resources that will be used. This "lesson workshop" is a key assessment opportunity for me. As I circulate from group to group, listening to their conversations, I am able to learn more about their current thinking about CPI discussions. In the large group discussion that follows the lesson workshop, we focus on problems that have arisen as the students develop the lessons and talk about how to tackle those problems. The students then revise their lessons, and I give them feedback before the lessons are used in their student teaching placements.

We devote a considerable amount of time and effort on the lesson design process for two reasons. First, in a study of teachers who were exceptionally good at teaching their students to participate in CPI discussions, I learned that the lesson design stage was a critical step in their teaching of skills (Hess 1998). These teachers developed elaborate lesson plans and directed the full battalion of their pedagogical content knowledge to the lesson planning process, which accounted for why their students were well prepared for the discussions. The materials the students had studied were wide-ranging, of high interest, and written at the appropriate grade level. Additionally, the discussion model these skilled teachers selected was carefully matched to the discussion skills they were helping their students develop.

There is a second reason why I encourage my teacher education students to not shortcut the lesson design stage. Remember that one of the misconceptions my students bring into the teacher education program is that discussions occur naturally, spontaneously, and without preparation. By focusing their attention on developing fairly elaborate lessons that will prepare their students well for the CPI discussion, I am purposely trying to counteract that misconception. My hope is that their preparation will pay off when they use the lesson with their students.

CPI Discussions in Their Classrooms. The teacher education students use the CPI lesson they have developed in their student teaching placement: either a middle or high school social studies class. Depending on the design of the lesson, it can range from a few class periods to a full week. In the past year, the CPI discussion topics ranged from whether tax money should be required to pass graduation tests to earn a high school diploma, to whether a federal hate crime law should be passed by Congress. The students teaching in middle schools tended to gravitate toward "Structured Academic Controversy" (see Figure 5.1) because of its structure, but other discussion models were used as well. I encouraged the students to make sure their cooperating teacher viewed the lesson and a few of the students were also able to teach the lesson when their university supervisor was observing. During and after the lesson, the students took notes about how the lesson worked, which they later relied on when assessing how the lesson met the standards for instruction that are in *Powerful and Authentic Social Studies* (Harris and Yocum 2000).

Powerful and Authentic Social Studies. Incorporated throughout both methods classes is a focus on the standards for instruction that are part of *Powerful and Authentic Social Studies* (PASS), a professional development program created by educators in Michigan (Harris and Yocum 2000) that was published recently by the National Council for the Social Studies. PASS combines NCSS standards for *powerful* teaching (1993) with standards for *authentic* instruction derived from National Center on Organization and Restructuring of Schools research (Newmann, Secada, and Wehlage 1995) to construct a set of expectations for social studies instruction, curriculum design, and assessment techniques. "Grounded in a vision of intellectual quality," PASS aims at "significant, meaningful" student achievement, which is made "evident in the mastery displayed by adults acting competently in their role as citizens" (Harris and Yocum 2000, 15-16).

I use these standards for their rich theoretical framework and because they focus my students' attention on what their students are learning (see Figure 5.2). Often novice teachers become so concerned about what they are doing that it is difficult to pay appropriate attention to what should matter most in the classroom—the students' experience and learning. As part of each major unit in the two methods classes, the teacher education students develop a lesson, teach it to their students, and then write a fairly elaborate reflection of it using the PASS instructional standards. Thus, my students are already familiar with the PASS standards and their rubrics before the discussion unit.

Assessing examples of classroom instruction using the PASS standards is an elaborate process because each of the six standards has a specific definition and its own rubric. For example, the definition of substantive con-

Figure 5.2
Standards for Instruction from Powerful and
Authentic Social Studies[1]

Standard 1. Higher Order Thinking: Instruction involves students in manipulating information and ideas by synthesizing, generalizing, explaining, hypothesizing, or arriving at conclusions that produce new meaning and understandings for them.

Standard 2. Deep Knowledge: Instruction addresses central ideas of a social studies discipline or topic with enough thoroughness to explore connections and relationships and to produce relatively complex understandings.

Standard 3. Substantive Conversation: Students engage in extended conversational exchanges with the teacher and/or their peers about subject matter in a way that builds an improved and shared understanding of ideas or topics.

Standard 4. Connections to the World Beyond the Classroom: Students make connections between substantive knowledge and personal experiences, social problems, or public policy.

Standard 5. Ethical Valuing: Students consider core democratic values when making decisions on matters of public concern or when judging personal conduct.

Standard 6. Integration: Instruction broadens the scope of learning by spanning social studies disciplines, linking social studies to other subject areas, bridging time or place, or blending knowledge with skills.

versation states: "In classes characterized by high levels of substantive conversation, there is sustained teacher-student and/or sustained student-student interaction about a topic; the interaction is reciprocal, and it promotes coherent shared understanding" (Harris and Yocum 2000, Handout H5-1). The low end of the standard for substantive conversation is that "virtually no features of substantive conversation occur during the lesson," while the high end requires that "all three features of substantive conversation occur, with at least one example of sustained conversation, and almost all students participate" (Harris and Yocum 2000, Handout H5-1). After explaining how their CPI discussion met each of the six standards, the students write a brief reflection about what they would change to improve the lesson or their approach to CPI discussion overall.

Electronic Portfolios. Throughout the two methods classes, the teacher education students construct a portfolio that demonstrates what they know and can do relative to the University of Wisconsin-Madison's Teacher Education Standards. In the first methods class, the portfolio is in draft form and on paper. Students include it in their CPI discussion lesson plan, preceded by an explanation of what the lesson and their experience teaching it illustrate about their teaching skills. In the second semester of the methods course, the portfolio is substantially expanded and revised, and then converted into electronic form and published on a password- protected Web site. Although students are not required to keep their CPI discussion lesson as an artifact in their final portfolio, virtually all of them do so. Additionally, the final portfolios tend to include additional experiences with CPI discussions that the students have used in their student teaching long after the CPI discussion unit.

Persisting Challenges in the Teaching of CPI Discussion

Given my earlier claim that it is difficult to teach secondary school students how to participate effectively in CPI discussions, it follows naturally that it is also challenging to teach teacher education students how to use CPI discussion teaching. While the curriculum I have been using has proved fairly successful, I continue to be faced with a number of challenges. They include: (1) my students' continuing problems with facilitating CPI discussions; (2) my own concern that CPI discussions are not nested powerfully in a comprehensive framework for democracy education; and (3) the degree to which the controversial pedagogical issue of choice (meaning whether students should or should not be given a choice about participating orally in classroom discussion) can, if not examined thoroughly, undermine how CPI discussions work in social studies classes.

As they gain experience, my students recognize and lament the difficulty of facilitating discussions (of all sorts, not just those that focus on CPI). As a result, they become more critical of their own facilitation skills. While the university supervisors who critique and provide feedback on their teaching in the field provide sophisticated and helpful advice about how they can improve their facilitation skills, it is clear to me that we need to attend to this more substantially in the methods classes. One way to do this would be through in-class "micro-teaching" where the students facilitate a discussion of other methods students and receive feedback from the group. While I know other methods professors have success doing this, class time is always in short supply, and the challenges of facilitating CPI discussions with middle and high school students are different (and greater) than those in a university classroom. A second way of helping students become more skilled at facilitating CPI discussions involves a combination of self-reflection and feedback from a critical friend. To that end, one major change I am planning to implement is to require the methods students to videotape the CPI discussions they lead in their student teaching, to view the tapes looking for certain characteristics of effective facilitation, and then to identify the problems that they would like to work on with the assistance of a critical friend (another student in the class), who would also view the tape.

A second persisting challenge in my CPI discussion teaching is ensuring that students see the connection such discussions have to democracy education. As you recall, the CPI discussion unit is toward the beginning of the first of two methods classes—before we have had much time to focus on democracy as a concept or the many different approaches to democracy education. I now think this is a mistake because it fails to sufficiently emphasize the relationship between CPI discussions and democracy—which, in my mind, is the most powerful rationale for such discussions. The correction is an obvious one: to precede the focus on CPI discussions with a larger emphasis on conceptualizing democracy and democracy education. As an example of how I may do this, Figure 5.3 illustrates a framework I am developing to represent various approaches to democracy education.

The schools of thought presented here illustrate a wide variety of overlapping approaches to democratic education. Although each school of thought has adherents, and its practical manifestations can be found in school curricula, there is often considerable overlap across these schools of thought. That is, teachers will often draw on several schools when designing and enacting their curricula because their goals for democracy education encompass the goals of more than one school. CPI discussions, for example, typically combine the skills and issues schools of thought. This "schools of thought" framework will now be used to create a curriculum that will precede the CPI discussion unit, with the goal of helping students understand the connections between CPI discussions and democracy.

Finally, I continue to be intrigued and challenged by the controversial pedagogical issue of choice I mentioned earlier: whether students should or should not be given a choice about participating orally in classroom discussion. Many of my teacher education students have contradictory opinions on the question. On one hand, they value discussions more when many students are participating verbally, but on the other hand, they are unsure whether it is educative or fair to require their students to do so. I do not find this surprising. I have observed that while most teachers are relatively sanguine about requiring students to do a number of other classroom tasks—from keeping journals to writing essays to watching films—there

Figure 5.3
Democracy Education in the U.S.: Six Schools of Thought

	Knowledge	Service	Skills	Issues	Values	Participation
Desired outcome	Develop knowledge of democratic history, principles, processes, and structures	Learn how to (and want to) provide voluntary service to communities to address civic/political problems	Improve thinking, research, deliberation, discussion, advocacy, and cooperative group skills	Learn how to form and advocate positions on political and social issues	Develop an understanding and appreciation of pro-democracy values	Vote and engage in other forms of political service and action (such as jury duty)
Focus	Democracy involves building knowledge	Democracy involves individuals working to help other people	Democracy involves investigating and solving problems	Democracy involves a "public" making decisions on issues	Democracy involves values and how you act on those values	Democracy involves using the "codes of power" to participate
Example	*We the People* (Center for Civic Education 2001)	*Community Service Learning* (Wade 1997)	*Public Issues Discussion* (Oliver & Shaver 1974)	*PPD Approach* (Parker & Zumeta 1999)	*Reasoning with Democratic Values* (Lockwood & Harris 1985)	*Kids Voting* (2001)

is something unique about classroom discussion that causes many teachers to feel uncomfortable about requiring verbal participation. There are a number of reasons that account for this discomfort.

For one, some teachers say that many students do not like having to talk in class discussions and it is unfair to force them to do so because of the public nature of discussion. Rahima Wade's (1994) research on preservice teachers' beliefs about oral participation in class shows that these teachers may be correctly interpreting the desires of their students. In Wade's study, 66% of preservice teachers agreed with this statement: "Participating in class discussions is a matter of personal choice. It is not essential that everyone contributes in this way" (1994, 235).

In a recent study of how high school students experience and learn from CPI discussions in secondary social studies, my colleague and I had similar findings (Hess & Posselt 2001). Specifically, we found an important tension between responsibility to the group and individual choice about verbal participation (see Figure 5.4). The high school students believe they have a responsibility to contribute to class discussions occasionally, that verbal participation is an essential skill to have, and that students should be taught how to participate effectively in discussions (#28, 29, and 31). They are divided over whether participation in class discussion is a matter of personal choice (#30), however, and on whether it is fair for a teacher to base a part of their grade on the quality of their participation (#32). As Figure 5.4 illustrates, many students say that while it is important to learn how to participate in discussions, actually doing so should be a matter of personal choice.

In addition to the argument that it is unfair to require students to participate verbally in discussion, some teachers say they believe that some students learn best by listening and should not be forced to speak if that is not the way they learn. Teachers also raise concerns about cultural hegemony, arguing that some cultures in which students are raised do not support mandatory participation in public discussions and that to do so in school denigrates the students' home culture. Underpinning many of these arguments against forced participation in classroom discussion in the sense that there is something inherently undemocratic about requiring students to speak publicly when it is not what they want to do. Ironically, this belief may be an offshoot of how values related to free speech have permeated the belief system of people in the United States. The constitutional right to freedom of speech implies to many the converse—the freedom not to speak.

Not all teachers, however, agree that students should be given a choice about whether to participate verbally in class discussions. Likening the learning of discussion skills to other educational outcomes, some teachers say that students will only get the message about the importance of learn-

Figure 5.4
Post-class Survey: Discussion as a Value (n=46)

	Agree	Disagree
	%	%
28. Every student in a class has the responsibility to contribute to class discussions occasionally.	84%	16%
29. Being able to speak up in a group of one's peers is an essential skill for a person to have.	95%	5%
30. Participating in class discussions is matter of personal choice. It is not essential that everyone contribute in this way.	53%	47%
31. It is important that students be taught how to participate effectively in class discussions.	87%	13%
32. It is fair for a teacher to base a part of the students' grade on the quality of their participation in class discussions.	55%	45%

ing how to participate verbally in classroom discussions if the teacher requires everyone in the class to do so. If only the already verbally proficient students are expected to participate in class discussions, then others will be deprived of the opportunity to learn how to do something which has cache in a democratic society. Appropriating the reasoning of Lisa Delpit (1995), verbal participation in classroom discussion is seen as both an avenue to important educational outcomes (such as enhanced critical thinking skills or the understanding of vital content) and a code of power in its own right that all students should be taught.

While I have always included the controversial pedagogical issue of choice in the methods classes, I do not think it has been given enough attention. Specifically, I have come to believe that the choice issue is a fundamental one—meaning that how it is decided will determine, by definition, many things about the role of classroom discussion in social studies. For example, if teachers do not require students to participate verbally in class discussions, then it is unlikely that any serious attention will be given to assessing or evaluating students' discussion skills. Moreover, if all students are not required to participate verbally, the need to provide explicit instruction on oral discussion skills diminishes. Therefore, the importance of this issue has convinced me that more attention should be devoted to analyzing it in the methods classes. In the future, I plan to do this by sharing the research on how other pre-service students and high school students think about this issue with the methods students (Hess and Posselt 2001; Schwingle 2000; Wade 1994). Additionally, I will ask them to develop a position on this issue over the course of the two methods classes. In short, I will make this issue a larger focus of our attention to CPI discussions in the methods classes.

Conclusion: Teaching to Controversy

By placing such a large emphasis on CPI discussions in secondary social studies methods courses I hope to influence the role such discussions play in democracy education. I do not mean to suggest that CPI discussions are the only necessary component of a robust democracy education curriculum. However, their role is critical and must be enhanced. Controversy about political and social issues is part and parcel of what occurs in every society. Learning how to confront controversy with civility and respect, however, is a distinguishing characteristic of a healthy democracy, and thus, should be embraced by those of us preparing the next generation of social studies teachers. Focusing explicitly and extensively on CPI discussions in teacher education provides a way of teaching to controversy—which holds potential for improving our democracy through broader and more sophisticated citizen participation.[2]

Appendix: Assessing Discussion Skills

Throughout this course you will work to improve your ability to participate effectively in small and large group discussions. The course focuses on this goal for two reasons. First, what we learn and create in this class will be influenced by the quality of our public talk. That is, we will form deeper and more sophisticated understanding of important events, ideas, issues, and one another if we have frequent high quality discussions. Second, your abilities as a discussant are connected to your efficacy in your various life roles: as a citizen, family member, colleague, neighbor, etc. Improving your discussion abilities will help you learn more and help you create more powerful and meaningful bonds with others. Thus, the course is structured to both teach *with* and teach *for* discussion.

There are three ways we will work toward the goal of creating high quality discussion and skills discussants in this course. First, we will identify and describe the characteristics of good discussion and ways to operationalize those characteristics in our class. Second, through immersion—learning by doing. We will have frequent discussions, each followed by an evaluation of the discussion itself. Third, you will identify at least one specific goal for improving your discussion abilities and will work toward that goal throughout the semester. On several occasions you will give and receive feedback from a "discussion critical friend" about the discussion skill you are working on. Your assessment of your improvement, coupled with my assessment of the same, will be combined to account for half of the class participation portion of your grade for this course. As the syllabus states, the other half of the class participation category is comprised of your demonstration of preparation for class (typically, the short papers you write evaluating the ideas in readings, or the questions you prepare for class activities).

To put this plan into practice, you need to identify and describe at least one specific discussion skill to work on throughout the semester and plan for improvement. The skill needs to be important enough to deserve your attention, and must have some meaningful connection to the overall quality of our group's discussion. For example, you may want to work on increasing the overall quantity and quality of your verbal participation. Conversely, if you overtalk in discussion, you may want to work on holding yourself in restraint and retargeting some of your verbal contributions to invite the participation of others. Although it is likely that some of you are already highly skilled discussants, I anticipate that each of you has some room for improvement. The point here is to identify explicitly what you want to work on and develop a plan to do so.

By the beginning of the third week of class, please answer the following questions. If you would like to schedule a meeting to discuss your plan, please do so. Or, we would communicate via e-mail if that would be more convenient.

1. What is the specific discussion skill you want to improve in this course?

2. In what ways is that discussion skill connected to the overall quality of our group's discussions?

3. Imagine that you became significantly better at this skill by the end of the course. Describe what this would look, sound, and/or feel like.

4. What evidence can I look for that will enable me to provide you meaningful feedback on this discussion skill?

5. What plan will you follow to improve this skill?

6. What can I and your "discussion critical friend" do to help you implement your plan?

Notes

1. Figure 5.2 is derived from *Powerful and Authentic Social Studies: A Professional Development Program* for Teachers by Harris and Yocum, which was published in 2000 by the National Council for the Social Studies.

2. Acknowledgments: Much of what I have learned about CPI discussion teaching in secondary social studies methods courses came from the three years in which I had the good fortune of working with Professor Walter Parker at the University of Washington. As his teaching assistant, I observed his masterful teaching and participated in numerous conversations with him about the issues of CPI discussion teaching. I also want to thank Julie Posselt and Sue Hess for their helpful editing of this chapter.

References

Barber, Benjamin R. "Public Talk and Civic Action: Education for Participation in a Strong Democracy." *Social Education* 53 (1989): 355-356, 370.

Costa, A. L., and B. Kallick. "Through the Lens of a Critical Friend." *Educational Leadership* (October 1993): 49-51.

Delpit, Lisa. *Other People's Children: Cultural Conflict in the Classroom*. New York, NY: W. W. Norton & Co., Inc., 1995.

Dillon, J. T. *Using Discussion in Classrooms*. Philadelphia: Open University Press, 1994.

Doble Research Associates, Inc. *A Report on People's Thinking in the 1998-1999 National Issues Forums*. Englewood Cliffs, NJ: National Issues Forums Institute, 1999.

Evans, Ronald W. and David W. Saxe, eds. *Handbook on Teaching Social Issues*. Washington, DC: National Council for the Social Studies, 1996.

Gall, J. P., and M. D. Gall. "Outcomes of the Discussion Method." In *Teaching and Learning through Discussion*. W. Wilen, ed. Springfield, IL: Charles S. Thomas, 1990.

Gray, Dennis. "Putting Minds to Work." *American Educator* 13 (1989): 16-23.

Grossman, P. L. *The Making of a Teacher: Teacher Knowledge and Teacher Education*. New York: Teachers College Press, 1990.

Gutmann, Amy. *Democratic Education*. Princeton, NJ: Princeton University Press, 1987.

Hahn, Carole L. "Research on Issues-Centered Social Studies." In *Handbook on Teaching Social Issues*. R. W. Evans and D. W. Saxe, eds. Washington, DC: National Council for the Social Studies, 1996, 26-39.

Hahn, Carole L. *Becoming Political: Comparative Perspective on Citizenship Education*. New York: State University of New York Press, 1998.

Harris, David. "Assessing Discussion of Public Issues: A Scoring Guide." In *Handbook on Teaching Social Issues*, R. W. Evans and D. Harris, eds., Washington, DC: National Council for the Social Studies, 1996, 288-297.

Harris, David, and M. Yocum. *Powerful and Authentic Social Studies: A Professional Development Program for Teachers*. Washington, DC: National Council for the Social Studies, 2001.

Hess, Diana. *Discussing Controversial Public Issues in Secondary Social Studies Classrooms: Learning from Skilled Teachers*. Unpublished doctoral dissertation, University of Washington, Seattle, WA, 1998.

Hess, Diana. "Developing Strong Voters through Democratic Deliberation." *Social Education* 64 (September 2000a): 293-296.

Hess, Diana. *The Controversial Pedagogical Issues of Controversial Public Issues Teaching*. Paper presented at the meeting of the American Educational Research Association, New Orleans, LA, April 24-28, 2000b.

Hess, Diana, and J. Posselt. *How Students Experience and Learn from Discussing Controversial Public Issues in Secondary Social Studies*. Paper presented at the meeting of the American Educational Research Association, Seattle, WA, April 10-14, 2001.

Johnson, David W., and Roger T. Johnson. "Conflict in the Classroom: Controversy and Learning." *Review of Educational Research* 49 (Winter 1979): 51-69.

Johnson, David W., and Roger T. Johnson. "Critical Thinking through Structured Controversy." *Educational Leadership* 45 (May 1988): 58-64.

Kettering Foundation. *Meaningful Chaos: How People Form Relationships with Public Concerns*. Dayton, OH: Kettering Foundation, 1993.

Kids Voting. Available on-line: <http://www.kidsvotingusa.org/>, 2001.

Kohlberg, Lawrence. *The Philosophy of Moral Development: Moral Stages and the Idea of Justice*. San Francisco: Harper and Row, 1981.

Lockwood, Alan, and David Harris. *Reasoning with Democratic Values: Ethical Problems in U.S. History*. New York: Teacher's College Press, 1985.

Lockwood, Alan. "Controversial Issues: The Teacher's Crucial Role." *Social Education* 60 (1996): 1, 28-31.

Lortie, D. *Schoolteacher: A Sociological Study*. Chicago: University of Chicago Press, 1975.

Mansbridge, J. "Democracy, Deliberation, and the Experience of Women." In *Higher Education and the Practice of Democratic Politics: A Political Education Reader*, B. Marchland, ed., Dayton, OH: Kettering Foundation, 1991, 122-135 (ERIC Document 350 909).

National Council for the Social Studies. Quoted in: *Expectations of Excellence: Curriculum Standards for Social Studies*. Washington, DC: National Council for the Social Studies, 1994.

National Education Association. *The Social Studies in Secondary Education: A Report of the Committee on Social Studies of the Committee on the Reorganization of Secondary Education*. (Bulletin 28). Washington, DC: Bureau of Education, 1916.

Newmann, Fred M. *Clarifying Public Controversy: An Approach to Teaching Social Studies*. Boston: Little, Brown, 1970.

Newmann, Fred M., W. G. Secada, and Gary G. Wehlage. *A Guide to Authentic Instruction and Assessment: Vision, Standards, and Scoring*. Madison, WI: Wisconsin Center for Educational Research, 1995.

Noddings, Nell. *Educating for Intelligent Belief or Unbelief*. New York: Teachers College Press, 1993.

Nystrand, M., A. Gamoran, and W. Carbonara. *Towards an Ecology of Learning: The Case of Classroom Discourse and Its Effects on Writing in High School English and Social Studies*. Albany, NY: National Research Center on English Learning and Achievement, 1998 (ERIC Document Reproduction Service No. ED 415 525).

Oliver, Donald W., and James P. Shaver. *Teaching Public Issues in the High School*. Logan, UT: Utah State University Press, 1974.

Parker, Walter, C., and Diana Hess. "Teaching with and for Discussion." *Teaching and Teacher Education* 17 (April 2001): 273-289.

Parker, Walter C., and William Zumeta. "Toward an Aristocracy of Everyone: Policy Study in the High School Curriculum." *Theory and Research in Social Education* 27 (Winter 1999): 9-44.

Schwingle, M. A. *High School Students' Attitudes about the Use of Graded Discussions in Social Studies*. Unpublished masters thesis, University of Wisconsin, Madison, WI, 2000.

Singleton, Laurel R., and James R. Giese. "Preparing Citizens to Participate in Public Discourse: The Public Issues Model." In *Handbook on Teaching Social Issues*, R. W. Evans and D. W. Saxe, eds., Washington, DC: National Council for the Social Studies, 1996, 59-65.

Torney-Purta, Judith, Rainer Lehmann, Hans Oswald, and Wolfram Schultz. *Citizenship and Education in Twenty-eight Countries: Civic Knowledge and Engagement at Age Fourteen.* Amsterdam: International Association for the Evaluation of Educational Achievement, 2001.

Wade, Rahima C., ed. *Community Service Learning.* Albany: State University of New York Press, 1997.

Wade, Rahima C. "Teacher Education Students' Views on Classroom Discussion: Implications for Fostering Critical Reflection." *Teaching and Teacher Education* 10: 2 (1994): 231-242.

Wilen, William W. and Jane J. White. "Interaction and Discourse in Social Studies Classrooms." In *Handbook of Research on Social Studies Teaching and Learning.* James P. Shaver, ed., New York: Macmillan, 1991. 483-495.

6

Teaching Teachers to Lead Discussions: Democratic Education in Content and Method

Walter C. Parker

Student teacher A: I like the part where King says that an act of civil dis-
obedience must be done "openly and lovingly."
Student teacher B: What do you mean?
Student teacher A: What do I mean or what does King mean?
Student teacher B: Both.
Student teacher A: I'm not sure. I think it makes this kind of law-break-
ing really different—um, religious.
Student teacher C: Religious?
Student teacher D: Different from what?

This is an excerpt from a discussion of Martin Luther King's *Letter from Birmingham City Jail* (1963), which I was facilitating in my social studies curriculum and instruction class. My purpose in leading the discussion, a seminar, was to deepen these student-teachers' understanding of the issues, values, and ideas raised by the *Letter*. I wanted also to teach them to facilitate such discussions with *their* students. They are my students, but they are in turn the teachers of other students. This is the strange, iterative world of teacher education where one pedagogic exchange is always conducted with an eye toward another that involves a different teacher and a different set of students somewhere and sometime in the future. "X" is teaching "Y" to "Z" in one setting so that "Z" can appropriate "Y" for use with "A" in another setting at a later date.

As the excerpt reveals, the discussion is going rather well. In a few turns, students are expressing themselves, challenging one another's statements, seeking clarity, and giving reasons. But while the discussion is successful enough, are the participants themselves learning to lead discussions with their students? This is another matter entirely.

I will share some of my recent efforts to teach social studies methods students to lead purposeful discussions. This work required me first to demonstrate purposeful-discussion leadership, as best I could, and to open these demonstrations to critique. It required me also to develop a topology of discussion that helped students distinguish among *kinds* of discussion. The typology was needed, I had learned, because students' critiques of the demonstrations often focused on marginal issues and missed the big picture, the discussion's purpose and whether or not it was achieved. For many students, discussion tended to be both monolithic and invisible; monolithic because they had only a general and singular conception of discussion; and invisible because while they no doubt had been involved in at least some purposeful discussions in their school experiences, they often could not describe their distinguishing characteristics well enough to appropriate discussion as a classroom tool. It was as though they hadn't actually seen the discussions in which they had participated. They had memories of them being "interesting," but little more. All this made it difficult for students to participate in, let alone lead, disciplined (purposeful, meaningful, respectful) and lively (interesting, challenging, exciting) discussions of academic topics or controversial public issues.

The typology distinguishes two discussions: seminars and deliberations.[1] Seminars are discussions aimed at enlarging students' understandings of select texts. "Select texts" here are powerful printed documents, such as some primary and secondary sources in history and social science, some works of historical fiction, and some transcribed speeches. Texts also are works of film and photography, painting and theater, social happenings and performances, and so forth. A text worthy of a seminar is a potentially mind-altering text—one that contains or gives rise to powerful issues, ideas, and values. A deliberation is a discussion aimed at making decisions about what a "we" should *do*. Deliberation helps participants weigh policy alternatives on a public (shared) issue on which action is needed. For this reason, deliberation is the most basic labor of democratic life. "Is it fair?" "Will it work?" With questions like these, participants in a deliberation look together at the problem, framing and reframing it, searching for an array of alternatives, then weighing them and eventually choosing a course of action. The issue itself is now the "text" along with the alternative courses of action that might be taken to address it and, perhaps, solve it. This may be a classroom issue (e.g., a kindergarten teacher asks students to decide whether a new rule is needed to remedy a classroom problem; a high school teacher asks students to decide whether tardiness should affect course grades), a school issue (e.g., student council members deliberate dress-code policies), or a community issue (e.g., students decide what stand they will take, as a group, on a non-school public issue—a taxation issue, a resource distribution issue, a war and peace issue, and so forth). Whenever a "we" is deciding what to do, and the decision is binding on all, then arguably a better decision will emerge when the parties to it have at least sought out one another's views and listened to and talked with one another seriously. (Voting, by contrast, can be done without listening or talking; it is a discussion-free decision-making method.) In summary, seminars deepen our understanding of the world while deliberations help us decide, together, when and what to change and how. One without the other is not desirable.

The two kinds of discussion cover a lot of ground, and for this reason alone they are widely useful instructional models in social studies classrooms. The ground they cover includes both the content of the discussions—the text or controversial issue at hand—as well as the civic outcomes of being involved with one another in these two modes of face-to-face communication. Students may be discussing material that requires them to deepen their understanding of democracy in a diverse society, such as King's *Letter*, or the issue of whether to disenfranchise ex-convicts.

These subject matters are themselves clearly related to democratic education, as is the method by which they are being considered: discussion. I will return to this point shortly, and it is an underlying theme of this chapter. But let me conclude this introduction by noting that discussion facilitation is not all I try to teach my students.

The course to which I will refer here is a two-quarter social studies curriculum and instruction course for future teachers of middle and high school students.[2] It begins with a unit on teaching and learning with inquiry, which is framed by John Dewey's "double movement of reflection" (Dewey 1991, 79-100; Fenton 1967; Parker 2001b), followed by a unit on concept development that relies on the work of Hilda Taba (1971). After these comes the seminar unit, which completes the first quarter of ten weeks. The second half of the course (the second quarter) begins with a deliberation unit and proceeds to a unit called "History Workshop," which lasts the rest of the quarter. This unit is dedicated to teaching and learning with various instructional methods that help students "do history" themselves rather than only "absorbing" the histories done by others (Levstik and Barton 2001).[3] It includes teaching students to puzzle through document sets (sometimes asking students to lead seminars on key documents), compose and assess original historical narratives, and collectively decide on (deliberate) sensible standards for historical reasoning and scoring rubrics for historical compositions, whether cause-effect essays, museum exhibits, or original biographies.

Seminar and deliberation facilitation are central units in the course, and both are featured in the culminating unit as a way to review them and put them to work. Let me turn now to the body of this chapter, which has three sections: (1) discussion, (2) seminar, and (3) deliberation.

Discussion

Discussion is the concept of which seminar and deliberation are sub-concepts. I begin with the understanding of discussion offered by David Bridges:

> The distinctive and peculiar contribution which discussion has to play in the development of one's knowledge or understanding . . . is to set alongside one perception of the matter under discussion the several perceptions of other participants . . . challenging our own view of things with those of others. (Bridges 1979, 50)

Bridges' definition points to the basic *circumstance* of discussion—that it is a shared situation—and the *potential* of that situation to encourage participants to consider others' interpretations of things and to reconsider their own interpretations of things and, thereby, to widen and deepen their own understanding. By being challenged, we might "snap out of it," as the saying goes—see around or through our taken-for-granted responses and stances. We might see the world and our place in it differently. The picture might widen; a window might open. We might spend a night in jail with King or Socrates or Gandhi and feel inspired rather than sorry or bored. We might feel both the resentment and the efficacy of the women who met at Seneca Falls and delight in the brilliant rhetoric of their *Declaration*. We might wonder seriously for the first time about the compromises of the Framers on the institution of slavery, or be pulled up short by a criticism that we had not before even imagined.

Discussion is a kind of shared inquiry the desired outcomes of which rely on the expression and consideration of diverse views. This in turn requires discussants to do something difficult and existential: to switch loyalties from justifying positions and winning arguments to listening intently to others, seeking understanding, and expressing ideas that are underdeveloped and "in progress." This is to switch from a defensive stance to an inquisitive stance. This potential prompted Donald Oliver and his associates (1992, 103) to call discussion an "occasion." Discussion widens the scope of each participant's understanding of the object of discussion by building into that understanding the interpretations and life experiences of others. Discussion results, therefore, in what could be called shared understanding. The occasion is both a situation and a method, and these have consequences. In Joseph Schwab's terms, discussion is "a species of activity" by which shared understanding can be achieved: "[D]iscussion is not merely a device, one of several possible means by which a mind may be brought to understanding of a worthy object. It is also the *experience* of moving toward and possessing understanding." (Schwab 1978, 126, 105).[4]

This is the promise of discussion. Discussion is important both as a way of knowing and as a democratic way of being with one another. Participation in sustained discussions of powerful questions can be both a mind-expanding and community-building endeavor. Discussion is relevant both to the pedagogical aim of creating intelligent, collaborative communities of inquiry and to the broad social aims of democracy in a diverse society.

Seminars and deliberations represent the distinction between the world-revealing and the world-changing functions of discussion. When we seek understanding together, we work to develop and clarify meanings. When we forge a decision together, we weigh alternatives and decide which action to take. These overlap. Decision making requires understanding, to be sure, but understanding is not its aim. Its aim is action. With this distinction, we can see why a social studies classroom should not be issue-centered—that is, deliberation-centered—anymore than it should be centered on achieving enlarged understandings—that is, seminar-centered. Given the aims of social studies education, courses routinely must try to do both in tandem. The horizon-broadening and knowledge-deepening promise of seminars helps to provide an enlightened platform for public deliberation and action, and visa versa. To decide solutions to public problems without the advantage of historical and cultural knowledge or of knowing what one another thinks is like trying to rearrange furniture in a dark room. *Understanding and decision making are functionally inseparable, like the two wings of an airplane.* Accordingly, seminar and deliberation are deservedly paired emphases in the project called social studies education. I cannot imagine serious work on one without the advantage provided by serious work on the other.

Here, then, is the typology. It should clarify the distinction between the two kinds of discussions I am describing and, thereby, help us participate in, lead, and teach discussion facilitation to others. (See Figure 6.1) A typology is a classification scheme and, like any ideal type should be handled gingerly. Typologies should not be believed, because they are not descriptions of reality. But they can be *used*; they are mental tools created to aid thinking and doing. Typologies delineate things—all sorts of things, from poetry (haiku, free verse) to governments (autocracy, democracy). They are helpful because they idealize distinctions, making boundaries artificially clear and, thereby, providing analytic power and precision.

This typology permits a rough, at-a-glance comparison of seminars and deliberations on four categories: (1) the aim or purpose, (2) the subject matter under question, (3) the opening question, and (4) exemplars. Let me unpack it by clarifying five of the central terms: deliberation, seminar, pow-

Figure 6.1
A Typology Distinguishing Seminar and Deliberation

Dimension	Seminar	Deliberation
Purpose	1. Reach an enlarged understanding of a powerful test. 2. Improve discussants' powers of undersanding.	1. Reach a decision about what "we" should do about a shared problem. 2. Improve discussants' powers of understanding.
Subject Matter	Ideas, issues, and values in a print or film selection, artwork, performance, political cartoon, or other test.	Alternative courses of actions related to a public (shared; common) problem.
Opening Question	What does this mean?	What should we do?
Exemplar	Socratic Seminar	Structured Academic Controversy

ers of understanding, opening question, and exemplar. Following that, I will outline my units on seminar and deliberation in the social studies curriculum and instruction course.

Deliberation. Deliberations are discussions aimed at deciding on a plan of action that will resolve a problem that a group faces. The essence of deliberation is clarifying the problem and weighing alternatives. Deliberating public issues is the most basic citizen behavior in democracies. Without it, citizens exercise power (e.g., voting; direct action) without having thought together about how to exercise it. The opening question is usually some version of, "What should we do about this?"

Seminar. Seminars are discussions aimed at developing, exposing, and exploring meanings. A seminar's purpose is an enlarged understanding of the ideas, issues, and values in or prompted by the text. The text may be a historical novel, a primary document, an essay, a photo, film, play, or painting. A seminar is not planning for action. There may be deliberative moments within seminars, particularly in the social studies curriculum where "What should we do about this?" is never far from consideration. The seminar's primary purpose, however, is not to repair the world so much as to reveal it with greater clarity. Seminars enrich deliberation, to be sure, and for social studies teachers they go hand in hand by widening students' knowledge and deepening their understanding of issues. Seminars and deliberations overlap, but their emphases and teaching/learning purposes are distinct.

Powers of Understanding. Improving discussants' "powers of understanding" is a secondary aim of both seminars and deliberations. Sometimes termed "habits of mind" (Meier 1995), these are the intellectual arts of interpretation, also called critical thinking or higher-order reasoning. We can think of them as the inquiry skills and dispositions needed to apprehend the world (the purpose of a seminar) and those needed to help us decide what changes should be made (the purpose of a deliberation).

Opening Question. The opening question begins the discussion and is aimed at the purpose of the discussion—toward a decision or an enlarged understanding of a text. When it is effective, the opening question helps the group get to the heart of the matter, whether directly or along a meandering route. And, the opening question is genuine. A question is genuine when the facilitator has not made up his or her mind as to the answer. The teacher doesn't have the answer, but infects students with the same sense of perplexity he or she feels.[5] The genuineness of the question allows the teacher to be actually curious about the students' responses because the teacher too, is grappling with them.

Exemplar. The purpose of any exemplar is to display vividly the critical attributes of the concept it represents. The typology gives one exemplar for each of the two kinds of discussion: Socratic Seminar for seminar and Structured Academic Controversy for deliberation. Each will be detailed in the sections that follow.

Seminar

The Socratic Seminar is the product of a number of interests and forces, but for present purposes we can trace it to the Paideia Group and its publication *The Paideia Proposal*, which advocated "the same course of study for all" and delineated three modes of teaching and learning, K12: recitation and lectures for the acquisition of organized knowledge, coaching and practice in project work for the development of intellectual skills, and discussion of texts (books, art, letters, etc.) for "enlarged understanding of ideas and values" (Adler 1982, 21, 23). Dennis Gray, who was a member of the Paideia Group, helped popularize the third of these, the Socratic Seminar, by conducting teacher training programs and writing a popular article in the *American Educator*.[6] Gray wrote:

> Seminars demand rigorous thinking by all the participants, not mere mastery of information. They require no predetermined notion of what particular understandings will be enlarged or what routes to greater understanding will be followed. The conversation moves along in accordance with what is said by the participants, rather then deference to a hard and fast lesson plan.

Seminars are inhospitable to competition for right answers, particularly given the principal aim in engaging students in critical thinking about complex, multisided matters. Instead, they join participants in a collaborative quest for understanding, in mutual testing of each other's responses to the text. (Gray 1989, 18)

I begin the seminar unit with a unit overview. It informs students that I will demonstrate a "Socratic Seminar" after which they will have two opportunities to plan and lead a seminar themselves. Those seminars will be "microseminars," that is, short seminars in small groups with each participant taking the facilitator role in turn, each with a different, short text. Each microseminar lasts about 20 minutes, including five minutes for participants to read the text on which the seminar will be conducted. Prior to the microseminars, students who will be leading a discussion of the same text but in different groups get together, "Jigsaw" style (Aronson et al.1978), to discuss that text and to prepare an opening question. Following the microseminars, they will go back to these planning groups to compare experiences and make facilitator notes. After they have each led two seminars, I tell them, I will lead one more and ask them to critique my facilitation based on what they have learned from their own experiences as a participant and facilitator up to that point.

Knowing all this in advance has advantages, of course. Students have the big picture in mind and, specifically, they are motivated to pay close attention to the facilitator role in the first seminar, the one I lead, rather than focusing only on the text and one another. They know they will be taking that role subsequently.

Debriefings play an important part, too, and one follows each seminar and microseminar. A debriefing keeps everyone's attention on what just happened while, at the same time, extending the "occasion," providing a reflective opportunity to scrutinize what happened and why, and to hone one's understanding of the facilitator role. Students reflect on the seminar model and address the many problems that come to mind—how to frame an effective opening question; what to do with some students who will not do the reading and other students who would do it if they could, but they cannot; what to do with students who are uncomfortable participating and students who talk too much and/or will not listen. Also during the debriefings, I provide direct instruction on a number of points: selecting a powerful text, preparing to lead a seminar, stating the purpose of the seminar, stating and/or eliciting norms and standards, keeping the discussion going and on focus, de-briefing a seminar, follow-up writing assignments, working with reading comprehension problems, and tolerating failed seminars and trying again.

By placing this instruction in the debriefing context, light is shed on the just-completed seminar or microseminar—back onto concrete experience.

This is reflection, from *reflectere*: bending backward to understand what happened and forward to imaginatively create one's behavior in the next seminar (Valli 1997). This is also the inductive/deductive "double movement of reflection" (Dewey 1991, 216): students move from experience to creating a working hypothesis about that experience, and back to experience again to test the working hypothesis, then back to revise the hypothesis, and so forth, creating a practical "working theory" of discussion facilitation.

Incorporated in these debriefings is the viewing of two videotapes. One is a 15-minute instructional video called *How to Conduct Successful Socratic Seminars*, featuring Boulder, Colorado, teacher John Zola and his high-school students.[7] While John instructs viewers on various elements of seminar planning and facilitation, he is shown leading a seminar with his students on a Supreme Court decision dealing with sexual harassment at the workplace (*Harris v. Forklift*, 1993). Here the seminar is focused on a primary document that deals with a difficult and controversial public issue on which the Court is rendering an opinion, which the students in the seminar are attempting to understand. The other video is one of a collection of videos that accompanies a teaching manual called *Preparing Citizens: Linking Authentic Assessment and Instruction in Civic/Law-Related Education.*[8] The segment I use shows Judy Still and her middle-school students in Cherry Creek, Colorado, having a seminar on Howard Fast's novel about the opening days of the American Revolution, *April Morning* (Bantam 1961). Here the seminar is focused on historical fiction, and the students are working to understand how its main character and the new nation both are developing.

Selecting a Powerful Text. Powerful texts can call out to us in any medium—print (e.g., King's *Letter*; a Supreme Court opinion), visual (a stature or mural; the Vietnam Memorial), auditory (a workers' song or national anthem), or theatrical (a scene from *The Crucible* or a musical). What makes them "powerful" is that they contain or arouse in participants mind-altering ideas, issues, and values. By "mind-altering" I mean texts that raise persisting or surprising human questions and lend themselves to conflicting interpretations. The exchange and clarification of interpretations should arouse the discussants both intellectually and morally and, thanks to the diversity of participants and disagreements among them, broaden their horizons. The ideas, issues, and values carried by these texts deal intimately with who we are and how we live together, how and who we are going to be, why we hate and love, why we suffer and hope, what we do and don't try to build. At least this is the aim. Of course, not every text does this. At one point in Anglo-American history, such texts were listed and collected and called *the* "Great Books of the Western World" (Hutchins 1952). With the broadening of the canon in recent decades, the group of texts that can be called "great" has been opened up dramatically. Still, this does not mean that all texts are equally powerful, as any teacher and any reader knows, and the chief task for a seminar facilitator is to select the most powerful text for the purpose and students at hand.

Typically in Socratic Seminars, we deal with text *excerpts*. This flies in the face of good literature practice, of course, but it has benefits that can outweigh these costs. Mainly, the class can concentrate more intently on, and dig more deeply into, a brief (1-4 pages) passage than an entire work. And, given the myriad reading ability problems in middle and high schools, the brevity of the passage lends itself to intensive work on a small area and, therefore comprehension.

In the social studies methods course, I try to select powerful texts that deal centrally with problems and principles of democracy. Of the two demonstration seminars I lead myself, recall that one comes at the beginning of the unit, the other after students have each facilitated two seminars and participated as discussants in six-to-eight more in microseminars. For these demonstrations, I often choose King's *Letter from Birmingham City Jail* for the first, which I have excerpted down to four pages from the twenty-page version that appears as a chapter in King's book, *Why We Can't Wait* (1963); and, for the second, Plato's *Crito*, which is an account of Socrates' time in jail prior to his drinking the hemlock. These make an unforgettable pair of seminars. I facilitate the first with the whole-class; in the second I demonstrate a "fishbowl" style seminar, with an inner and outer circle of students who trade places midway through the seminar (students may speak only when in the inner circle).

I choose an additional eight-to-ten texts for the two rounds of microseminars. (Two microseminars with four participants each requires eight texts; if groups are of five students, then ten texts are required.) These texts must be very brief, as students in the microseminars are given only five minutes to read the text prior to the seminar. Typically these are not more than one page long, and my selections often include the following, excerpted: James Baldwin's *A Talk to Teachers*,[9] Machiavelli's *The Prince*, the "Melian Dialogue" in Thucydides' *History of the Peloponnesian War*, Toni Morrison's *Playing in the Dark*,[10] *The Declaration of Independence*, the *Seneca Falls Declaration*, *Federalist No. 10*, Jane Addams' *Democracy and Social Ethics*,[11] Tocqueville's *Democracy in America*, John Kenneth Galbraith's *The Affluent Society*,[12] John Dewey's *Democracy and Education*, and *The Pledge of Allegiance* (this short text in its entirety).Below are the Tocqueville and Addams excerpts. Later, I provide the opening questions I use for each.

> *Alexis de Tocqueville*: There is, indeed, a most dangerous passage in the history of a democratic people. When the taste for physical gratifications among them has grown more rapidly than their education and their experience of

free institutions, the time will come when men are carried away and lose all self-restraint at the sight of the new possessions they are about to obtain. In their intense and exclusive anxiety to make a fortune, they lose sight of the close connection that exists between the private fortune of each and the prosperity of all. It is not necessary to do violence to such a people in order to strip them of the rights they enjoy; they themselves willingly loosen their hold. The discharge of political duties appears to them to be a troublesome impediment which diverts them from their occupations and business. If they are required to elect representatives, to support the government by personal service, to meet on public business, they think they have no time, they cannot waste their precious hours in useless engagements; such idle amusements are unsuited to serious men who are engaged with the important interests of life. These people think they are following the principle of self-interest, but the idea they entertain of that principle is a very crude one; and the better to look after what they call their own business, they neglect their chief business, which is to remain their own masters.[13]

Jane Addams: Women who live in the country sweep their own dooryards and may either feed the refuse of the table to a flock of chickens or allow it innocently to decay in the open air and sunshine. In a crowded city quarter, however, if the street is not cleaned by the city authorities, no amount of private sweeping will keep the tenement free from grime; if the garbage is not properly collected and destroyed a tenement house mother may see her children sicken and die of diseases from which she alone is powerless to shield them, although her tenderness and devotion are unbounded. As society grows more complicated it is necessary that women shall extend her sense of responsibility to many things outside of her own home if she would continue to preserve the home in its entirety.[14]

Certainly a comment is needed about my rationale for choosing the texts I do. My selection is surely limited to the extent of my own knowledge, which results from a combination of my social position, education, and individual dispositions. Generally, I try to choose texts that force my student teachers and me to grapple with how we are wanting to live together, that is, with the arrangement of private and public life. I choose the Tocqueville and Addams texts because they go to the heart of what is arguably the most important issue in educating for democratic living: the tension between individual interests, and the common good (or independence and community; negative and positive liberty). Moreover, Tocqueville connects this tension to the problem of affluence, as does Galbraith, and Addams blurs the boundaries between domestic life and public life. I choose the *Letter* and *Crito* because both feature (a) great moral philosophers, (b) who are in jail, and (c) on purpose—for reasons of conscience, love of justice, and respect for law/community. Together, they provide a dramatic comparison. I choose *The Prince* and the *Melian Dialogue* because they deal centrally with the tension between right (justice) and might (power) and with equality and inequality. Madison's *Federalist 10*, Morrison's *Playing in the Dark*, and Baldwin's *A*

Talk to Teachers each deals with diversity: Madison with the need to limit majority power, Morrison and Baldwin with the depth, persistence, and consequences of racism and prejudice. A good seminar on the *Pledge* spurs some participants for the first time to contemplate the idea of allegiance to a way of living together (a republic) rather than to a person (e.g., the Prince) or a place (e.g., a "fatherland").

Preparing To Lead A Seminar. Preparing to lead a whole-class or fishbowl seminar, or a microseminar, involves numerous decisions and serious consideration of the text to be discussed. How will the class be arranged for seminar? (One large circle? Two concentric circles for alternating "fishbowl" discussions? Small groups?) Will participation be required? Will the seminar be evaluated? How will homework reading, if assigned, be checked prior to the seminar? Will students who haven't done the reading be allowed to participate? How will the seminar purpose be stated and communicated? What norms will be posted (or proposed or elicited from the group)? What question will open the seminar? Here, I deal with the last three questions concerning purpose, norms, and the opening question.

As for purpose and norms, I ask student teachers to prepare a poster that can be taped to the wall each time a seminar is held:

Purpose:

To enlarge your understanding of the ideas, issues, and values in this text.

Norms:

1. Don't raise hands.

2. Address one another, not the discussion leader.

3. Use the text to support opinions.

Communicating with students about the purpose and norms requires knowledge of the students, their discussion experience in and out of school, and the norms by which they usually interact with one another. The adolescents I have worked with often do not have language for challenging or clarifying one another's statements easily or courteously; accordingly, we teach them phrases such as these: "I have a different opinion. . . ." (then state it); or, "I disagree. Let me explain." And, for clarification: "I think I understand, but let me be sure. . . ." (then rephrase); or "What do you mean by. . .?" In the videotape (Social Science Education Consortium 2001) of Judy Still's middle-school seminar on *April Morning*, we see her post the following norms:

1. Don't raise hands.

2. Listen to and build on one another's comments.

3. Invite others into the discussion.

4. Support opinions by referring to passages in the book.

5. Tie what you know about the history of the revolution into your interpretation of "April Morning."

Preparing the opening question for a seminar is the most important aspect of seminar facilitation, without which the purposes and norms have nothing in particular to realize. The key here is reading and re-reading (viewing and re-viewing; listening and re-listening) the text the students will be reading (viewing, listening) and discussing. I indicated earlier that my student teachers participate in two rounds of microseminars, facilitating once in each round. Prior to this, they prepare, Jigsaw style, in planning groups with others who will lead a microseminar on the same text. This is an enormously important planning session, for here they discuss the ideas, issues, and values in the text, and then frame several opening questions and decide on one to try out. (This decision is actually a deliberation since group members are weighing the suggested questions and deciding on one that all will use to open their seminars—that is, they are reaching a decision that will be binding on all.)

Opening questions usually should be interpretive, rather than factual or evaluative. An interpretive question concerns the meaning of the ideas, issues, and values in a text. It has no single correct answer as does a factual question, so the discussion will be text-based as students use the text to marshal evidence for and against particular interpretations. Of course, there will be disagreement. An evaluative question also has no single correct answer, but it is less about interpreting the text and more a matter of making value judgments about something in the text or related to it.[15] Here are some examples. First, I give opening questions I have used with the two texts printed earlier by Tocqueville and Addams. Both are interpretive.

- What does Tocqueville mean in the last sentence of the paragraph, where he writes: but the idea they entertain of that principle (the principle of self-interest) is a very crude one?
- What would be a good title for this paragraph, one that captures Addams' key concerns?

And, here are opening questions I have used with *Letter* and *Crito*. I provide an interpretive, then an evaluative question for each.

- How does King distinguish between just and unjust laws?
- Should social studies teachers urge their students to follow King's example?
- Why didn't Socrates escape when he had the chance?
- Would you have tried to escape if you were in Socrates' place?

De-Briefing A Seminar. A common approach to debriefing a seminar, which I model for my students in the demonstration seminars on *Letter* and *Crito*, is to go around the circle of participants and ask, "In your opinion did we achieve the purpose? Was your understanding enlarged?" Or, ask each participant to make an observation about the seminar: "What is one thing you noticed about the seminar we had today?" Either is a good assessment opportunity for both facilitator and participants, and either should suggest problems that can be addressed immediately or in the next seminar. In the two videotapes, teachers are shown asking these questions, and viewers have the opportunity to listen to students' responses.

Deliberation

Deliberation is discussion with an eye toward deciding what "we" should do (Dillon 1994; Fishkin 1991; Mathews 1994; Young 1997). This "we" is a community that shares a problem. Deliberation is a community-building enterprise because it brings people together around a problem they share and creates a particular kind of democratic culture among them: listening as well as talking, forging decisions together rather than only defending positions taken earlier, and coming to agreement or disagreement (Parker, Ninomiya, and Cogan 1999).

Selecting an exemplar for deliberation is more difficult than for seminar because there are more possibilities. The Public Issues Model (Oliver, Newmann, and Singleton 1992; Evans and Saxe 1996; Oliver and Shaver 1974; Hess 1998) is probably the most venerated in the social studies education field, and for good reason. Students are engaged in large- and small-group discussions of an enduring public issue; they study the issue in depth, including its instantiation across analogous cases; they learn to distinguish between *kinds* of issues (those involving value conflicts as opposed to definitional disputes of disagreements over the facts); and they are taught numerous skills of civic discourse, such as clarification, stipulation, and drawing analogies. However, for the unique pedagogical circumstance of teaching new social studies teachers to lead deliberations, I have come to appreciate Structured Academic Controversy (SAC) as developed by the cooperative learning researchers David and Roger Johnson (1985; 1988). I believe it provides a working platform from which the Public Issues Model can be explored later, if desired.

This "unique pedagogical circumstance" involves (a) novices, not experienced teachers, (b) whose own 16-year "apprenticeship of observation" (Lortie 1975, 61) has taught them a great deal about the IRE (initiate-respond-evaluate) pattern of teacher-student recitation but little about orchestrating purposeful student-student discussions of controversial issues, and (c) who worry, understandably, about their performance as student teachers before their students, peers, cooperating teachers, and university supervisors. This is no ordinary circumstance. My attempts at teaching new teachers to lead deliberative discussions have taught me that Structured Academic Controversy is the better place to begin the journey, while the Public Issues Model allows plenty of room for growth later. In other words, SAC scaffolds student teachers successfully into controversial issues deliberations, after which they may (and I urge them to do so) work toward what I believe is the more ambitious and nuanced Public Issues Model.

Johnson and Johnson (1988) call the strategy "structured academic controversy" in order to emphasize, first, the structured or scaffolded nature of the discussion and, second, the academic or subject-matter controversies, as opposed to nonacademic or interpersonal controversies, that are at issue. A brief excerpt from a SAC discussion should be helpful. Here students are discussing a controversy concerning crime, race, and citizenship: whether ex-felons should be disenfranchised. Value conflicts and disagreements over facts arise in only a few turns.

Terrell: You're absolutely right they should be allowed to vote. They paid their time didn't they? If you don't let them vote you're saying they haven't paid their time.

Sara: But shouldn't we have more respect for the ballot box?

Terrell: Now what does that mean?

Sara: Show a little respect for the victims why don't you.

Angie: Wait. You switched reasons. Let's go back to the ballot box. I think you're right there. Most states don't let ex-cons vote once they're let out of prison, and the reason is that the felons disqualified themselves from citizenship when they violated community norms. It's like they broke the social contract. Sorry, Terrell, but that makes complete sense to me. You can't treat citizenship as cheap.

Sara: Some states, I think. Not more states.

Byron: Do you know who most of those felons are? Maybe not most, but lots? Black. It says right here (pointing to article) that 13 percent of all Black men can't vote today because of current or prior felon convictions. Now what do you really think this issue is about? Crime? Race?

Sara: Now I know why Democrats want the voting restrictions lifted and Republicans don't.

Angie: Why's that?

There are at least two good reasons for teaching the SAC method to preservice students. First, it encourages them to uncover and feature the controversies that suffuse the subject matter they are planning to teach, and doing so improves the quality of their curriculum swiftly and surely. Scholars, recall, are in continual disagreement about the nature of their fields and the claims they are advancing. Scholarship, in fact, is defined by one's participation in these disagreements: A scholar's grasp of the questions and conflicts that mark her field, combined with her willingness to subject her understandings to the criticism of peers, is in large measure what constitutes her as a scholar. Historians disagree fundamentally about why Rome fell, why the tyrannies of Hitler and Mussolini arose in democracies, why women were executed as witches in Salem, why slavery in North America wasn't abolished sooner, and which of these questions is most important. None are settled matters, especially not among the people who know a great deal about them. Competing accounts are adjudicated differently, evidence is evaluated differently, and arguments are made, interpreted, and deployed differently.

Second, along with this uncovering function whereby teachers bring genuine academic controversy to the forefront of their curriculum, SAC sponsors a unique kind of classroom discourse. It involves students in safe, focused discussions with one another during which competing ideas and values are set alongside one another. Moreover, it does this in a way that, in my experience at least, is feasible for the novice teacher who is worried, understandably, about the commonplaces of student teaching: classroom management, relating with students, teaching subject matter, and appearing competent before supervisors.

The discussion excerpt above is, all things considered, quite good. It is a small-group discussion. Students are expressing positions, challenging positions, seeking clarity, giving reasons, and following the reasoning (Angie noted Sara's "switch"). Moreover, they are addressing one another, and each student contributes. These objectives are not easily achieved, as any teacher knows. It is important to note that the discussion occurred with no explicit instruction on how to have such a discussion; instead, careful prompts were given in a particular sequence, which is what earns SAC the adjective "structured" in its name. In this way, SAC scaffolds students into impressively demanding discussions which otherwise may be beyond their reach.

Briefly, here is the SAC procedure as I've adapted it (Parker and Hess 2001). Students read, in groups of four, background material (e.g., historical narrative; journalism) on the issue at hand (e.g., Should states be permitted to disenfranchise ex-felons? Was WWII the second half of WWI? Why was slavery abolished so late in U.S. history? Should physician-assisted suicide be permitted in our state?). Then, each group breaks into two pairs. Each pair is assigned a different position on the issue, affirmative and negative, and given a set of primary and secondary sources in order to study the position and its supporting arguments. This period of text-based study can take anywhere from twenty minutes to several hours or days, depending on the amount and depth of material involved. (Hence, a SAC can be adapted to a single lesson or a whole unit.) Following study, each pair plans and presents its position and arguments to the other pair. Then, the pairs reverse perspectives: each pair feeds back the other pair's position and reasoning until each is satisfied that its case has been heard and understood. All this discussion, recall, is occurring with the relatively safe settings of, first, a pair of students, and then two pairs together in a small group of four students. Following the presentation of the affirmative and negative cases and the subsequent reciprocity, the pairs are asked to dissolve themselves so that the group of four can become one deliberative body. The pairs are asked to drop the positions to which they were assigned. Individuals are encouraged now to be genuine, drawing not only on the readings but also on their life experiences and emotions. "See if you can forge a position, together. Feel free to change your mind." The small group's task now is to reason together in the direction of a consensus on the question; if not consensus, then to "come to disagreement," clarifying the nature of the disagreement.

This small-group discussion is the culminating activity of SAC and the source of the discussion excerpt above. To speak of it as a culminating activity is to say, in linear terms, that it is the final activity setting in the sequence of activity settings that constitutes SAC. Students have been prepared for it not only by studying the issue but by discussing it with a partner, then representing it to an audience (the opposing pair), then reversing perspectives, and then studying it again—now through small-group discussion, setting one perspective alongside others, "challenging our own view of things with those of others" (Bridges 1979, 50).

The SAC procedure may strike some readers as too structured, yet in the culminating discussion students typically change their minds as they see fit, not necessarily clinging to initially assigned positions; and they are listening to and challenging one another, and each of them is contributing. This is not magic. *It was the earlier work in the sequence of settings that scaffolded students successfully into this culminating discussion.* The work done in pairs developed whatever students' initial understanding of the issue might have been, and students were able to broaden that knowledge thanks to the dynamics of presenting and reversing positions and then discussing the issue in the group of four. The scaffold, in other words, has the desired consequences. When we recall the stubborn persistence of recitation in classrooms across the nation and through the grade levels, this is no small feat. Walking around the classroom, listening to the discussions in each group of four, is routinely a satisfying moment.

But my objective here is to teach these preservice teachers to facilitate SAC deliberations with *their* students, which requires more than their engagement in this one demonstration lesson. If I did only this, much of the pedagogy would remain invisible and, therefore, unusable. To appropriate it as a tool in their own teaching, they need not merely to be involved in it while their attention and intellectual effort is focused on the issue being deliberated; they need also to place their attention and intellectual effort on the pedagogy itself. What to do? Following the strategy described earlier for seminars, I could move from the SAC demonstration lesson to "micro-SACs," which students would take turns leading themselves. That would not be feasible, however, because of the large amount of study time needed for the pairs to prepare adequately for their presentations. Instead, I require each student to develop a full SAC lesson plan and to append the affirmative and negative readings their students will study at the outset.

As with the seminar, a good deal of the direct instruction on SAC occurs during the debriefing of the demonstration lesson, but a significant portion of it occurs also during the question-and-answer portion of class sessions in which they are sharing their work on their own SAC plans. The array of problems and considerations needing attention is similar to those for seminar: selecting a powerful issue, articulating to students the purpose of the deliberation, stating and/or eliciting norms and standards for the deliberation, deciding whether to reveal one's own position on the issue, keeping the discussions going and on focus (in pairs; in small groups), de-briefing a SAC, follow-up writing assignments, working with reading comprehension problems, and tolerating failed deliberations and trying again.

Each is important, but due to space limitations I will just touch upon the first four of these.

Selecting a Powerful Issue. The SAC plan my students develop includes a written rationale for the selected issue, which requires them to wrestle with (as they must with seminars) the selection of subject matter. I stipulate that to be powerful, the selected issue should be central—not peripheral—to the course of study at hand (e.g., in a history course, central to the historical era or unit theme), *and it should represent one or more larger, enduring issues*. An enduring issue arises again and again in human affairs, across time and place. The issue of felon disenfranchisement, for example, is central to a civics or government course that deals with voting rights, voter behavior, and such values as liberty, justice, and equality. It represents a number of enduring issues about crime and deviance in any society, especially a society where justice, equality, one-person-one-vote, and the rights *and* responsibilities of citizens are espoused ideals. Similarly, a SAC deliberation on the causes of the American Revolution and whether its instigators were "traitors" or "patriots" is central to a U.S. history course. Here, an enduring issue might be: when is rebellion justified?[16]

Articulating the Purpose of a SAC Deliberation. At this point in debriefing the demonstration lesson on ex-felon voting rights, I introduce the typology presented earlier in this chapter (Figure 6.1). In order to perceive the purpose of deliberation and use it appropriately as a tool in their own classrooms, teachers need a differentiated (rather than monolithic) understanding of discussion. Then, teachers can distinguish among different purposes, tailoring the discussion to different kinds of subject matter. Do students need to deepen and broaden their understanding of the ideas, issues, and values in a particular text? Or do they need to reach a decision? I have found that the typology is not helpful until after the second discussion framework, deliberation, is introduced. At that point, the problem of distinguishing between the two arises.

Norms. Because discussions in SAC are being conducted within small groups, it is unnecessary to establish the hand-raising and address-one-another norms of the seminar. Needed instead are norms related to reaching decisions on controversial issues through civilized disagreement and deep exploration of the issue itself. A videotape I show at this point displays a high-school class in Denver deliberating the issue of physician-assisted suicide.[17] The discussion leader, Diana Hess, elicits from students and writes on the chalkboard the following norms:

1. *Hear all sides equally.*
2. *Listen well enough to respond to and build upon each other's ideas.*
3. *Talking loudly is no substitute for reasoning.*
4. *Back up opinions with clear reasons.*
5. *Speak one at a time.*

The Teacher's Role During Deliberation. The question my student teachers wrestle with more than any other, once they begin to facilitate deliberations on actual controversies (or imagine themselves doing so) is this: what should I do with my own position and reasons on the issue? Should I disclose? When the question is raised, I ask a student to facilitate a brief deliberation. The opening prompt: "See if you can come to a consensus on this issue, or at least clarify the disagreement." Listening to this discussion is invariably a good, informal assessment of students' reasoning on the issue and their background assumptions about the politics of teaching. I follow up by distributing Thomas Kelly's (1989) brief article. He weighs carefully the alternatives, then recommends a particular form of disclosure. If time permits, Kelly's article makes for a good seminar discussion.

Conclusion

Seminars are discussions aimed at enlarging students' understandings of select texts, while deliberations are discussions aimed at making decisions about what a "we"—a community—should do. Deliberation is the basic labor of democratic life, for it addresses common problems and at the same time forges a democratic community of those deliberating such problems together. Yet, it requires not only a "we" with a problem but a "we" with knowledge. A social studies classroom, therefore, should not be deliberation-centered anymore than it should be seminar-centered. Social studies courses, to reiterate the position I took near the beginning of this chapter, must routinely try to do both in tandem. The depth of understanding promised by the seminar helps to provide an enlightened mental and social platform for public action. The reverse is true, too. To take bold social action without the advantage of deep social understanding reeks of action for its own sake, mindlessness; and to take no action, preferring contemplation and theory, is the exemplar of social irresponsibility, cruel inaction in the face of cruel circumstances. Understanding and decision making are functionally inseparable in the project called social studies education.

Pedagogical tools—scaffolds—tailored to the two emphases are needed. Seminar and deliberation are two such tools. Inquiry, concept development, and history workshop (the topics of the other three units in this course) are three more. They support the understanding side of the coin more than the deliberative side, I suppose, except when the inquiries, concepts, and original historical narratives are directed toward public problems such as the enduring tensions between individual interests and the common good, might and right, and *pluribus* and *unum*. Accordingly, the subject matters of the two emphases overlap significantly, and the distinction between the world revealing and the world-changing functions of social studies education is blurred. Still, the two tools we have been considering here—seminar and deliberation—are distinct, and each is worth honing by new and experienced teachers alike. This honing entails something more than participating in them as discussants. It requires also knowledge of both, the sort of knowledge that results from two activities in addition to participation: planning (with others) to lead them and studying (with others) the distinctions between them.

Acknowledgment

I am grateful to Denee Mattioli, Margaret Branson, and Wendy Ewbank for their comments on an earlier draft of this chapter.

Notes

1. The typology, along with a study of some problems that arise when teaching discussion facilitation to others, are detailed in Parker and Hess, 2001. See also Parker 2001a.

2. I sometimes teach the elementary social studies course as well, in which I use the text I authored (2001b). In the present chapter, I focus on the secondary course because it lasts two quarters rather than one and, therefore, I delve further into discussion facilitation.

3. This distinction is detailed in Parker, 2001b, Chapter 4.

4. See also Burbules (1993, 21): "The participants are caught up; they are absorbed."

5. Socrates provides the classic role model. See Plato's *Meno*, in *Protagoras and Meno*, 1956.

6. The Great Books Foundation in Chicago, with which Adler was connected, also has done much to popularize the seminar mode of discussion, conducting teacher trainings across the nation and publishing collections of seminar texts, such as *Introduction to the Great Books*,

a series of texts (with leaders' guides) ranging from Tocqueville's *Democracy in America* to Virginia Woolf's *A Room of One's Own*. Also, the National Paideia Center supports a network of "Paideia schools" (see T. Roberts et al., *The Power of Paideia Schools*. Alexandria, VA: ASCD, 1998). See the work of Sophie Haroutunian-Gordon in high schools, reported in her book, *Turning the Soul* (1991), and her examination of the Socratic method itself in "Was Socrates a 'Socratic' Teacher?" (1988). The Socratic Seminar is used in higher education as well: Undergraduates at St. John' College (Annapolis, MD and Santa Fe, NM) experience seminars as one of the instructional staples in each of the four years of undergraduate study.

7. Alexandria, VA: Association for Supervision and Curriculum Development, 1999.

8. The teaching manual is authored by Barbara Miller and Laurel Singleton, 1997. I analyze two of the videotaped discussions in this collection in Parker, 2001a. These videotapes are available separately (Social Science Education Consortium, 2001).

9. In R. Simonson & S. Walker, ed. *Multicultural Literacy* (St. Paul, MN: Graywolf Press, 1988), 1-15.

10. New York: Random House, 1992.

11. New York: Macmillan, 1902.

12. Boston: Houghton Mifflin, 1998 (40th anniversary edition).

13. In Alexis de Tocqueville, (1969, Vol. II, Part II, Chapter 14, "Physical Pleasures...Freedom and ...Public Affairs").

14. In Frances Maule, ed. *Woman Suffrage: History, Arguments, and Results*. New York: National American Woman Suffrage Association, 1913.

15. This distinction among question types is given concisely in the discussion leader's handbook of the Great Books Foundation (1999).

16. The U.S. history booklets published as the *Public Issues Series* by the Social Science Education Consortium in Boulder, Colorado, carefully tie case issues to enduring issues. Other curriculum materials that lend themselves to deliberative discussions are the issues booklets developed for the *National Issues Forum* (Dubuque, IA: Kendall/Hunt) and for *Choices for the 21st Century* (Center for Foreign Policy Development, Brown University). A public-policy model for deliberating issues is detailed in Parker and Zumeta, 1999.

17. This video is available from the same source as the *April Morning* seminar discussed earlier (Social Science Education Consortium, 2001). See my analysis in Walter C. Parker, "Classroom Discussion: Models for Leading Seminars and Deliberations." *Social Education* 65 (March 2001): 111-115.

References

Addams, Jane. *Democracy and Social Ethics*. New York: Macmillan, 1902.

Adler, Mortimer J. *The Peideia Proposal*. New York: Macmillan, 1982.

Aronson, E. et al. *The Jigsaw Classroom*. Beverly Hills, CA: Sage, 1979.

Bridges, D. *Education, Democracy and Discussion*. Atlantic Highlands: Humanities Press, 1979.

Dewey, John. *How We Think*. Buffalo, NY: Prometheus Books, 1991/1910.

Dillon, James T., ed. *Deliberation in Education and Society*. Norwood: Ablex, 1994.

Evans, Ronald W., and David W. Saxe, eds. *Handbook on Teaching Social Issues*. Washington, D.C.: National Council for the Social Studies, 1996.

Fenton, Edwin. *The New Social Studies*. New York: Holt, Rinehart and Winston, 1967.

Fishkin, James S. *Democracy and Deliberation*. New Haven: Yale, 1991.

Fraenkel, Jack R. *Helping Students Think and Value: Strategies for Teaching the Social Studies*. 2nd ed. Englewood Cliffs, NJ: Prentice-Hall, 1980.

Gray, Dennis. "Putting Minds to Work: How to Use the Seminar Approach in the Classroom." *American Educator* 13 (Fall 1989): 16-23

Great Books Foundation. *An Introduction to Shared Inquiry: A Handbook for Junior Great Books Leaders*. 4th ed. Chicago: Great Books Foundation, 1999.

Haroutunian-Gordon, Sophie. "Was Socrates a 'Socratic' Teacher?" *Educational Theory* 38 (Summer 1988): 213-224.

Haroutunian-Gordon, Sophie. *Turning the Soul*. Chicago: University of Chicago Press, 1991.

Hess, Diana. *Discussing Controversial Public Issues in Secondary Social Studies Classrooms: Learning From Skilled Teachers*. Unpublished dissertation, University of Washington, Seattle, 1998.

Hutchins, Robert M. *The Great Conversation: The Substance of a Liberal Education*. Chicago: Encyclopedia Britannica, Inc., 1952.

Johnson, David W., and Roger T. Johnson. "Classroom Conflict: Controversy vs. Debate in Learning Groups." *American Educational Research Journal* 22, (Summer 1985): 237-256.

Johnson, David W., and Roger T. Johnson. "Critical Thinking through Structured Controversy." *Educational Leadership* 45 (May 1988): 58-64.

Kelly, Thomas E. "Leading Class Discussions of Controversial Issues." *Social Education* 53 (October 1989): 368-370.

King, Martin Luther, Jr. "Letter from Birmingham City Jail." In *Why We Can't Wait*. New York: Mentor, 1963, 79-95.

Levstik, Linda S., and Keith C. Barton. *Doing History: Investigating with Children in Elementary and Middle Schools*. 2nd ed. Mahwah, NJ: Lawrence Erlbaum Associates, 2001.

Lortie, Dan C. *Schoolteacher*. Chicago: University of Chicago Press, 1975.

Mathews, David. *Politics for People: Finding a Responsible Public Voice*. Urbana: University of Illinois Press, 1994.

Meier, Deborah. *The Power of Their Ideas*. Boston: Beacon, 1995.

Miller, Barbara, and Laurel Singleton. *Preparing Citizens*. Boulder: Social Science Education Consortium, 1997.

Oliver, Donald W., Fred M. Newmann, and Laurel R. Singleton. "Teaching Public Issues in the Secondary School Classroom." *The Social Studies* 83 (May/June 1982): 100-103.

Oliver, Donald W., and James P. Shaver. *Teaching Public Issues in the High School*. Logan: Utah State University Press, 1974.

Parker, Walter C. "Classroom Discussion: Models for Leading Seminars and Deliberations." *Social Education* 65 (2001a): 111-115.

Parker, Walter C. *Social Studies in Elementary Education*. 11th ed. Upper Saddle River, NJ: Merrill/Prentice Hall, 2001b.

Parker, Walter C., and Diana Hess. "Teaching With and For Discussion," *Teaching and Teacher Education* 17 (2001): 273-289.

Parker, Walter C., Akira Ninomiya, and John Cogan. "Educating World Citizens Toward Multinational Curriculum Development." *American Educational Research Journal* 36 (Summer 1999):117-145.

Parker, Walter C., and William Zumeta. "Toward an Aristocracy of Everyone: Policy Study in the High School Curriculum." *Theory and Research in Social Education* 27 (Winter 1999): 9-44.

Plato. *Protagoras and Meno* (W. K. C. Guthrie, Trans.). New York: Penguin Classics, 1956.

Roberts, Terry, and the Staff of the National Paideia Center. *The Power of Paideia Schools*. Alexandria, VA: Association for Supervision and Curriculum Development, 1998.

Schwab, Joseph. "Eros and Education: A Discussion of One Aspect of Discussion." In *Science, Curriculum, and Liberal Education: Selected Essays*, Ian Westbury and Neil Will, eds. Chicago: University of Chicago Press, 1978, 105-132.

Social Science Education Consortium. *Preparing Citizens Video and Guide*. Boulder, CO: Social Science Education Consortium, 2001.

Taba, Hilda, et al. *A Teacher's Handbook to Elementary Social Studies: An Inductive Approach.* Reading, MA: Addison-Wesley, 1971.

Tocqueville, Alexis de. *Democracy in America.* In J. P. Mayer, ed., *Democracy in America.* Garden City: Doubleday, 1969/1839.

Valli, Linda. "Listening to Other Voices: A Description of Teacher Reflection in the United States." *Peabody Journal of Education* 72:1 (1997): 67-88.

Young, Iris M. "Difference as a Resource for Democratic Communication." In *Deliberative Democracy: Essays on Reason and Politics*, James Bohman and William Rehg, eds. Cambridge, MA: The MIT Press, 1997, 383-406.

7

Civic Intelligence and Liberal Intelligence in the History Education of Social Studies Teachers and Students

Lynn R. Nelson and Frederick D. Drake

For the past two decades educational reform in the United States has recalled liberal education to its civic role in a democratic society. Numerous proponents of liberal and civic education have emphasized the renewal of democratic citizenship in the curriculum of elementary and secondary schools plus colleges and universities.[1] Ernest L. Boyer and Fred M. Hechinger, for example, observed that higher education "should create a climate in which the values of the individual and the ethical and moral issues facing society can be thoughtfully examined" (1981, 60). Charles F. Bahmueller and Charles N. Quigley remind us that instructional programs in our schools need to promote civic competence, civic responsibility, and widespread participation of youth in the civic and political life of their communities and the nation (1991, 1). We argue that historical study focused upon the principles and practices of citizenship in a democracy should be in the core curriculum of elementary and secondary schools and in the civic foundations of university-based programs for prospective social studies teachers.

This chapter is framed by the recent attempts to reinvigorate the civic mission of social studies in elementary and secondary schools and university-based programs for teacher education. We confront the reflective practitioner of history and the social studies with the problem of translating theory into practice and considering *historical knowledge, historical inquiry,* and *democratic deliberation* as the heart of the social studies. At the same time, we challenge educators who argue that decision-making about current public issues or social problems, which eschews context-based inquiry, ought to be the heart of social studies education (Engle and Ochoa 1988,

61-77).[2] Further, we propose a history-centered model of education for citizenship in a democracy, which involves students in making decisions about issues within the confines of historical time periods and stresses the critical importance of socio-cultural contexts. (See Figure 7.1: Frameworks of Civic Intelligence, which is the first of seven figures presented in the Appendix to this chapter; see page 155.)

Three significant principles inform our preference for history-centered education for democratic citizenship in elementary and secondary school social studies courses and in the university-based education of social studies teachers. **First**, a popular culture that magnifies the importance of both individuals and groups in the present necessitates a counterbalance that will contextualize the lives and decisions of individuals and groups with the dimensions of time and place (Lasch 1991; Lasch 1995; Schlesinger 1998). Decisions analyzed within time and place include opponents of those choices and unintended consequences of them. For example, the actions of Rosa Parks in the mid-1950s would be diminished in meaning without reference to time, place, and circumstances of her decisions and without an understanding of the interrelated decisions of civil rights activists and southern and northern politicians that resulted from her actions. As reported in Richard Niemi and Jane Junn's summary of the 1988 NAEP results, students may be able to identify Rosa Parks as the person who initiated the Montgomery bus boycott without explaining the legality of the boycott (1998, 30). We suggest historical context would provide a meaningful framework to examine the significance of particular events and enable the students to understand and apply a particular concept, for example boycott, in other historical circumstances.

Second, and intertwined with the first principle, when we constantly "background" or marginalize people and events in the past (as does the decision-making on social issues model), we diminish their status and dangerously elevate our own. History "foregrounds" individuals in the time period in which they lived, while the decision-making social issues model backgrounds all individuals except those living in the present. Rosa Parks' heroism can better be appreciated when one realizes that she could not foretell the consequences of her decision. Too often, the political actor in the past is viewed as possessing prescience for what flows later from her actions. Little regard is paid to the anguish and risks that accompanied her decisions.

Third, the decision-making on social issues model more often than not results in a debate to score points rather than a deliberation to fully understand ideas, values, and beliefs. We believe historical inquiry, historical knowledge, and deliberation are the heart of the social studies. We believe deliberation more clearly conveys the democratic nature of the process in which individuals gather information, analyze values, and reason together in order to understand and evaluate events that occurred in the past and present. Deliberation calls upon an individual to willingly suspend initial inclinations to action in order to present her ideas and to carefully consider the ideas of others.

Since the first publication of *A Nation at Risk*, released by the National Commission on Excellence in Education in 1983, academic disciplines in the school curriculum have received on-going scrutiny from their respective professional organizations and from other interested groups that have proposed content standards and learning goals (Gagnon 1989). History is no exception and standards have emerged at national and state levels. History teachers must be aware of these standards and use them to organize the content and skills of their instruction. While the standards provide general guidelines for school districts and teachers, they require interpretation by teachers and curriculum specialists to guide classroom instruction and to create curriculum documents for school districts.[3]

The Ideal of Citizenship Education

The ideal of citizenship education is an enduring belief and value in public education as old as the republic. Such individuals of the American founding era as Benjamin Rush argued that the primary purpose of schools was the creation of good citizens (Kaestle 2000, 48). The theories of citizenship education coincided with the rise of schools as important institutions. Perhaps the earliest popular theory was a framework that merged history and fiction to teach good character through narratives. During the decades following the founding of the republic, American publishers issued readers and spellers that included such stories as Parson Weems's tale of George Washington. These narratives provided generations of children with examples of character that were worthy of emulation as well as engaging them in an interesting story. Proponents of this theory of instruction would conjoin history and fiction to achieve their paramount purpose of character development (Kaestle 1983, 92-94).

Another popular theory of citizenship education was that of faculty psychology and mental discipline. Proponents of faculty psychology used the metaphor of the mind as a muscle, so the mind needed to be exercised through memorization and other intellectual gymnastics. For students of history this theory was put into practice by generations of students who memorized large sections of historical narrative (Kliebard 1995, 4-6). Hard work and the rigorous exercise of the mind, advocates argued, would lead to good character and intellectual development.

In contrast to previous theories, William Torrey Harris translated the principles of Hegelian philosophy into a theoretical framework for education with his five "windows of the soul," namely grammar, literature and art, mathematics, geography, and history. The schools, by imparting knowledge to students, provided them with the means to individual improvement throughout their lives and a mechanism to establish a common culture. Knowledge, including historical knowledge, served as the foundation for both individual fulfillment and social progress. Harris' humanistic, liberal curricular vision was challenged by early Progressives whose perspective focused on the changing nature of American society and the problems of youth in America's new industrial order. Harris' ideas, initially supported by the influential President of Harvard University Charles W. Eliot, were betrayed as Eliot shifted in 1908 from being a proponent of a common liberal education to a supporter of a differentiated curriculum at the high school and new junior high school (Kliebard 1999, 42-43).

Modern educational theory was born in the competing world views of Progressive education and resulted in a shift in the goals for schooling. Clearly, a turning point occurred as competing interests contested the important position held previously by liberal and civic education. All variants of Progressive education focused on what was perceived as the changing nature of American society in the last decade of the nineteenth century and first decades of the twentieth century. Changes in immigration, urbanization, and industrialization worried Progressive educators. Such curricular interest groups as child-centered advocates, social efficiency proponents, pedagogical progressives, social meliorists, and social reconstructionists contested the purposes and practices of education (Kliebard 1995; Tyack 1975). These various groups of Progressive educators challenged the liberal, humanist view of education that was articulated by William Torrey Harris. While Progressives in education agreed on the radical change that American society was undergoing, individuals in these various curricular camps differed widely in their prescriptions for educational reforms. For example, the ideas of G. Stanley Hall influenced theorists and practitioners to adapt curriculum and instruction to the needs and interests of students at their various stages of development. By contrast, such vocational educators as David Snedden argued that modern industrial America and the need for social efficiency required vocational education involving students in manual training, and later vocational training, for specific jobs. While the followers of Hall and Snedden vied with one another for support, they agreed upon the relative **unimportance** of history as a school subject (Kliebard 1999, 171, 231). Each camp posed challenges to liberal and civic education, and the programs that these groups developed undermined the importance of both civic and liberal education in the twentieth century.

Perhaps the least radical challenges came from the followers of John Dewey, who have been labeled "pedagogical progressives" by the historian David Tyack and "social meliorists" by curriculum historian Herbert Kliebard. Pedagogical progressives and social meliorists embraced the civic purpose for education while calling for a new curriculum and teaching methods organized around decision-making and scientific inquiry. These individuals broadly agreed that the process of reflective thought should be the core of the curriculum.

Divisions among Progressive educators contributed to battles that are fought by history and social studies educators today. On one side, the divisions that separate history and the social studies emanate from the belief among some social studies educators that decision-making and a focus on contemporary social problems should be the comprehensive organizer of curriculum and instruction. In contrast, history and social science educators argue for the integrity of their academic disciplines as a superior means to curricular organization (Gagnon 1989; Ravitch 2000; Wineburg 2001).

Beyond history, social science, and social studies educators, the battle lines are clearly drawn. Unlike the dispute that involves how best to organize the curriculum for citizenship education, the argument with vocational and technological educators is drawn around the issue of the purposes for elementary and secondary education. Following the prescriptions of David Snedden and Charles A. Prosser, vocational educators have called for schools to "train-up" individuals as human capital for an increasingly technical and specialized workforce (Kliebard 1999; Ravitch 2000). Both history and social studies educators are under siege from vocationalists who question whether civic and liberal knowledge are important enough to warrant a prominent place in the curriculum. Arguments both familial and foreign will continue into the future. While differences between history, social studies, and vocational educators are clearly delineated, the familial disagreements are no less real and no less important. History and social studies educators, who agree in opposition to the vocationalists will nonetheless continue to disagree on issues about organization of the curriculum. Should academic disciplines or interdisciplinary social problems and issues be the focus of curriculum and instruction? Is there one form of curricular organization, based on interdisciplinary study of social issues or problems, that is sufficient to the social and civic education of students? Or is the study of academic disciplines, history and the social sciences, a better way for students to achieve an accurate and elaborate comprehension of social reality in the past and present?

Reflective Practice: History Education and Social Issues

Conditions of the twentieth century have not been favorable to advocates of history and social studies education. Essays in the popular press have portrayed American education as inadequately preparing youth to

take advantage of vocational opportunities. In the years immediately following the Second World War, this argument was most often framed in
terms of the scientific and mathematical deficiencies of American children
vis-á-vis their Soviet counterparts. Since the end of the Cold War, this argument has focused on America at risk, with the risk perceived as American
children's technological deficiencies to assume their places in the "high-
tech" workforce. Advocates of liberal and civic education face considerable challenges, having ceded the playing field of public discourse regarding
the purposes and practices of American education to vocational educators.
National and state standards help to an extent, but they are not enough.
Several generations of American citizens have come to consider *the* purpose of America's schools to be the training of the workforce.

Given the marginalization of history and the social sciences in current
debates that surround education, a detailed and refined rationale must be
developed if history and the social sciences are to muster public support
regarding their position in the curriculum. These are challenging responsibilities for the reflective practitioner of history, who has much to offer
students concerning civic and liberal intelligence as foundations for democratic citizenship education in elementary and secondary schools and university-based teacher education programs.

The common roots of history and social studies education for the purposes of liberal and civic learning rest in the ideas of John Dewey. He
informs us that reflective thought is, "Active, persistent, and careful consideration of any belief or supposed form of knowledge in the light of the
grounds that support it, and the further conclusions to which it tends"
(Dewey 1910, 6). This dictum has influenced several generations of social
studies theorists and teachers. These individuals argue that social studies
education should focus on the decision-making process through which students inquire into the factual information and the values required to arrive
at a reasoned decision within a social and political context. For Dewey, a
democratic education is an on-going process. Discussion is both the beginning and end of inquiry.

The potential of individuals to make sense out of instruction is described
by Dewey and others as "natural intelligence." Yet, it is insufficient as an
end in itself. "Natural intelligence," Dewey reminds us, "is no barrier to
the propagation of error, nor large but *untrained experience* [emphasis added]
to the accumulation of fixed false beliefs" (Dewey 1910, 21). An intelligent
person may well be able to decipher arguments regarding a contemporary
social issue and not be able to deliberate as a citizen in public discourse.
The antecedents and context of the social issue, however, must be a fundamental part of the inquiry and discourse of students. If not, teachers and
students may be unable to evaluate cogently the quality of evidence and

arguments supporting various positions on an issue. The degree to which education has a responsibility to prepare future citizens for deliberative discussion, which includes both support and criticism of the existing political order, can no longer be taken for granted. Thus, history must be at the core of the curriculum, because it provides a fund of knowledge, which enables the individual to understand the past as it relates to the present and to exercise a degree of discrimination in the examination of public issues and events.

John Dewey made an early distinction between unreflective and reflective teaching. The former, dominated by impulse and the authority of traditions, embraces the everyday reality in schools, presuming undiscriminatingly that only the technical practices of pedagogy should be considered when planning for instruction (Dewey 1938). Reflective teaching is distinguishable from technical teaching. The reflective practitioner is the teacher who thinks systematically about how to integrate significant content with sound pedagogical practices, about how best to adapt content and methodology according to the experiential levels and interests of students, and about how to exercise the teacher's collateral responsibilities toward students and the community.[4] The history teacher who practices reflectively recognizes that history is an integrative discipline that informs the reflective thinking of students.

History, first, allows students to understand events and historical debates in the context of their time. Second, history enables each student and citizen to argue for the continuation of warranted political, economic, and social policies and traditions as well as provide students with the knowledge and skills to argue for necessary political, economic, and social change. Student intelligence is an ingredient that along with the quality of the materials one studies and the quality of the instruction that one receives results in the acquisition of both knowledge and skills *either* elegant, elaborate, and durable or rudimentary, primitive, and ephemeral.

Mortimer Adler in *The Paideia Proposal* (1982, 23) argued that subjects in the curriculum should be taught and learned so that students organize knowledge, develop intellectual skills, and enlarge their understanding of ideas and values. In particular, history teachers should employ three pedagogical skills: didactic or telling instruction, coaching or supervising instruction, and Socratic or maieutic questioning instruction. These teaching skills contribute to the greater purpose of student learning, which is to develop the knowledge and skills necessary to contribute to the deliberation of social and political issues within historical and contemporary contexts.

The study of history must extend beyond the acquisition of discrete pieces of information. Richard Niemi and Jane Junn, however, report that just the opposite is true in most classrooms (1998, 77-82). Teachers need to help students master the contours of a given narrative, whether a macro-history or a microhistory, and know about significant individuals, their ideas, and key political and social events that reflect continuity and change in a society. Moreover, the intellectual products of this study should be retained by the individual and be joined with related ideas to form the fabric of his or her historical memory.[5]

Students should also know about universal themes and ideas that cut across the human experience. These themes and ideas serve as filters that help students differentiate between what is significant and unimportant in the historical record. The National Council for History Education identified six "Vital Themes and Narratives" (see Figure 7.2 in the Appendix to this chapter) to assist teachers as they organize the knowledge domain of a history curriculum (Gagnon 1989, 26-27). Developers of *The National Standards of History* (1996, 15-16) have identified five "Standards in Historical Thinking": chronological thinking, historical comprehension, historical analysis and interpretation, historical research capabilities, and historical issues-analysis and decision-making.[6]

History instruction within the reflective practice framework considers the worth of knowledge both now and in the future. The reflective practitioner of history must know and understand the structure of history. That is, the teacher must know that history is organized around seminal vital themes and narratives that are punctuated by key turning points in the story of the human adventure. (See Figure 7.4: The Reflective Practitioner and the Teaching and Learning of History, which can be found at the end of this chapter.) The teacher must have command of historical content, both the main ideas and supporting details, and understand history's pivotal role as an integrative discipline among other school subjects (Wilson and Wineburg 1988; Wineburg 2001, 150-154, 170). History's power of synthesis enables the teacher and her students to draw upon ideas contributed by a number of disciplines to develop an understanding of the actions of people and the importance of events over a period of time. The social science disciplines are analytical. They provide powerful concepts that analyze the behavior of individuals and groups under varying circumstances. Thus, the reflective practitioner of history should possess knowledge of content and pedagogy, ability to implement her knowledge in the classroom, and desire to be a life-long learner about both the past and the present.[7]

The reflective practitioner, who occupies the position opposite the closed-minded individual, must also recognize the importance of having an open spirit of inquiry and curiosity about the past and present. At the same time, the thoughtful teacher must know the findings of research about effective teaching and must keep abreast of current issues on the teaching of history, geography, and social science or social studies. These are challenging responsibilities for the reflective practitioner of history.

Perhaps an all too common practice is for teachers of history to impose one fact after another, or to destroy the integrity of history by thoughtlessly transporting students across centuries and cultures to arrive at flawed generalizations that violate both the uniqueness of historical time and the particularity of culture and place. Decision-making activities that involve students in making untenable generalizations across time and place force students into simplistic, distorted conclusions in which they fail to recognize the uniqueness of historical circumstances and the uniqueness of historical periods.[8] Ultimately, if students are left with the impression that generalizations can be drawn facilely across the boundaries of time and place, then their distorted picture of the past has an impact on their self-perception in the present. The practice of making sweeping and unwarranted generalizations allows individuals to remove themselves from a specific context and to abrogate their responsibilities in current civic life.

We challenge the reflective practitioner of history and social studies education with the task of ensuring that all students develop a rich tapestry of historical knowledge; this tapestry should recognize the unique patterns of history within particular periods of time and cultures. We challenge history and social studies educators to develop in their students a nuanced understanding of the relationship between historical literacy and civic participation which is based upon the appreciation that events and ideas are perishable when transported across time periods. One cannot require, without doing significant damage to unique historical circumstances, the making of generalizations that sweep rashly across centuries of time and cut carelessly across cultural circumstances. Generalizations must be qualified, and they always must consciously recognize the uniqueness of events and the cultural frameworks or contexts in which these historical events occurred.[9]

History, when well taught, provides students with durable knowledge that informs the ideas individuals bring to their conversations as citizens. This knowledge provides individuals with a sense of humility that precludes superficial and unwarranted generalizations across time and cultures. Durable historical knowledge is neither immutable nor immune from challenge and reconstitution. After all, historians give meaning to the past through interpretations, which are acts of intellectual synthesis. The challenges to and the changes in one's durable knowledge are products of compelling evidence, interpretation, and reflection.

History's durable knowledge rests in "doing history"and "understanding ways historians think." It recognizes the dangers of making generalizations. While Hegelian schemes of metahistory and historical causation have been discredited among many professional historians, they continue to be used by some teachers in order to provide a degree of unity for the tapestry of history. However, the damage done to the uniqueness of historical circumstances is considerable and outweighs any benefits that might accrue to students who view the past in a comprehensible picture, but one that grotesquely distorts historical circumstances.

The decision-making model advocated by such curricular theorists as Engle and Ochoa (1988), we caution, is akin to combining measures drawn from varying scales and then drawing conclusions from the accumulated data. Historical facts, historical circumstances, however, are perishable entities that do not travel easily across the dimensions of time and space. Thus, history and social studies educators need to balance two countervailing tendencies. The first is the tendency to over-generalize from the past; the second is to act as the antiquarian and to value the past for its own uniqueness. Civic literacy involves the careful and qualified comparisons of the circumstances and actions of human beings across time and space. We offer a framework for a history education that balances countervailing tendencies and emphasizes both civic and liberal intelligence.

Liberal Intelligence and History Education

History education can be powerfully linked to the ideas of a liberal society. A society is liberal to the extent that its citizens possess a sense of justice that regulates individual actions to secure rights of individuals equally throughout society (Rawls 1971, 454). That sense of justice tied to protection of individual rights rests on a foundation of knowledge, a good part of which is historical. Unlike an absolute monarchy or dictatorship, a liberal democratic society draws upon knowledge and a use and disposition toward reason as the means of resolving disputes and establishing courses of action. Historical study contributes to the individual's creation of this framework of justice. History offers examples of the laudable and acceptable as well as the reprehensible behavior of individuals and groups over the span of years.

Historical knowledge and inquiry skills invite the individual to participate in deliberations that have been ongoing since the founding of the American republic. The student who is considering contemporary race relations, for example, is informed by the discussions of indentured servitude and slavery in seventeenth-century Virginia, the give-and-take compromises during the founding era, the meetings of abolitionists in the 1830s, disagreements between Booker T. Washington and W. E. B. Du Bois, and the actions of Lester Maddox as the racist owner of a restaurant in Georgia in the 1960s. The liberally educated individual can draw upon multiple ideas and images to engage in deliberative discourse.

Liberal intelligence appreciates the uniqueness of the past. A student who reads about and discusses the ideas and life of W. E. B. Du Bois, the entrepreneur Madame Walker in Indianapolis, and countless African Americans throughout the United States in the years following the Civil War appreciates the uniqueness of the historical circumstances that defined their lives and contributed to their ideas in the latter part of the nineteenth century and first half of the twentieth century. Du Bois' ideas were forged in his upbringing in Boston, as a witness to the aftermath of Reconstruction and *Plessy v. Ferguson* (1896), and his experiences in German seminars as a scholarship student during the 1890s (Herman 1997, 194-198). Students of history appreciate the tentative nature of judgments when examining Du Bois' recommendations and reactions to these ideas in African American and white communities. Historians and their students perceive past events and issues as Du Bois and others experienced them at the time, and they develop historical empathy as opposed to an excessive present-mindedness (Gagnon 1989, 25-26).[10]

Such examples of historians' habits of the mind are the intellectual property of liberally educated individuals. These important ways of thinking serve as a foundation for liberally educated individuals to distinguish Du Bois, Walker, and other African Americans and their circumstances from the circumstances of the Reverend Dr. Martin Luther King Jr., Rosa Parks, and civil rights activities of the mid-twentieth century. The Reverend King's public life was informed by the opportunities for black Americans to promote racial equality in the context of racial segregation and the Cold War struggle between the United States and then Soviet Union. Also contributing to Reverend King's understanding of the condition of African Americans were such Supreme Court decisions as *Sipuel v. University of Oklahoma* (1948), *McLaurin v. Oklahoma State Regents* (1950), *Sweatt v. Painter* (1950), *Brown v. Board of Education of Topeka, Kansas* (1954), and *Bolling v. Sharpe* (1954), and the legal leadership of African-American lawyers Charles Houston and Thurgood Marshall.

Liberal intelligence requires the cautious use of historical periods, often far removed in time and even geographic distance, to support ideas and arguments. However, the examples drawn upon in conversation are fragile exports. The ideas exported out of their time periods may be damaged and changed when brutally joined to what appear to be similar ideas and examples drawn from a different time period. Historical knowledge travels best when packaged in detailed understanding that includes a realization of each historical period's unique qualities. Liberal intelligence takes satisfaction in knowledge regarding the past and informs individual judgment regarding the meaning of past events; it pursues a natural curiosity to understand an idea or event for it own sake. Liberal intelligence balances two opposing forces: (1) antiquarianism, the love of historical knowledge for its own sake, and (2) presentism, the rush to use ideas across time and place and eschew context-based inquiry. This form of intelligence is the product of an intellectual foundation nurtured by the students of history and other disciplines. As we conceive the curriculum, liberal intelligence is both a pre-requisite and a co-requisite to the development of civic intelligence.

Civic Intelligence and History Education

Civic intelligence draws upon historical knowledge as a foundation for democratic deliberations. Americans must be cognizant of the key principles that historically have been fundamental to civic life in their country. As students deliberate the meaning of these principles in contemporary society, they must understand that accurate construction of past events is more important than making convincing arguments. Evidence that counters their existing position on issues should result in a refining of their position, not a discarding of evidence. Deliberation among citizens in a democracy requires intellectual honesty in the use of information, not the use of biased information to win points in a debate. The purpose of studying history and placing deliberations in an historical context is to help students engage in historical thought processes rather than prepare them for the mere regurgitation of facts.

David Mathews reminds us that civic intelligence is not a singular intellectual entity; rather, it comprises no less than four distinct levels of intellectual construction.[11] (See Figure 7.1: Frameworks of Civic Intelligence, which is presented at the end of this chapter.) The first and most basic level is to amass facts and gather information. Mathews cautions, however, that unorganized information is not very useful by itself (Mathews 1985, 678-681).

A second level of civic intelligence is the ability to sort and categorize information, which is a process in the creation of theories. By joining facts into larger structures the individual sees parts in relationship to wholes. A third level of intelligence is the ability to invent, to innovate, or to imagine. This level of civic intelligence joins theories to empirical realities. This third level of civic intelligence calls upon the creative and imaginative capacities of a liberally educated person.

Mathews notes that the three aforementioned levels of civic intelligence are privatized. That is, an individual can collect and gather facts; an individual can theorize; and an individual can invent and create. The fourth level of civic intelligence is deliberation in which the highest purposes are the creation of "good public philosophies" and "good public practices." Mathews notes that citizens thinking together in public is essential to a democratic republic. It is necessary if public policy issues are going to be carefully and thoughtfully addressed in cities, states, and the nation.

Citizenship has a moral agency in which the common good shares a stage with individual liberty. History plays a most significant role because of its power to stimulate creation of images and models of the actions taken by free individuals and collectives to grapple with issues in the past. History offers students, in the words of historian Peter Stearns, a "laboratory" of human experiences, a place where the individual measures perceptions of the world against the background of prior ideas and events.[12] Civic intelligence can draw upon history as a foundation of our common interests.[13]

Liberal and civic intelligences are overlapping constructs that share many of the same characteristics. They are grounded in the use of rational thinking and in the collection of evidence to support assertions, and they are based upon such principles as honesty in the analysis of evidence that runs counter to the individual's preferred ideas. The historian who uncovers or is presented with ideas that challenge or modify his scholarly positions is bound by the canons of his craft to reflect and recant his positions if warranted. Participants in political deliberation continuously reflect upon the tenability of their positions on issues in light of the evidence and arguments presented by others during discourse.

Deliberative Discussion and the Teaching of History

We draw upon the ideas of Amy Gutmann and Dennis Thompson, Walter C. Parker, and John J. Patrick to inform our proposal for deliberative discussion as a foundation for the teaching of history. Gutmann and Thompson (1996) provide an alternative to the excessive individualism of John Rawls and other liberals with their call for deliberative democracy, which seeks to establish a balance between the extremes of individualism and communitarianism. Gutmann, writing in 1999, notes that democratic education must foster and encourage deliberative democracy. She describes deliberative democracy as affording citizens opportunities to engage one another in "morally defensible reasons for mutually binding laws in an ongoing process of mutual justification" (Gutmann 1999, xii). Public schools, she observed, are responsible for educating citizens in the methods necessary to participate actively in their government. "Deliberation," Gutmann explains, is more than a single virtue because it includes "veracity, nonviolence, practical judgment, civic integrity, and magnanimity" as qualities necessary for a democratic society to "secure both the basic opportunity of individuals and its collective capacity to pursue justice" (Gutmann 1999, xiii). Both Gutmann and Thompson recognize the necessary joining of individual rights and the common good (see Figure 7.1: Frameworks of Civic Intelligence). Accordingly, deliberative democracy establishes a conceptual structure for discussion that is inclusive of various moral positions on public issues (Gutmann and Thompson 1999, 243-279). The principles articulated by Gutmann and Thompson provide directions for teachers as they consider instructional methods to involve students in deliberations of historical or contemporary issues.

Deliberation, Gutmann and Thompson observe, is democratic in two ways. It is both a democratic principle and a process of democratic discussion. Both aspects of deliberation are necessary in a democratic forum. Deliberation requires a disposition to give up time and energy to become informed and to consider and respect the ideas of others. Deliberation, in a sense, implies self-discipline and a commitment to respect the ideas of others. When defined as a process of discussion, deliberation is a practice of reflection on several different levels. First, when individuals gather information, they consider the validity and reliability of sources of their information. Second, as they engage in democratic deliberation, the process involves individuals in reflection upon the ideas and values of others with whom they may agree or disagree. Third, deliberation encompasses the thoughtful establishment of a course of action regarding public policy. Deliberation, Gutmann and Thompson (1996, 83-85) point out, requires reciprocity, which they define as "the capacity to seek fair terms of cooperation for its own sake," and economy of moral disagreement, which they explain as giving careful consideration to the ethical and moral positions of all participants in the deliberative process. Even the positions of individuals that we might initially find objectionable are neither rejected nor given cursory examination.

Discussion is a necessary component of learning in history and social studies classrooms. The quality of classroom discussion varies greatly in terms of the intellectual engagement of teachers and students in the process. At one extreme, discussion may merely be recitation, which involves students in the regurgitation of textbook information in response to predictable questions asked by the teacher. At the opposite pole, teachers and students are engaged in a rigorous conversation in which ideas, values, and conclusions are held up to analysis through discourse. Walter C. Parker (1997, 18-22) elaborates on discussion relative to democracy. He points to the necessity of the "art of deliberation" in social studies classrooms. We apply his ideas to the history classroom by stressing that deliberative discussion is dependent upon the quality of primary sources selected for subsequent discussion. The teacher needs to attend carefully to working with students in order to enhance their abilities to analyze documents. We propose a two-tiered system of deliberation. We caution the reader that this is not a single method of instruction; rather, deliberations serve as the focus for a variety of instructional strategies.

The theoretical framework, as we conceive it, is comprised of two concentric circles. The first-order deliberation focuses on analysis of a seminal document introduced by the teacher who carefully crafts questions designed to involve students in historical analysis (see Figure 7.5: Deliberative and Evaluative Discussions, which is presented at the end of this chapter). The second-order deliberation surrounds the core of the document first deliberated upon. The second order is less clearly defined because, in part, the deliberations that follow are a product of the inquiry completed during primary order deliberations along with the interests of students as they extend their deliberations to deal with related issues. The second-order deliberations provide students and the teacher with the opportunity to consider larger issues that are related to history's vital themes and narratives and standards.

All documents require analysis that calls upon the teacher and her students to interpret the meaning of the primary source. We offer this model as a guideline (see Figure 7.6: Primary Source Analysis Guide) for the analysis of documents realizing that an analysis guide, like any other guide, is always subject to permutations and that teachers will be able to use their judgment as to best practices. First, the teacher directs students to identify the document (author, title, date, and type of document). Second, the teacher asks students to analyze the document by discussing with students central ideas and purposes for the document, which includes summarizing the main ideas of the document, identifying antecedent conditions which prompted the author to write the document, identifying the audience the author wishes to inform, and identifying biases of the author as well as questions students would ask of the author. Third, the teacher and students describe the context and the time frame of the document both locally and nationally along with the comparative conditions in other places in the world community. Fourth, students identify a vital theme and narrative as represented in the document and provide evidence of the connection to this source. And fifth, students identify evidence in the document that relates to one of the social science disciplines in the social studies curriculum. One must keep in mind that this process is essentially non-linear. As the deliberation progresses, students and teacher may revisit the previous questions and modify or elaborate upon their initial thoughts.

During the primary-order deliberation, the teacher asks questions and provides written frameworks, which guide students in the analysis of sources. Throughout this analytical process, the teacher calls upon students to suspend their evaluation of the document based upon contemporary standards. Students synthesize historical information from the documents introduced in class along with other sources that may be encountered as they engage in research. The issues inherent in the documents and questions raised by the teacher and her students in the course of their inquiry shape the primary and secondary deliberations. Primary-level deliberations will continue as teachers and students examine questions that are raised in the course of their deliberations and research. The teacher and her students ask questions that are prefaced by "what," "how," and "why" during deliberation as a catalyst to understanding multiple causation. Questions that are prefaced with "should" are reserved for evaluative discussion.

Evaluation occurs as students gain expertise sufficient to evaluate the documents within their appropriate time frame. Evaluation comes subsequent to the analysis of a number of documents that pertain to a particular historical issue or problem, which motivates historical inquiry. Ultimately, students engage in evaluation when they make judgments about meaning in the past and bind together individual events into a larger framework of civic concerns.

Social studies teachers can adapt materials already existing from the Amherst History Project, Harvard Social Studies Project, the Center for Civic Education's *We the People*. . . programs, and Brown University's program of the Thomas J. Watson Jr. Institute for International Studies. They offer the potential to emphasize deliberation, and they are distinguished by their respective use of primary sources and historical context for contemporary issues (see Figure 7.7: Instructional Models Involving Decision-Making). The project from Brown University addresses contemporary and historical issues; the historical materials engage students within the particular historical period being examined. For example, students might analyze issues regarding "Russia's Uncertain Transition" following the end of the Cold War (contemporary) or come to grips with such historical turning points as "A More Perfect Union: Shaping the American Government," (constitutional history in the founding era) and "Coming to Terms with Power: U. S. Choices After World War II" (the historical context of Cold War origins).[14]

We believe that our framework for history-based inquiry fits the ideas of John J. Patrick and others who emphasize a discipline-based foundation for civic education. Patrick states (1999, 47) that "Well-designed and delivered courses in civics, government, and United States history—based on key ideas, information, and issues of democracy in the past and present—enable students to acquire a fund of civic/political knowledge that can be called upon to comprehend, cope, and otherwise interact successfully with the issues, problems, and challenges of civil society and government." Decision making about public issues can be embedded effectively within the framework of history or a social science discipline to teach knowledge, skills, and dispositions of democratic citizenship.

Patrick (1999, 45-50) describes the changes that have taken place in the organization of the high school history course since the 1960s, namely that political/constitutional history has been diminished by social and cultural history. He strongly argues that political and constitutional history should be reinstated as the organizing framework for history courses so that history can provide a fund of intellectual capital for students to become constructively engaged in democratic political and civic life.

In another essay, Patrick points to a key strategy all schools and teachers of history should consider, which treats tensions and accommodations between civic unity and multicultural diversity in response to core constitutional principles and issues in United States history. "The core curriculum," he states, "that conjoins civism and multiculturalism emphasizes diverse perspectives and interpretations of the key turning points in the history of constitutional democracy" (Patrick 2000, 124).

Patrick's proposal emphasizes inquiry about principles and issues of constitutional democracy in primary documents of the founding era and subsequent periods of United States history. To carry out his proposal, history teachers first need to identify and make known to their students the constitutional issues at key turning points in the nation's experience in representative democracy. Second, teachers must engage students with knowledge of constitutional principles in core documents connected to turning points and issues in United States history. Third, teachers and students should examine and evaluate alternative viewpoints and diverse perspectives on constitutional issues and turning points in United States history (Patrick 2000, 124-125).

In another essay, Patrick stresses the importance of continuous and systematic teaching and learning of core ideas and issues about the meaning and practice of a constitutional representative democracy. As students move from lower to higher grades in school, they should encounter the core principles and issues repeatedly in increasing cycles of depth, complexity, and breadth. Patrick writes: "A key to better teaching and learning of founding-era conceptions of constitutionalism and their subsequent development in American and world history is emphatic, detailed, and recurrent treatments of these ideas in the classroom. The core ideas and issues must be introduced early in the curriculum and visited again and again, in cycles of increasing complexity and depth, if students are to develop a deep understanding of the ideas and reasoned commitments to them as first principles of constitutional democracy" (Patrick 1996, 100).

Toni Marie Massaro concurs with Patrick. Writing in favor of constitutional-political history, Massaro points out that "an historical dimension to life . . . is extremely useful, perhaps essential." She continues, "Chronology and context—time and space—are the most basic means by which one locates events, things, and lives. Without them, students feel and are quite lost." Constitutional history and constitutional language, Massaro states, are the best ways to address "competing meanings of equality" and to preserve those values regarded by all as "values worth preserving" (Massaro 1993, 149-151).

Historian Pauline Maier broadens the effects of document-based teaching when she asserts that documents have a "centripetal role." That is, as students carefully examine such principles as "equality, rights, popular sovereignty, limited power, and rule of law" in important historical documents they should apply their common understanding of these ideas to various circumstances throughout American history. The potential benefit of analyzing documents both contextually and comparatively moves students beyond consideration of themselves as isolated individuals and moves them into the role of individuals whose lives are contextualized in a fabric of historical ties (Maier 1996, 45-64).

Linda Kerber may have touched to a degree upon this fabric of historical ties when she wrote her 1997 essay, "The Meanings of Citizenship," published in the *Journal of American History*. Kerber's essay, written for a symposium on the history of American citizenship, suggested we have a "braided" narrative of citizenship history. That is, that citizenship must be seen from different eyes, perhaps the eyes of African-American slaves and their descendants and women. Ronald Takaki reminds us of the expansiveness of the historical memory. According to Takaki (1998, 353), we need to share "our varied stories" in order to "create a community of larger memory."

Toni Marie Massaro strongly suggests that when students understand the "national constitutional tradition" they will better appreciate the "perpetual struggle to balance multiple competing concerns." This tradition within a liberal democracy, she states, must emphasize "solidarity in respecting democratic processes" and majority rule and "accommodate our ideological, religious, racial, gender, ethnic, and multiple other differences" as well as "the right to dissent" (Massaro 1993, 127).

While many civic educators prefer a history that emphasizes political and constitutional elements, social history has a natural potential to include constitutional issues. Social history has a nexus with political and constitutional history. Further, the study of social conditions connected to constitutional issues offers students opportunities to analyze social conditions of the founding era and other turning points in constitutional history contextually and comparatively.

Document-based deliberative discussions afford students opportunities to practice deliberation on moral and factual issues. However, students suspend moral judgments while they seek to understand thoroughly the ideas and principles embedded within the documents prior to making evaluation. This practice is common to both liberal intelligence and civic intelligence. Students encountering historical documents will place the documents within the time period and with practice suspend the temptations of imposing present values on individuals in the past. So too, they will attempt to thoroughly understand the position of others before engaging in critique and debate.

Deliberative discussion, while distinct from the common classroom discussion that teachers typically hold, is not completely alien to the practices of teachers. The teacher who practices deliberation sets a tone that encourages open dialogue initially with no judgments. Open dialogue enables the teacher and her students to understand the positions of various individuals prior to evaluation. Concomitantly, the clarification of positions without judgments fosters a spirit of mutual trust. In contrast to decision-making, which we view as focused on the individual, deliberation involves students collectively in their careful consideration of historical or contemporary issues with the primary purpose being the development of the best possible solution without scoring debating points. Deliberative discussion is both a generator of inquiry and a stimulator of ongoing reflection about important issues. Thus, it should be at the core of social studies education in elementary and secondary schools and university-based programs for prospective social studies teachers.

Conclusion

We conclude that citizens grounded in historical literacy have a foundation of common knowledge they can call upon when engaged in the responsibilities of democratic civic and political life. However, the importance of historical knowledge tends to be placed at the margins of concern when decision-making about current issues or problems is the heart of the social studies. So we propose a history-centered curriculum that emphasizes content pertaining to citizenship in a democracy and involves inquiry and deliberation about public issues.

We conclude that history education unifies liberal and civic intelligence in the consideration of issues that are of on-going importance to citizens in a democratic republic. It introduces the learners to questions and positions that have framed and informed the constitutional and political debates throughout American history.

We conclude that *historical inquiry* and canonical *historical knowledge* are essential to democratic deliberations; and *deliberation* about ideas and issues, based on this kind of inquiry and knowledge, is the heart of the social studies. Such deliberation, however, is not confined to the discipline of history. It is carried out in the social sciences as well, which with history comprise the federation of subjects we label the social studies.

We recognize that there is an on-going debate about whether social studies is a unified field focused on decision-making about social issues or a federation of subjects in history and the social sciences. However, we believe very strongly that the goal of democratic citizenship education is best served when students are engaged in studies of history and the social science disciplines, which emphasize concepts and issues about government and politics.

The recent empirical research of Sam Wineburg, a cognitive scientist and historian, supports our advocacy of domain-specific or discipline-based inquiry in history. Like us, he recommends that history, taught and learned in schools as a separate subject with a distinctive way of thinking and knowing about reality, is a key to effective education for citizenship in a democracy. And he urges emphasis in the education of history teachers on the core concepts and ways of thinking in the discipline, because "expert teaching entails not a selection of methods but a transformation of knowing" among learners (Wineburg 2001, 82).

If the rich potential of a varied social studies education is reduced to one method of curricular organization and instruction, a comprehensive issue-centered social studies, then students will lack the intellectual frameworks and historical knowledge to understand themselves as citizens of their constitutional representative democracy. Instead of an interdisciplinary issue-centered social studies, we propose a history-centered curriculum, augmented by courses in different social sciences, which stresses education for citizenship in a democracy through context-based inquiry and deliberation about public issues. We would have a curricular synthesis of content and processes that can yield civic intelligence, liberal intelligence, and skills in democratic deliberation about public issues of the past and present. In our scheme for the reform of civic education, this curricular synthesis would prevail in programs of social studies teacher education and in social studies courses for students in elementary and secondary schools. Thus, the core of the elementary and secondary school social studies curriculum and the civic foundations of university-based programs for prospective social studies teachers would in concert be connected to the time-honored democratic purposes of education.

Appendix: Figures 7.1-7.7

Figure 7.1
Frameworks of Civic Intelligence

David Mathews' Taxonomies of Civic Intelligences	Amy Gutmann's Theoretical Framework for Civic Education

1. Amass facts and gather information
2. Assign meaning to facts by theorizing
3. To invent, innovate, and create
4. To think together
   Levels 1, 2, and 3 are private
   Level 4 is the creation of publics.
	1. Proceduralism: Fair procedures and value of majority rule
	2. Constitutionalism: Constitutional rights and constraits
	3. Deliberation: Moral deliberation to reach a justifiable resolution

Engle and Ochoa's Model of Decision-Making	**Historical Issues-Analysis and Decision-Making**
1. Recognizing a predicament 2. Defining or stating a problem 3. Gathering and evaluating relevant data 4. Identifying and analyzing values 5. Hypothesizing as to what might remedy the situation 6. Checking out each hypothesis for its plausibility 7. Deciding 8. Acting	1. Identify problems and dilemmas people faced in historical settings (context) 2. Analyze the interests, values, and points of view 3. Identify causes of the problem or dilemma 4. Propose alternative ways of resolving the problem or dilemma 5. Formulate a position or course of action on an issue 6. Identify the issue 7. Evaluate the consequences of the actions taken

Figure 7.2
Vital Themes and Narratives

In the search for historical understanding of ourselves and others, certain themes emerge as vital, whether the subject be world history, the history of Western civilization, or the history of the United States. To comprehend the forces for change and continuity that have shaped—and will continue to shape—human life, teachers and students of history must have the opportunity to pursue many or most of the following matters.

1. Civilization, cultural diffusion, and innovation

2. Human interaction with the environment

3. Values, beliefs, political ideas, and institutions

4. Conflict and cooperation

5. Comparative history of major developments

6. Patterns of social and political interaction

This figure is derived from The Bradley Commission on History in Schools, *Building A History Curriculum: Guidelines for Teaching History in Schools* (Washington, DC: Educational Excellence Network, 1988), 10-11.

Figure 7.3
History's Habits of the Mind

- Understand the significance of the past to our own lives.

- Distinguish between the important and the inconsequential, to develop the discriminating memory needed for a discerning judgment in public and personal life.

- Perceive past events and issues as they were experienced by people at the time, to develop historical empathy as opposed to present-mindedness.

- Acquire at one and the same time a comprehension of diverse cultures and of shared humanity.

- Understand how things happen and how things change in a tangle of purpose and process.

- Comprehend the interplay of change and continuity, and avoid assuming that either is somehow more natural, or more to be expected, than the other.

- Prepare to live with uncertainties, realizing that not all problems have solutions.

- Grasp the complexity of historical causation, respect particularity, and avoid excessively abstract generalizations.

- Appreciate the often tentative nature of judgments about the past, and thereby avoid the temptation to seize upon particular "lessons" of history as cures for present ills.

- Recognize the importance of individuals who have made a difference in history, and the significance of personal character for both good and ill.

- Appreciate the force of the nonrational, the irrational, the accidental in history and human affairs.

- Understand the relationship between geography and history as a matrix of time and place, and as context for events.

- Read widely and critically in order to recognize the difference between fact and conjecture, between evidence and assertion, and thereby to frame useful questions.

This figure is derived from The Bradley Commission on History in Schools, *Building A History Curriculum: Guidelines for Teaching History in Schools* (Washington, DC: Educational Excellence Network, 1988), 9.

Figure 7.4

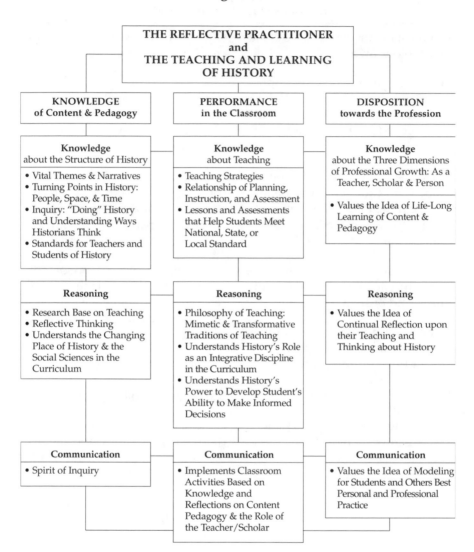

THE REFLECTIVE PRACTITIONER
and
THE TEACHING AND LEARNING
OF HISTORY

| KNOWLEDGE of Content & Pedagogy | PERFORMANCE in the Classroom | DISPOSITION towards the Profession |

Knowledge
about the Structure of History

- Vital Themes & Narratives
- Turning Points in History: People, Space, & Time
- Inquiry: "Doing" History and Understanding Ways Historians Think
- Standards for Teachers and Students of History

Knowledge
about Teaching

- Teaching Strategies
- Relationship of Planning, Instruction, and Assessment
- Lessons and Assessments that Help Students Meet National, State, or Local Standard

Knowledge
about the Three Dimensions of Professional Growth: As a Teacher, Scholar & Person

- Values the Idea of Life-Long Learning of Content & Pedagogy

Reasoning

- Research Base on Teaching
- Reflective Thinking
- Understands the Changing Place of History & the Social Sciences in the Curriculum

Reasoning

- Philosophy of Teaching: Mimetic & Transformative Traditions of Teaching
- Understands History's Role as an Integrative Discipline in the Curriculum
- Understands History's Power to Develop Student's Ability to Make Informed Decisions

Reasoning

- Values the Idea of Continual Reflection upon their Teaching and Thinking about History

Communication

- Spirit of Inquiry

Communication

- Implements Classroom Activities Based on Knowledge and Reflections on Content Pedagogy & the Role of the Teacher/Scholar

Communication

- Values the Idea of Modeling for Students and Others Best Personal and Professional Practice

© Frederick D. Drake and Lawrence W. McBride, "The Summative Teaching Portfolio and the Reflective Practitioner of History," *The History Teacher* 34 (November 2000): 53.

Figure 7.5
Deliberative and Evaluative Discussions

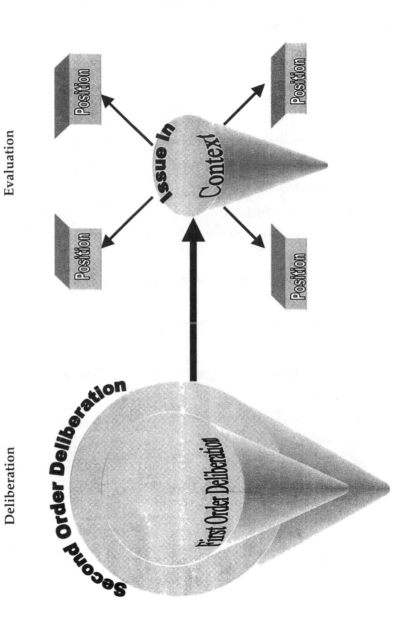

Figure 7.6
Primary Source Analysis Guide

1. Identify the Document

Author(s) or source: _____

Title: _____

Date: _____

Type of document: _____

Relationship to other documents (first order/second order): _____

_____

2. Analyze the Document

Main idea of the document: _____

Relationship to other documents (first order/second order): _____

_____

Preceding conditions that motivated the author: _____

Intended audience and purpose: _____

Biases of the author: _____

Questions to ask the author: _____

3. Historical Context; Important people, events, and ideas at time of document

Local: people, events, and ideas of the time: _____

National: people, events, and ideas of the time: _____

World: people, events, and ideas of the time: _____

Conclusions about local, national, and world at the time: _____

4. Identify the Vital Theme and Narrative Represented

Theme and Narrative: _____

Evidence document represents this VTN _____

5. Relationship to discipline in social sciences

Discipline: _____

Evidence of relationship: _____

Figure 7.7

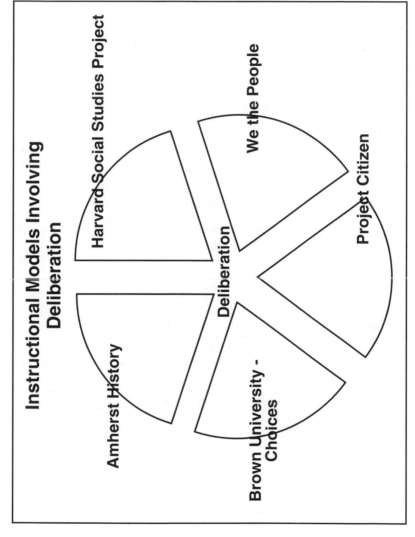

Instructional Models Involving
Deliberation

Harvard Social Studies Project

We the People

Amherst History

Deliberation

Project Citizen

Brown University -
Choices

Notes

1. Several publications emphasized the renewal of civic education in higher education and in pre-college education. See Ernest L. Boyer and Fred M. Hechinger, *Higher Learning in the Nation's Service* (Washington, D.C.: Carnegie Foundation for the Advancement of Teaching, 1981); Frank Newman, *Higher Education and the American Resurgence* (Princeton: Carnegie Foundation for the Advancement of Teaching, 1985); R. Freeman Butts, *The Civic Mission in Educational Reform: Perspectives for the Public and the Profession* (Stanford, California: Hoover Institution Press, 1989); Bernard Murchland, ed., *Higher Education and the Practice of Democratic Politics: A Political Education Reader* (Dayton, Ohio: Kettering Foundation, 1991). The Center for Civic Education published *National Standards for Civics and Government* as part of the National Education Goals 2000: Educate America Act of 1994. See Charles N. Quigley et al., eds., *National Standards for Civics and Government* (Calabasas, California: Center for Civic Education, 1994). Several other works have emphasized citizenship education, among them Walter C. Parker, *Educating the Democratic Mind* (Albany: State University of New York Press, 1996). History is noted by Paul Gagnon as the precondition for civic intelligence; see Paul Gagnon, "History's Role in Civic Education: The Precondition for Political Intelligence," in *Educating the Democratic Mind*, ed. Walter C. Parker (Albany: State University of New York, 1996), 241-262.

2. An alternative view of the central components of the social studies was provided by Shirley H. Engel and Anna S. Ochoa; see Shirley H. Engle, "Decision Making: The Heart of Social Studies Instruction," *Social Education* (November 1960): 301-304, 306 and Shirley H. Engle and Anna S. Ochoa, *Education for Democratic Citizenship: Decision Making in the Social Studies* (New York: Teachers College Press, 1988), 139-141. They have recognized, however, that social studies education based on the study of issues in history can be an acceptable alternative to their preferred curricular model.

3. See various curricular frameworks and guides to content standards, such as The Bradley Commission on History in the Schools, *Building a History Curriculum: Guidelines for Teaching History in Schools* (Washington, DC: Educational Excellence Network, 1988); The National Commission on Social Studies in the Schools, *Charting a Course: Social Studies for the 21st Century* (National Commission on Social Studies in the Schools, 1989); The National Center for History in the Schools, *National Standards for History for Grades K-4: Expanding Children's World in Time and Space; National Standards for World History: Exploring Paths to the Present; National Standards for United States History: Exploring the American Experience* (Los Angeles: National Center for History in the Schools, 1994). Additionally, see state standards as reported in David Warren Saxe, "The State of State Standards in History," *The State of State Standards 2000* (Washington, D.C.: The Thomas B. Fordham Foundation, 2000) <http://www.edexcellence.net/library/soss2000/2000soss.html#History>. Also see *National Standards for Civics and Government* (Calabasas, California: Center for Civic Education, 1994).

4. We are not suggesting that John Dewey would have advocated the current emphasis on prescribed methodological standards. Dewey recognized "general methods" of teaching, but he distinguished "general methods" from "a prescribed rule." Dewey advocated "intelligence, and not through conformity to orders externally imposed." See John Dewey, *Democracy and Education* (New York: Macmillan, 1916), 178. For further discussion see James W. Garrison, "Style and the Art of Teaching," in James W. Garrison and Anthony G. Rudd Jr., eds., *The Educational Conversation: Closing the Gap* (Albany, NY: State University of New York Press, 1995), 41-60. Nor are we suggesting that Dewey would have advocated the contemporary preoccupation with standards-based education. Dewey's "theory of experience" and his thoughts on resisting the extremes of "objective and internal conditions" may well challenge arguments for national curriculum standards. For further discussion see John Dewey, *Experience and Education* (New York: Collier, 1938).

5. Since the 1970s historians have moved away from social science history and the optimistic belief in modernization. Macrohistory and its emphasis upon conventional political history of elites was challenged methodologically by microhistory proponents who focused on everyday life of the neglected and on small social units. The subject matter of historians moved from the "center" of power to the "margins," to individuals regarded by many historians as lacking in resources and civil rights and suffering from exploitation. The grand narrative, which hid common people as well as the marginalized under one history, was abandoned in favor of multiple histories and stories. The grand narrative is deemed near impossible to achieve; microhistories are often criticized for trivialization and a decline toward anecdotal history and antiquarianism. See George G. Iggers, *Historiography in the Twentieth Century: From Scientific Objectivity to the Postmodern Challenge* (Hanover, New Hampshire: Wesleyan University Press, 1997), 101-105. Also see a discussion over trends in history in an "AHR Forum: The Old History and the New," *The American Historical Review* (June 1989): 654-698. Five historians tease out the distinctions in separate essays: Theodore S. Hamerow, "The Bureaucratization of History," 654-660; Gertrude Himmelfarb, "Some Reflections on the New History," 661-670; Lawrence W. Levine, "The Unpredictable Past: Reflections on Recent American Historiography," 671-679; Joan Wallach Scott, "History in Crisis? The Others' Side of the Story," 680-692; and John E. Toews, "Perspectives on 'The Old History and the New': A Comment," 693-698. Additional important essays include Dorothy A. Ross, "Grand Narrative in American Historical Writing: From Romance to Uncertainty," *American Historical Review* (June 1995): 651-677; Linda Kerber, "The Meanings of Citizenship," *Journal of American History* 84 (December 1997): 833-54; and Joyce Appleby, "The Power of History," *AHR* (February 1998): 1-14.

6. The Bradley Commission on History in Schools also presents thirteen habits of mind for historical thinking (See Figure 7.3: History's Habits of Mind) in their indispensable pamphlet, *Building a History Curriculum: Guidelines for Teaching History in Schools* (Washington, DC: Educational Excellence Network, 1988, 1989), 9.

7. Many states have adopted standards developed by the Interstate New Teachers Assessment Support Consortium (INTASC), which emphasize knowledge of content and pedagogy, performance in the classroom, and disposition towards teaching.

8. A particular weakness of the decision-making model that Engle and Ochoa (1988) put at the "heart" of the social studies, which involves a comprehensive interdisciplinary curriculum based on inquiry about public issues, is its disregard of historical knowledge rooted in particular contexts.

9. We have emphasized the flaws of facile and unwarranted generalizations in the study and practice of history. There are no universal laws of history that determine human behavior. However, we also recognize the problem of an extreme historicism, which reduces and confines all knowledge claims and values to particular contexts. An outcome of this kind of extreme historicism leads to radical cultural relativism, which we reject as unwarranted. Further, we recognize that some transcultural generalizations are warranted by evidence in history. Civic cultures that stress constitutional democracy, for example, are more likely to protect human rights than cultures in which there are despotic or autocratic regimes.

10. The Bradley Commission on History in Schools also presents thirteen habits of mind for historical thinking, two of the thirteen, irrationality and present-mindedness, were incorporated in this text, (See Figure 7.3: History's Habits of Mind) in their indispensable pamphlet, *Building a History Curriculum: Guidelines for Teaching History in Schools* (Washington, DC: Educational Excellence Network, 1988), 9. *The National Standards for History* (Basic Edition, 1996), had identified five Standards in Historical Thinking: Chronological Thinking; Historical Comprehension; Historical Analysis and Interpretation; Historical Research Capabilities; and Historical Issues-Analysis and Decision-Making. See *National Standards for History* (Los Angeles: National Center for History in Schools, 1996), 15-16.

11. We borrow from Bernard Murchland whose essay, "Civic Education: Parsing the Problem," summarizes David Mathews' four levels of civic intelligence. See Bernard Murchland, "Civic Education: Parsing the Problem," in *Civic Learning for Teachers: Capstone for Educational Reform, Proceedings of the Seminar on Civic Learning in the Education of the Teaching Profession*, ed. Alan H. Jones (Ann Arbor, Michigan: Prakken Publications, 1985), 34-35. Also see David Mathews, "Civic Intelligence," *Social Education* 49 (November/December 1985): 678-681.

12. See the ideas of Peter N. Stearns, "Why Study History," American Historical Association, <http://www.theaha.org/pubs/stearns.htm>.

13. See David Mathews, "The Liberal Arts and the Civic Arts," *Liberal Education* 68 (Winter 1982): 269-275 and Mark H. Curtis, "The Liberal Arts as Civic Arts: A Historical Perspective," *Liberal Education* 68 (1982): 277-280. This entire volume of *Liberal Education* was devoted to "civic purposes of liberal learning."

14. See instructional materials developed through the *Choices for the 21st Century Education Project* at Brown University.

References

Adler, Mortimer J. *The Paideia Proposal: An Educational Manifesto*. New York: Macmillan, 1982.

Bahmueller, Charles F., and Charles N. Quigley, eds. *Civitas: A Framework for Civic Education*. Calabasas, CA: Center for Civic Education, 1991.

Boyer, Ernest L., and Fred M. Hechinger. *Higher Learning in the Nation's Service*. Washington, DC: Carnegie Foundation for the Advancement of Teaching, 1981.

Bradley Commission on History in Schools. *Building a History Curriculum: Guidelines for Teaching History in Schools*. Washington, DC: Educational Excellence Network, 1988.

Butts, R. Freeman. *The Civic Mission in Educational Reform: Perspectives for the Public and the Profession*. Stanford, CA: Hoover Institution Press, 1989.

Center for Civic Education. *National Standards for Civics and Government*. Calabasas, CA: Center for Civic Education, 1994.

Dewey, John. *Democracy and Education*. New York: MacMillan, 1916.

Dewey, John. *Experience and Education*. New York: Collier, 1938.

Dewey, John. *How We Think*. Boston: Heath, 1910.

Engle, Shirley H., and Anna S. Ochoa. *Education for Democratic Citizenship: Decision Making in the Social Studies*. New York: Teachers College Press, 1988.

Gagnon, Paul, ed. *Historical Literacy: The Case for History in American Education*. Boston: Houghton Mifflin Company, 1989.

Gagnon, Paul. "History's Role in Civic Education: The Precondition for Civic Intelligence." In *Educating the Democratic Mind*. Walter C. Parker, ed. Albany: State University of New York Press, 1996, 241-262.

Garrison, James W. "Style and the Art of Teaching." In *The Educational Conversation: Closing the Gap*, James W. Garrison and Anthony G. Rudd Jr., eds. Albany: State University of New York Press, 1995, 41-60.

Gutmann, Amy. *Democratic Education*. Revised Edition. Princeton: Princeton University Press, 1999.

Gutmann, Amy, and Dennis Thompson. *Democracy and Disagreement*. Cambridge: Belknap Press of Harvard University Press, 1996.

Gutmann, Amy, and Dennis Thompson, "Democratic Disagreement." In *Deliberative Politics: Essays on Democracy and Disagreement*. Stephen Macedo, ed. New York: Oxford University Press, 1999.

Herman, Arthur. *The Idea of Decline in Western History*. New York: The Free Press, 1997.

Kaestle, Carl F. *Pillars of The Republic: Common Schools and American Society, 1780-1860*. New York: Hill and Wang, 1983.

Kaestle, Carl F. "Toward a Political Economy of Citizenship." In *Rediscovering the Democratic Purposes of Education*, Lorraine M. McDonnell, P. Michael Timpane, and Roger Benjamin, eds. Lawrence: University Press of Kansas, 2000.

Kerber, Linda. "The Meanings of Citizenship." *Journal of American History* 84 (December 1997): 833-854.

Kliebard, Herbert M. *Schooled to Work: Vocationalism and the American Curriculum, 1876-1946*. New York: Teachers College Press, 1999.

Kliebard, Herbert M. *The Struggle for the American Curriculum 1893-1958*. New York: Routledge, 1995.

Lasch, Christopher. *The Culture of Narcissism: American Life in an Age of Diminishing Expectations*. New York: W. W. Norton, 1991.

Lasch, Christopher. *The Revolt of the Elites and the Betrayal of Democracy*. New York: W. W. Norton, 1995.

Macedo, Stephen, ed. *Deliberative Politics: Essays on Democracy and Disagreement*. New York: Oxford University Press, 1999.

Maier, Pauline. "Nationhood and Citizenship: What Difference Did the American Revolution Make?" In *Diversity and Citizenship: Rediscovering American Nationhood*. Gary Jeffrey Jacobsohn and Susan Dunn, eds. Lanham, Maryland: Rowman and Littlefield Publishers,1996, 45-64.

Massaro, Toni Marie. *Constitutional Literacy: A Core Curriculum for a Multicultural Nation* Durham: Duke University Press, 1993, 149.

Mathews, David. "Civic Intelligence." *Social Education* 49 (November/December 1985): 678-681.

Mathews, David. "The Liberal Arts and the Civic Arts." *Liberal Education* 68 (Winter 1982): 463-465.

Murchland, Bernard. "Civic Education: Parsing the Problem." In *Civic Learning for Teachers: Capstone for Educational Reform*. Alan H. Jones, ed. Ann Arbor, MI: Prakken Publications, 1985.

Murchland, Bernard, ed. *Higher Education and the Practice of Democratic Politics: A Political Education Reader*. Dayton, OH: Kettering Foundation, 1991.

National Center for History in Schools. *National Standards for History*, Basic Edition. Los Angeles: National Center for History in Schools, 1996.

National Commission on Excellence in Education. *A Nation at Risk: The Imperative for Educational Reform*. Washington, DC: United States Department of Education, 1983.

Newman, Frank. *Higher Education and the American Resurgence*. Washington, DC: Carnegie Foundation for the Advancement of Teaching, 1985.

Niemi, Richard G., and Jane Junn. *What Makes Students Learn*. New Haven, CT: Yale University Press, 1998.

Parker, Walter. "The Art of Deliberation." *Educational Leadership* (February 1997): 18-21.

Parker, Walter C., ed. *Educating the Democratic Mind*. Albany: State University of New York Press, 1996.

Patrick, John J. "Constitutionalism in Education for Democracy." In *Can Democracy Be Taught?*, Andrew Oldenquist, ed., Bloomington, IN: Phi Delta Kappa Educational Foundation, 1996, 91-108.

Patrick, John J. "Education for Constructive Engagement of Citizens in Democratic Civil Society and Government." In *Principles and Practices of Education for Democratic Citizenship: International Perspectives and Projects*, Charles F. Bahmueller and John J. Patrick, eds., Bloomington, IN: ERIC Clearinghouse for Social Studies/Social Science Education, 1999, 41-60.

Patrick, John J. "Multicultural Education and the Civic Mission of Schools." In *Research Review for School Leaders*. William G. Wranga and Peter S. Hlebowitsh, eds. Mahwah, NJ: Lawrence Erlbaum Associates, 2000, 103-33.

Ravitch, Dianne. *Left Back: A Century of Failed School Reform*. New York: Simon & Schuster, 2000.

Rawls, John. *A Theory of Justice*. Cambridge, MA: Harvard University Press, 1971.

Schlesinger, Arthur M. Jr. *The Disuniting of America: Reflections on a Multicultural Society*. New York: W. W. Norton, 1998.

Takaki, Ronald. *A Larger Memory: A History of Our Diversity with Voices*. Boston: Little, Brown and Company, 1998.

Tyack, David B. *The One Best System: A History of American Urban Education*. Cambridge, MA: Harvard University Press, 1974.

Wilson, Suzanne M., and Samuel S. Wineburg. "Peering at History through Different Lenses: The Role of Disciplinary Perspectives in Teaching History." *Teachers College Record* 89 (Summer 1988): 526-539.

Wineburg, Sam. *Historical Thinking and Other Unnatural Acts: Charting the Future of Teaching the Past*. Philadelphia: Temple University Press, 2001.

8

Using *We the People. . .* Programs in Social Studies Teacher Education

Nancy Haas

This chapter describes the use of *We the People. . . The Citizen and the Constitution* and *We the People. . . Project Citizen* as course materials for pre-service education students in a social studies methods course. Both *We the People* programs are sponsored by the Center for Civic Education and are funded by the U.S. Department of Education by an act of Congress.[1] Hereafter, for brevity *We the People. . . The Citizen and the Constitution* will be referred to as *We the People* and *We the People. . . Project Citizen* will be referred to as *Project Citizen*.[2]

At the outset, it is important to state that this chapter is a description of the principles embodied within the two programs that make each of them viable training materials for social studies methods courses at both the secondary and elementary levels. In this chapter, I first describe the overall organization of my methods course; second, I describe *We the People* and *Project Citizen*; third, I describe the learning strategies employed in the programs; fourth, I discuss the framework for civic education; and, finally, I discuss the need for building partnerships to enhance civic education in social studies methods of teaching courses.

Organization of the Methods of Teaching Course

The social studies methods course structure one chooses should attend primarily to learning principles and the content that pre-service teachers perceive to be valuable. This is not to imply that pre-service teachers should choose the content and control the curriculum. Rather, it is meant to convey the notion that methods instructors should be able to explain the value of what they are teaching and how the concepts can be directly applicable to the teachers' future classrooms. When information is valued, it more likely will be retained (Niemi and Junn 1998).

Second, the social studies methods course should be well organized. We know that information is learned and retained when presented in an organized and meaningful context (Snowman and Biehler 2000). There is a greater rate of retention when students are required to pursue learning in an active rather than passive manner. Students learn more when put in situations that require them to exercise their judgment as compared to merely recalling disconnected bits of information (Kintisch and Cordero 1993). Strengths of *We the People* and *Project Citizen* include active learning strategies and the relevance to the school curriculum built into the materials.

In a typical social studies methods course, there often are students with majors in such academic specializations as history, political science, geography, and economics. Thus, methods instructors should consider selecting teaching strategies and materials that can be generalized across the content areas.

I devote two three-hour sessions to the *We the People* and *Project Citizen* programs and students have an additional twelve to fifteen hours of independent and group work to complete assignments. In addition to content associated with civics, I address teaching strategies in history (American and world), geography, and economics. The transfer of specific strategies for each of the other three areas (history, geography, and economics) to civics are discussed and reinforced.

Students are introduced to *We the People* and *Project Citizen* early in the semester; specific learning activities and principles are reinforced throughout the semester. For example, students use principles of constitutional democracy to conduct historical research in local and national archives, analyze primary resources, and discuss public policy issues. The culminating project for *We the People* is participating in a simulated congressional hearing. The culminating project for *Project Citizen* is an oral team-presentation of a public policy issue that would be appropriate for investigation. For *Project Citizen*, students do not complete a presentation portfolio; rather, they describe the steps they would go through to complete the process and the governing body to whom they would present the issue. Given the time constraints, it is not feasible for the students to complete the portfolio.

Although the two programs have some shared core principles, there are enough differences to warrant treating them separately, as each also contributes uniquely to the outcomes of education for democracy. Keep in mind that if specific published curricular materials are incorporated into a methods course, they should be done so with the purpose of demonstrating principles and techniques that can then be transferred to a variety of settings. Toward that end, many organizational structures and teaching techniques could be incorporated into methods courses as part of the training preservice teachers receive. I have chosen *We the People* and *Project Cit-*

izen because they allow me to make abstract principles more concrete in order to help preserve teachers get a handle on teaching methods.

We the People. . . Project Citizen

Project Citizen is a civic education program designed for students in the middle school grades six through nine that introduces students to the field of public policy. Larry Gerston (1997, 6-7) provides a succinct definition of public policy "as the combination of basic decisions, commitments, and actions, made by those who hold or affect government positions of authority." He further states that those arrangements result from the interaction of those who demand changes in public policy, the decision makers, and those who are affected by the public policy. Gerston's definition describes the processes that students experience during *Project Citizen*. Students identify a public policy issue selected through consensus, then proceed with the following phases of the program:

- gathering data related to the problem;
- examining solutions to the public issue;
- developing a public policy to address the issue;
- developing an action plan that addresses the appropriate level of government;
- assessing the consequences of their actions, which includes recognition of limitations imposed by federal and state constitutions;
- presenting their portfolio, which contains a public policy recommendation, and finally;
- reflecting on their learning experience.

Through this process, students learn about the role of government in public policy; but more essential to democracy education, they learn their roles and responsibilities as citizens in the process.

Teachers can choose to have their students enter their portfolios into competition at local, state, and national levels. The processes embedded in *Project Citizen* provide teachers with strategies for investigating other issues in the social studies classroom. *Project Citizen* is an example of making concrete those abstract concepts that we want students to put into place as active citizens.

We the People. . . The Citizen and the Constitution

We the People is a Center for Civic Education program that introduces students to the U. S. Constitution in a way that helps them to understand how this document relates to their lives. The program is designed with developmentally appropriate learning strategies for upper elementary school through high school. *We the People* is divided into the following units of instruction, with each unit having key topics to guide the learning:

- Historical and Philosophical Foundations of Constitutional Government
- Creation of the Constitution
- Organization of the National Government
- Development of the Constitution
- Expansion of Rights During the Last 200 Years
- Roles of Citizens in American Democracy

The key topics and essential questions related to them guide the study of each unit and help students focus on the critical elements of the unit. For example, see the guiding questions for unit one of *We the People*, which are presented in Figure 8.1.

Often the quality of a discussion is dependent upon the caliber of the questions asked (Gunter, Estes, and Schwab 1999). Questions can promote lively discussions, but many novice teachers find it difficult to ask thought-provoking questions, opting rather for superficial rather than deep-probing questions. Therefore, it is important to guide new teachers in the art of asking and answering questions, since high-level questions tend to elicit higher-level responses for students and are correlated with student achievement (Klinzing, Klinzing-Eurich, and Tish 1985). Materials that help teachers develop questioning skills by providing good models for them help them gain expertise in questioning skills.

In addition to the overall guiding questions in *We the People* units, each lesson has questions that focus on narrower content within the unit. For example, within unit one, the *Historical and Philosophical Foundations of Constitutional Government*, the first lesson asks students to "describe how the natural rights philosophy is to preserve our natural rights to life, liberty, and property" (Center for Civic Education 1995, 31). These questions serve to increase the depth of processing for complex topics and require students to "learn" as compared to "cover" the material. Material that is merely covered can be forgotten easily, especially if it was never integrated into long-term memory or connected to prior learning (Caine and Caine 1999).

Civic Education Framework

The principles for the civic education portion of the methods course were adapted from the work of R. Freeman Butts (1996) in his *Morality of Democratic Citizenship* and by the *Civics Framework for the 1998 National Assessment of Educational Progress* (NAEP Civics Consensus Project 1996). Both documents provided the impetus for including civic education into my social studies methods class. I selected *We the People* and *Project Citizen* as examples of curricular material, because they have many of the components generally agreed upon as necessary for civic education.

Figure 8.1

**Example of *We the People*, Unit 1 Guiding Questions for
High School Students**

Units	Guiding Questions
1. Historical and Philosophical Foundations of Constitutional Government	• What would life be like in a state of nature? • How does government secure natural rights? • What did the founders learn about republican government from the ancient world? • How did modern ideas of individual rights develop? • What were the British origins of American constitutionalism? • How did representative government begin in England? • What basic ideas about rights and constitutional government did colonial Americans have? • Why did the American Colonists want to free themselves from Britain? What basic ideas about government did the founders put in the Declaration of Independence? • What basic ideas about government did the state constitutions include? How did the new states protect rights?

R. Freeman Butts (1988) suggests that civic education has two major goals: (1) to enable students to know about government, its history, values, principles, and institutions; and (2) to enable students to participate in their communities, states, nation, and the world.

The goals that Butts proposes and the essential questions posited in the standards are illuminated in both *We the People* and *Project Citizen*. The first goal I consider the **knowing** goal and the second the **doing** goal. Both *We* *the People* and *Project Citizen* provide a strong knowledge base (*knowing*) and the transfer of that knowledge to civic action (*doing*). In order for students to become *active* rather than *passive* citizens, they must have a firm knowledge base from which to take action. There must be a balance between a civic knowledge base and a capacity for action.

A civic knowledge base is incomplete if it does not relate to the learners or invite them to participate in civic life. Conversely, sounding a clarion call to action without the firm grasp of civic knowledge and skills will unlikely result in deeply ingraining civic dispositions that are keys to responsible civic action. We must strike a balance (see Figure 8.2).

Figure 8.2

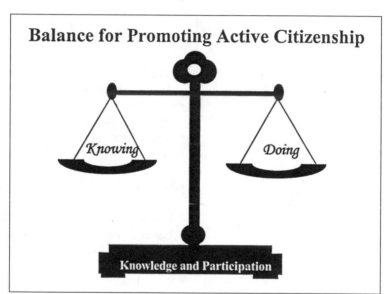

Balance for Promoting Active Citizenship

Knowing   *Doing*

Knowledge and Participation

Project Citizen provides the knowledge and strategies to take action on a problem identified by middle school children; thus they are educated in the foundations of responsible citizenship. In *We the People*, students take an *active* role in classroom citizenship by collaborating in learning and in the mock congressional hearing, which is the culminating activity. *We the People* students gain a strong knowledge base and conceptualize the relationship between the U.S. Constitution and their lives.

The *doing* goal requires some proposed civic action in order to evaluate the achievement of students. The mock congressional hearing gives teachers the opportunity to assess students' ability to apply concepts and principles from the Constitution to new situations and to evaluate their knowledge of the Constitution, in addition to evaluating their skills in research, collaboration, organization, and presentation.

In both *We the People* and *Project Citizen*, essential questions for **civic knowledge** are at the core of the curriculum. The essential questions that guide the programs are consistent with questions posed in the *National Standards for Civics and Government* and in the framework for the *National Assessment of Educational Progress*. Here are the five key questions.

1. What are civic life, politics, and government?
2. What are the foundations of the American political system?
3. How does the government established by the Constitution embody the purposes, values, and principles of American democracy?
4. What is the relationship of the United States to other nations and to world affairs?
5. What are the roles of citizens in American democracy?

In addition to **civic knowledge**, *We the People* and *Project Citizen* also teach **civic skills**, and **civic dispositions** highly valued in civic education and embodied in the *National Standards for Civics and Government*. Note that in Figure 8.3, I have added the words *and collaborative* to the first civic disposition because both of these programs promote high levels of collaboration. Also note that I have added *in a diverse society* to the second item in the list of dispositions. I believe that we have to take a more vocal stance to acknowledge the changing demographics in the United States. Figure 8.5 displays some ways in which both *We the People* and *Project Citizen* operationalize the fundamentals of civic education.

Active Teaching and Learning Strategies

There is a plethora of teaching models that have nuances to make each somewhat unique. However, the best instructional methods have their common characteristic of encouraging active learning of the lesson's objectives.

Engagement in relevant activities helps to bridge the gap between abstractions and students' actual experiences (Freiberg and Driscoll 2000). Movement along the instructional continuum in Figure 8.4 is expected in the learning cycle. Although there is nothing inherently wrong with a lecture, teachers should be encouraged to also incorporate more student-centered strategies into their repertoire. Instructional strategies should be chosen based on the learner, the context, and the content (Freiberg and Driscoll 2000).

In addition to teaching civic knowledge, civic skills, and civic dispositions, *We the People* and *Project Citizen* include many historical research and analytical skills, which are consistent with the requirements of civic knowledge, skills, and dispositions.

Figure 8.3

**Civic Skills and Civic Dispositions in the National
Standards for Civics and Government**

Civic Skills	Civic Dispositions

<u>Intellectual</u>
  Identifying
  Describing
  Explaining
  Evaluating
  Analyzing
  Taking Positions
  Defending Positions
 	
<u>Participatory</u>
  Interacting
  Monitoring
  Influencing
	• Becoming an independent **and collaborative** member of society
	• Assuming the personal, political, and economic responsibilities of a citizen **in a diverse society**
	• Respecting individual worth and human dignity
	• Participating in civic affairs in a thoughtful and effective manner
	• Promoting the healthy functioning of constitutional democracy

Figure 8.4

Instructional Continuum								
Teacher Centered							Student Centered	
Lecture	Demonstration	Questioning	Discussion	Practice	Grouping	Role Playing	Simulation	Inquiry
Modified from Freiberg and Driscoll, 2000								

It is incumbent upon methods instructors to help pre-service teachers to construct ways to operationalize the skills, knowledge, and dispositions of civic education. (See Figure 8.5.) Otherwise, they are going to remain in a textbook, journal, or digest untouched and unused by social studies teachers, if they are not viewed as important for developing a citizenry. We can make a significant impact on current calls for renewal for civic education by helping students in pre-service teacher education programs see the relevance of the tenets of sound civic education and seek ways to operationalize them in the classroom.

We the People and *Project Citizen* include problem solving and higher-order thinking among the instructional strategies. In the high school version of *We the People*, students are asked to contemplate the following questions about the rights of groups compared to the rights of individuals:

1. What is meant by the rights of groups as opposed to the rights of individuals?
2. What are the advantages and disadvantages of viewing rights as being possessed by individuals rather than groups?
3. Give some contemporary examples of claims for group rights. What arguments can you make for and against these claims?
4. Should certain individuals in our society be given special rights and privileges because they are members of a particular social group?

Engaging in civil discourse on public policy reinforces students' civic dispositions and increases their knowledge of a subject. These discussions also may help students to participate in and understand their role in a democratic society (Hess 1999).

A strength of both programs, *Project Citizen* and *We the People*, is the transfer of civic skills, knowledge, and attitudes accomplished through active learning strategies. Transfer, critical for learning, is classically thought of as the application of learning in one setting to a new situation (Joyce, Weil, and Calhoun 2000). In the final analysis, it is the transfer of civic skills, knowledge, and dispositions to the student's lifelong role as a citizen that must make a difference, or civic education will be for naught. Therefore, it is important for teachers to teach for transfer or we will be having another call for civic renewal in the not too distant future. One of the ways that teachers can teach for transfer is to place the learning in an authentic situation so that students can see how it applies to their lives.

Assessment in *We the People* and *Project Citizen*

There is an unsettling adage in education that suggests "what gets tested gets taught." If that is true, it may bode poorly for social studies since the current trend across the country is for high-stakes, standardized achieve-

Figure 8.5
Civic Skills and Dispositions in *Project Citizen* and *We the People*

Project Citizen	*We the People*
Intellectual Skills	**Intellectual Skills**
Identifying Public Policy Issues	Defending their Position
Analyzing How Decisions Affect the Public	Gaining Research and Information Retrieval Skills
Taking a Stand on Public Policy Issues	Speaking in Public
Gathering Data	Writing Persuasive Papers
Analyzing Data	Reading from a Historical Perspective
Synthesizing Data	Using and Assessing the Credibility of Primary Sources
Reporting Data	Using Logic and Organization
Developing a Presentation Portfolio	Framing Historical Questions
Defending their Portfolio	Examining Different Points of View
Identifying Primary and Secondary Resources	Determining the Context in Which Statements Were Made
	Constructing Timelines
	Constructing and Interpreting Data
	Determining Opinions versus Facts
Participatory Skills	**Participatory Skills**
Participating on a Team	Contributing to the Team by Doing Quality Work
Monitoring Progress on an Issue	Contributing to the Team by Meeting Deadlines
Influencing Public Policy	Providing Feedback to Team Members
	Achieving Consensus
Dispositions	**Dispositions**
Becoming an Independent **and Collaborative** Member of Society	Becoming an Independent **and Collaborative** Member of Society
Assuming the Personal, Political, and Economic Responsibilities of a Citizen in a Diverse Society	Assuming the Personal, Political, and Economic Responsibilities of a Citizen in a Diverse Society
Respecting Individual Worth and Human Dignity	Promoting the Healthy Functioning of Constitutional Democracy
Participating in Civic Affairs in a Thoughtful and Effective Manner	Promoting and Protecting the General Welfare and Common Good
Promoting the Healthy Functioning of Constitutional Democracy	

ment testing in the basic skills of reading, writing, and mathematics. In addition to these standardized achievement tests, many State Departments of Education require more testing to assess mastery of state standards in language arts and mathematics. Given that few states administer tests in the area of social studies, during "testing season," usually in the spring, social studies content is often relegated to a low priority. The practice of abandoning the regular curriculum in favor of test preparation is becoming more widespread as the stakes become higher and higher (Haladyna, Allison, and Haas 1998). Although increasing achievement is a worthy goal for all students, the measure of achievement should be directly correlated to curriculum goals rather than to a published standardized achievement test. In other words, we should be measuring how well students have learned the content and have integrated that knowledge into civic dispositions. Testing should also be used as a tool for evaluating and adjusting curriculum goals and instructional practices (Parker 1996).

Social studies educators in grades K-12 and higher education should continue to send a resounding caution against high-stakes testing that reduces the content to the lowest common denominator, which in turn, would force the curriculum to follow suit with an emphasis on names, dates, faces, and places rather than on more historical analysis or civic knowledge and dispositions. On the other hand, we must not sound like anti-accountability advocates either. Measuring learning can be very relevant in the social studies using a combination of traditional and performance-based assessment.

Both *We the People* and *Project Citizen* provide for a comprehensive evaluation of student achievement in traditional and performance-based assessment. The portfolios students develop in *Project Citizen* present an opportunity to evaluate a student's work in an authentic setting. Students present their portfolios as a team and each team is held accountable for the quality of the work. In *We the People*, students take a rigorous multiple choice test and participate in a mock congressional hearing.

Responding to Individual Differences

Teachers are faced with many challenges. Among the biggest challenges is responding to the wide range of individual differences within groups. In any given class teachers can have students with limited skills in English or students who come from a culture very different from the mainstream and do not have the fundamental civic understandings as, presumably, students born and raised in this country would possess. *We the People* and *Project Citizen* present high-level content at a reasonable level of text density, so that students who are challenged by the English language can read the material. *We the People* has textbooks at three different levels, which can facilitate the achievement level of students with disabilities. *Project Citizen* has many tasks that contribute to the completion of the portfolio. Not everyone has to write the final report; students can contribute in a significant way by helping to put the portfolio boards together.

In addition to differences in reading and writing skills, teachers must face differences among students in motivation. Students who are not motivated in traditional social studies classes are often very motivated in classes using *We the People* and *Project Citizen* because of the interactive strategies used to learn the content. Students have the opportunity to collaborate and support one another, which typically increases continuing achievement motivation. We know that students learn best and are motivated with active learning strategies. Both programs have activities that are interesting and promote active participation. Preservice teachers need help in coming up with motivating lessons and *We the People* and *Project Citizen* teacher's guides suggest activities for the teacher to use to help students bring relevance to the learning.

Program Effectiveness

Both *We the People* and *Project Citizen* have been studied and have been shown to be effective in regard to students' civic attitudes and civic knowledge. In 1993 Richard Brody, a political science professor at Stanford University, conducted a study that focused on political tolerance and political attitudes. His findings support the use of these materials for democracy education and, although Brody did not discuss using *We the People* in preservice education social studies courses, the results of this study suggest that they carry credibility with them that make them appropriate to be introduced to future teachers to consider for their classrooms.

Brody's findings showed the students in the *We the People* program display more political tolerance than the average American and are more tolerant than students using other curricula. He also reported that students' use of *We the People* was related to higher levels of confidence and a deeper understanding of political freedom.

Project Citizen has also been evaluated for effectiveness in the United States and internationally. One of the most rigorous evaluations of the program examined *Project Citizen* in Indiana, Latvia, and Lithuania. In all three political units, the program had statistically significant and positive effects on students' civic knowledge, self-perceived civic skills, and propensity to participate in civic and political life (Vontz, Metcalf, and Patrick 2000). In another study, Tolo (1998) reported that 97% of the teachers using *Project Citizen* reported it to be an effective way to teach democratic citizenship.

Collaboration for Civic Education

There is a growing recognition of the benefits of building and strengthening collaborative relationships between the faculty in arts and sciences and education programs in the preparation of teachers. Social studies teachers must have a strong grounding in history and the social sciences in order to make the content relevant for their classrooms. Accrediting agencies such as the National Council for Accreditation of Teacher Education and Teacher Education Accreditation Council are encouraging the collaboration in their accrediting documents for greater integration of content and methods (NCATE 2001; TEAC 2001).

Project 30 Alliance is a national organization funded by the Carnegie Corporation that brings together faculty from the Schools of Education with faculty in Arts and Sciences in a collaborative approach for the education of pre-service teachers. This collaboration is done for the purpose of improving teacher education (Project 30 2000). The five themes identified by Project 30 are "important to clarifying the intellectual underpinnings of teacher education and to developing more fully the teaching profession . . . and are well beyond the particular expertise of either the arts and science faculty or the education faculty to solve alone." A major goal of Project 30, implied by the five themes, is to involve faculty across colleges and schools in the education of preservice teachers. The themes are (1) subject matter understanding, (2) general and liberal education, (3) pedagogical content knowledge, (4) international, cultural, and other human perspectives, and (5) increasing representation of under-represented groups in teaching.

It is incumbent upon methods instructors to build a bridge between the content of the liberal arts and sciences in order to guide teachers in the design of meaningful learning opportunities in the social studies. It is the social studies methods class where content and pedagogy converge, and students are taught the processes and strategies for making the content meaningful to diverse learners.

A further justification for building partnerships between the faculty in education and the faculty in arts and sciences is the current movement in standards-based learning. Each state has developed academic standards in the content areas for which teachers must plan their lessons. In order for students to be well-prepared for teaching to the standards, they must get the content from the arts and sciences curriculum. In addition, most states now have professional teaching standards which include content knowledge as well as pedagogical knowledge. Again, the content knowledge is gained from programs in the arts and sciences. In many states, teachers are required to pass a content knowledge test in order to obtain teacher certification.

This correlation to the standards is a salient issue because we are hearing more and more from teachers that if it's not tied to the standards, we are not supposed to teach it. Teachers all over the country are now having to demonstrate that their lesson plans directly reflect the state or district standards.

Collaboration with the public schools and learning from gifted teachers cannot be overlooked if faculties in higher education are serious about building partnerships for the betterment of civic education. In the past there has been an emphasis in putting theory into practice but the trend now is to build theories from successful practice (Brendtro, Brokenleg, Van-Bockern 1998). This way of conceptualizing collaboration between K-12 faculty and university faculty flip the former model on its side and the two-way communication becomes horizontal rather than one-way, top-down.

This reconceptualization of collaboration is at once promising and potentially dangerous. We have to use caution as we adopt new practices that we do not abandon effective teaching methods in favor of adopting new and untested "fads." On the other hand, we have to make certain that strategies used with preservice teachers are effective and can transfer to teaching K-12 students. Collaborative partners work together to inform each others' dispositions and practice; one ideology does not dominate the other. Perhaps through collaboration, higher education faculty can shed their "ivory tower" persona.

Conclusion

Students in pre-service teacher education programs benefit from having concrete examples for promoting active participation and meaningful learning for their students. Novice teachers do not begin their careers having a collection of materials and strategies to use for helping students create meaning for understanding of and participation in a democratic society. The Center for Civic Education's programs, *We the People* and *Project Citizen*, provide the foundations and strategies for learning civic knowledge, civic skills, and civic dispositions. The materials provide a springboard for using the strategies in other facets of the social studies such as history, geography, economics, sociology, anthropology, etc. The materials were never intended to and neither should they be used as the sole teaching materials in a social studies methods course. What they do provide are exemplary instructional materials and strategies that have been evaluated as effective for teaching about democracy.

Any materials chosen for demonstration in a methods course should carry credibility in terms of effectiveness and applicability to practice based on sound instructional principles and developmentally appropriate activ-

Figure 8.6
Higher Education and K12 Collaboration

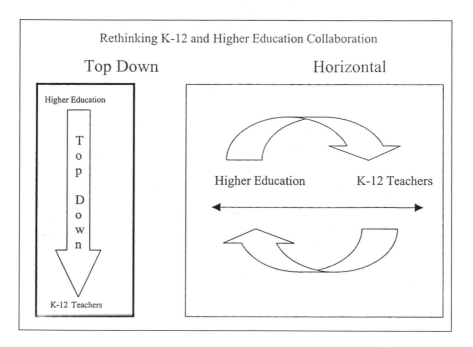

ities. There are many materials on the market that can be used, but criteria for their selection and use should be developed so that preservice teachers are introduced to quality programs that have been shown to increase student achievement of civic knowledge, civic skills, and civic dispositions, which are foundations of citizenship in a constitutional democracy.

Finally, collaborative partnerships among Arts and Sciences, Colleges of Education, and Pre K-12 teachers can serve to strengthen the respective knowledge bases of content and pedagogy. We have outgrown a top-down approach to collaboration among these educational entities and now recognize that collaborative approaches with the intent of informing each other's discipline is in the best interest of learning at all levels.

Notes

1. *We the People. . . The Citizen and the Constitution* is a three-level program involving six units of instruction on the history, principles, and practices of the U.S. Constitution. There are three textbooks that cover the same type of content with increasing depth and complexity from the first to the third book in the series. The "level one" book is for upper-elementary school students; the "level two" book is designed for middle-school students; the "level three" book is for high school students.

2. *We the People. . . Project Citizen* is an instructional module for middle school students, which teaches democratic citizenship by requiring students to practice it. Students participate in processes of democracy by selecting a community-based issue of interest to them; doing research about the antecedents and conditions of the issue; examining alternative responses or resolutions on the issue; choosing the best response; and justifying the best response.

References

Brody, R. A. *Secondary Education and Political Attitudes: Examining the Effects on Political Tolerance of the We the People. . . Curriculum.* Calabasas, CA: Center for Civic Education, 1994.

Caine, G., R. N. Caine, and S. Crowell. *Mindshifts.* Tucson, AZ: Zephyr Press, 1999.

Center for Civic Education. *An International Framework for Education in Democracy.* Calabasas, CA: Center for Civic Education, 2001.

Center for Civic Education. *National Standards for Civics and Government.* Calabasas, CA: Center for Civic Education, 1994.

Center for Civic Education. *We the People. . . Project Citizen.* Calabasas, CA: Center for Civic Education, 1995.

Center for Civic Education. *We the People. . . The Citizen and the Constitution.* Calabasas, CA: Center for Civic Education, 1995.

Freiberg, H. Jerome, and Amy Driscoll. *Universal Teaching Strategies.* Boston: Allyn & Bacon, 2000.

Gerston, Larry N. *Public Policy Making: Process and Principles.* New York: M. E. Sharpe, 1997.

Gunter, M.A., T. H. Estes, and J. Schwab. *Instruction: A Models Approach.* Boston, MA: Allyn and Bacon, 1999.

Haladyna, Thomas M., Jeanette Allison, and Nancy S. Haas. "Continuing Tensions in Standardized Testing." *Childhood Education* 74:5 (1998): 262-273.

Hess, Diana. *Discussing Controversial Public Issues in Secondary Social Studies Classrooms: Learning from Skilled Teachers.* Paper presented at the annual meeting of the College and University Faculty Association of the National Council for the Social Studies, 1999.

Joyce, Bruce, Marsha Weil, and Emily Calhoun. *Models of Teaching.* Boston, MA: Allyn and Bacon, 2000.

Kintisch, S., and W. Cordero. *Breaking Away from the Textbook.* Lancaster, PA: Technomic Publishing, 1993.

Klinzing, N. G., Klinzing-Eurich, G. and R. Tisher. "Higher Cognitive Behaviors in Classroom Discourse: Congruencies Between Teachers' Questions and Pupils' Responses." *Australian Journal of Education* 29 (April 1985): 63-75.

Snowman, J., and R. Biehler. *Psychology Applied to Teaching.* Boston, MA: Houghton Mifflin Company, 2000.

NAEP Civics Consensus Project. *Civics Framework for the 1998 National Assessment of Educational Progress.* Washington, DC: National Assessment Governing Board, 1996.

National Council for Accreditation of Teacher Education. *Interim Policies and Procedures for OSASB Approval of Specialized Professional Association Standards.* Washington, DC: NCATE, 2001.

Niemi, Richard G., and June Junn. *Civic Education.* New Haven: Yale University Press, 1998.

Parker, Walter C. "Assessing Student Learning of an Issue-Oriented Curriculum." In *Handbook on Teaching Social Issues*, Ronald W. Evans and David Warren Saxe, eds. Washington, DC: National Council for the Social Studies, 1996.

Project 30 Alliance. <http://www.project30.org/news.htm>, 2001.

Teacher Accreditation Council. *Accreditation Goals and Principles of the Teacher Education Accreditation Council.* Washington, DC: TAC, 2001.

Tolo, Kenneth. *An Assessment of We the People. . . Project Citizen: Promoting Citizenship in Classroom Publics and Communities.* Austin: Lyndon B. Johnson School of Public Affairs of the University of Texas, 1999.

United States Department of Education. *Teacher Quality Enhancement Program FY2000 Partnership Grants.* <http://www.ed.gov/PressReleases/09-2000/0921a.html>, 2000.

University of Northern Colorado. Collaborative Partnership with Arts and Sciences. <http://asweb.unco.edu/Newsletter/Current/article3.htm>2000.

Vontz, Thomas S., Kim K. Metcalf, and John J. Patrick. *Project Citizen and the Civic Development of Adolescent Students in Indiana, Latvia, and Lithuania.* Bloomington, IN: ERIC Clearinghouse for Social Studies/Social Science Education, 2000.

9

Democratic Teacher Education through Multicultural Service Learning

Marilynne Boyle-Baise

> If only we would endorse one perspective, so the argument goes, whether it be communitarianism, public work, social capital, or strong democracy, we could more easily revitalize democratic civic practice in America. We need, however, to be open to a greater diversity of perspectives about what it means to be a democratic citizen. (Battistoni 2000, 33)

Richard Battistoni (2000) argues that service learning is a powerful vehicle for civic education. However, he poses several caveats. First, service learning is not a cure for political apathy. Service learners often perceive community service as something apart from civic engagement. Second, civic learning does not accrue automatically from community-based learning. Service learning programs often fail to correlate community experiences with dispositions and skills needed for democratic citizenship. The proposals in this chapter relate to the second caveat.

Why is there a disconnection between service learning and civic education? According to Battistoni, part of the problem is conceptual: meanings for civic education are muddy and multiplistic. Part of the problem is pedagogical: service learning programs usually are not structured to teach civic values and skills. Rather than rhetorically limit definitions of service and citizenship, Battistoni argues for recognition of diverse meanings, and for all disciplines to contribute to discourse around civic education. He sets forth several integrations, possibly fruitful for civic education and meaningful for students, including exploration of service learning/civic education/multicultural education agendas. Battistoni also urges stronger linkages between service learning and democratic civic education. In this chapter, I propose three distinctive paradigms for service learning, each a different translation of democratic education. I sketch multicultural service learning, locate it within one of the three paradigms, and consider it as a form of democratic teacher education. Then, I describe multicultural service learning in practice, as a structure that emphasizes views, values, and skills for multicultural, democratic education.

Different Standpoints

Consider the following quotes from a preservice teacher and a college student who participated, respectively, in service learning as part of a multicultural education or a political science course.

> Before I took part in the service learning project, I never really associated myself with the community and sheltered myself within the confines of the university. When I first attended the Boys and Girls Club, I was a little apprehensive. I actually thought that these children were going to be like the teens in the movie "Dangerous Minds." Growing up all my life in predominately white middle class neighborhoods, this was a common stereotype that I made. Through community service learning, I gained a positive attitude toward all children and the community they live in. I learned the more diverse I am as a person, the more knowledgeable and understanding I will be as an educator. I am now more comfortable being around a diverse group of children and, in fact, welcome it. This experience has helped prepare me for the future challenges that I will face as a multicultural educator. (R. M. essay, 10/20/2000)

For this White, male, middle class prospective teacher, service learning kindled cross-cultural community connections. It jarred him from comfortable university environs. It spurred him to work with culturally diverse people in a low-income neighborhood. The experience challenged his stereotypes and his previous "we-they" distinctions. This preservice teacher rethought what it meant to serve the public through teaching. He readied to learn more about cultural diversity in order to become a better teacher. He welcomed the chance to work further with youth and adults like those he met during service learning.

Arguably, this preservice teacher gained a democratic education through service learning. He functioned as a thinking citizen; he critically analyzed his life, social position, and views of others. He developed a broader sense of community, discarded narrow views, and affirmed cultural diversity. He engaged civically through working with and learning from youth and adults different from himself. He committed to future involvement with diverse populations, to continual attention to perspectives of students and their communities. This preservice teacher's democratic education focused on building community with people previously distanced from himself.

Contrast this second quotation to the first. This college student recalls his/her service learning experience as part of Battistoni's political science course.

> Over the course of this semester, I have become a citizen of New Brunswick. It could be argued that I was a citizen here well before registering for this course, but I did not feel as if I were one. Having taken the course, I now know why I felt as I did. A citizen must play an active role in his or her community. A citizen must work for change and never accept the status quo... I see the city differently. I'm no longer scared walking to my service site—far from it. I feel like I know that small portion of the city now. Now, when I pass people in the street, some say hello to me, and call me by name. Through my work, I've gotten to know individual people, and they've gotten to know me. I enjoy my community service. It has opened my eyes to the role I play as a citizen in my community. (Battistoni 2000, 29)

What kind of democratic education did this student receive? What is *not* said is revealing. The student did not expressly address issues of culture, race, or power. The student gained better acquaintance with people in the community, but whether relationships cross race, cultural, or social class boundaries is unclear. The student greeted residents, and they acknowledged him in return, but there is little sense of working with residents for social change. There is no clue as to the meaning of a challenge to the status quo. Citizenship is perceived as a role rather than as a relationship with members of diverse communities.

The second recollection is more common to service learning than the first one. Service learning usually is not portrayed as an effort to build community. Instead, it is discussed as an opportunity to realize civic responsibility and to practice "arts" of civic participation, such as communication, deliberation, cooperation, and problem-solving (Barber 1998; Battistoni 2000). Values, skills, and civic dispositions often are discussed in a politically neutral way, as universally appropriate. Impacts of culture, race, and power on service learning and democratic education are addressed peripherally. Social change is stimulated by enlightened individuals, supposedly from all cultural/social groups.

These reflections, arguably, stem from and represent distinctive orientations to service learning. I suggest three paradigms for service learning: charity, civic education, and community-building. Stances center around and demonstrate particular values and views of service and citizenship. Service learners make meaning from within various paradigms, and movement from one to another requires a vigorous, conceptual shift. Impacted by their diverse backgrounds and idiosyncratic outlooks, service learners usually feel more comfortable in one of the three domains of thought. Moreover, educators tend to situate their teaching paradigmatically. They are most at home in one paradigm or another (Morton 1995). In the examples above, the preservice teacher perceives and practices service learning from a community-building stance, the political science student from a civic education position.

Before I delineate three paradigms, a counter claim is in order. Not every-one agrees that there are distinctive orientations to service learning. Instead, continua for teaching and learning are posed. Service learners presumably progress from a focus on charitable activities to involvement in social action. They move from personal connection with someone in need, to under-standing social problems, to concern for social justice (Eyler and Giles 1999). Practitioners supposedly stress alternate ends of a "student-community development continuum" (Stanton, Giles, and Cruz 1999, 96). They either emphasize student learning through service to communities, or act as com-munity allies, extending academic resources to local organizations.

These proposals acknowledge divergent perceptions and aims, but fail to construct frameworks of thought and action for learners or practitioners. Fur-ther, a learning continuum overlooks "where learners are," or what ideas and values they bring to service learning. It assumes linear, progressive learn-ing, from one step to another. These positions do not speak to my experience. Instead, I notice that ideological positions undergird my teaching and influ-ence community programs. Sometimes, my views contradict those of com-munity organizations with whom I work. For example, a Girl Scout program considers some teens "at-risk," whereas I suspect that label. Tensions such as these indicate divergent interpretations of youth advocacy, community improvement, service, and learning. Also, service learners often experience community work as an emotional jolt toward new understandings, rather than as a neat progression from charitable to social change views. Their per-ceptions of local conditions and concerns depend upon their prior life expe-riences with cultural diversity and poverty. In the continuum proposition, service learners might be viewed as entering at various points along a line. A paradigmatic argument, alternatively, situates instructors and learners within intricately interwoven sets of beliefs, meanings, and preferred actions. To shift from one view to another is an unsettling, uneasy, unusual event.

A number of scholars have suggested paradigmatic orientations to serv-ice learning. I integrate their proposals into three paradigms for charity, civic education, and community-building. As part of my presentation, I consider "thin" or "thick" paradigmatic interpretations. A thin translation lacks integrity and depth, a thick translation demonstrates both (Morton 1995, 21). In Figure 9.1, paradigms are introduced and distinctions among them are made.

The Charitable Paradigm

There is a broad consensus that charity is a major paradigm for com-munity service and for service learning (Chesler and Scalera 2000; Harp-er 1999; Kahne and Westheimer 1996; Morton 1995). A charitable position centers around giving of the well-off to the poor. There is a recognition of

Figure 9.1
Diverse Interpretations of Service Learning as Democratic Education

Paradigm of Service Learning	View of Service Learning	Form of Democratic Education	Relation to Multicultural Service Learning
Charity	Provide direct assistance to needy individuals. Meet immediate needs. Act as "good Samaritan" or give monetary support to social services. Enact humanism or foster altruism.	Compassion is modeled. Service is a moral imperative, not a dimension of citizenship. Social status is accepted. Some citizens are benefactors, others are second class citizens. Charity functions as an aside to government. At best, it sponsors humanistic dispositions which underpin democracy.	Promotes altruism, volunteerism, and philanthropy. Usually leaves deficit views intact, but compassion as unconditional love can support human dignity and worth. Glosses over root causes of need.
Civic Education	Teach citizenship education. Practice civic involvement. Provide equal opportunities for individuals. Work toward justice as full access to equal rights and opportunities. Aid to others supports enlightened self-interest.	Vigorous, participatory citizenship is modeled. Liberal social contract is enacted. Individual rights do not come for free. Service is a form of civic responsibility which secures individual freedoms. Service is in self and public interest. Arts of civic participation are stressed.	Extends democratic ideals to all cultural and social groups. Advances justice as equal rights and opportunities. Hold that justice is color-blind, sameness can obscure significant differences. Focus on individual agency can disregard cultural ties. Fosters social betterment through individual enlightenment.
Community-building: Communitarian View	Communicate with others, develop mutual interests, work toward common goals. Rethink own interests in relation to broader society. Challenge narrow and exclusive views.	Communal association is cultivated. Collaborative, deliberative participation is emphasized. Civic engagement means work with others to build and achieve common purposes. Communal interchange might or might not attend to cultural diversity in group make-up, central issues, and activities.	Builds community. Practices direct democracy. Supports mutualism. Seeks consensus about common good. A diverse community can sponsor a "hearing" for different views. Singular notions of common good can mask diversity and reflect dominant views.
Community-building: Social Change View	Empathize with others as equals, foster dialogue across differences, reduce we-they distinctions, expand definition of "us." Take action to improve welfare of marginalized groups.	Equality and equity are emphasized. Issues of difference and power are integral to democracy. Racism and other forms of prejudice are challenged. Multiple perspectives are valued. Social critique and activism are expected. Individual change is fostered. Change-making in schools is promoted. Builds community. Affirms cultural diversity and pluralism.	Underscores equality and equity. Develops sense of empathy. Fosters cross-group relationships. Practices shareholding. Supports multiple views of the common good. Advances social change toward greater humaneness, equality, fairness.

one's obligation to help and satisfaction of the opportunity to do so. Service learners often relish the chance to make a difference in the life of an individual. Charity is based on a moral sense of giving. It does not challenge the status quo. Instead, it helps marginalized people "deal better with" (Chesler and Scalera 2000, 19) their disadvantage or oppression. Charitable efforts usually maintain a sense of distance between provider and recipient and exoticize people who are different.

A thick view of charity is defined by Niles Harper (1999) in his discussion of urban community redevelopment. Deeply felt charity is spiritually based, as unconditional love for all humankind. Deeds of personal mercy or acts of mutual aid demonstrate this love. People act to meet a person's immediate needs or to support a blighted community—without counting the cost. A thin approach to charity is estranged from its spiritual base. Individuals give lightly of their time and energy as a hand-out to the less fortunate. If perceived as a form of benefaction, it can be little more than "noblesse oblige."

Harper (1999) describes social service as another paradigm. He describes social service as a mass version of charity, suited to busy citizens who can give their money, but not their time. Social service programs meet immediate needs, in an efficient, coordinated, accountable manner. Social service agencies typically implement policies developed at a distance from people served. Unemployment compensation, aid to dependent children, and food stamps exemplify social service. As this position echoes charitable intentions, writ large, I locate social service within the charitable paradigm. Social service is a thin form of charity when it creates dependency and dehumanizes individuals. It is a thick form of charity when it offers programs that build capacities for those in need.

What type of democratic education do preservice teachers receive from charitable service learning endeavors? Preservice teachers practice compassion; they give to others out of love or concern, but not out of civic responsibility (Barber 1998). Altruism is fostered. Service is a moral imperative, rather than an aspect of citizenship. Service functions alongside government, as a private substitute for public welfare. Momentary giving is a weak form of civic participation and can be perceived as apart from it. Social stasis is accepted; some citizens remain in second class categories, as the less fortunate, or less able. Others retain power as benefactors. This position allows a dominate/subordinate structure of power and powerlessness to stand. At best, charity sponsors humanistic dispositions which underpin democracy.

The Civic Education Paradigm

Civic education is the paramount paradigm for service learning (Battistoni 2000; Ehrlich 1997; Eyler and Giles 1999; Gabelnick 1997; Myers and

Pickeral 1997; Vadeboncoeur, Rahm, Aguilera, and LeCompte 1996; Wade 1997). Four themes resonate through literature on service learning for civic education: collaboration with community, importance of reflection, active learning, and development of empathy. The knowledge and skills service learning enhances supposedly strengthen social awareness, promote civic responsibility, and foster action to meliorate social problems.

Discussions of service learning embedded in this paradigm seem politically neutral. The four themes usually are discussed in technical, rather than in ideological terms. Notions like civic engagement and social responsibility are not problematized. Readers seem to know what is meant: service learning educates all students to be participatory citizens who serve the public good as part of their own good. Dimensions which curtail individual liberty or constrain public involvement for some students, like racism or poverty, are barely mentioned. Concern with diversity and power seem like side issues within this service learning discourse.

This position, arguably, is not apolitical. Rather, it is so ubiquitous that its political bases are difficult to detect. Varlotta (1997) submits that Rawls' liberal contract theory (1971) underpins the service learning/civic education stance. According to Rawls, if rational people imagine themselves randomly born in society, they will act to ensure the rights and opportunities of the least advantaged. Justice depends upon equal rights to basic liberties and upon equal access to scarce resources, such as education. Actions which safeguard rights and open opportunities benefit the most and the least advantaged. For example, service as a tutor helps low-income youth take advantage of their right to public education. To the extent that tutoring helps to develop educated, productive citizens, it promotes the self-interest of provider and recipient.

The liberal contract theory places personal liberty, and defense thereof, at its center (Macedo 2000). In return, a liberal democracy channels individual freedom in ways which lend it support. As examples, people should respect the rights of others and act to secure their own. People should participate in self-government and govern in ways that tolerate difference and advance shared goals. Currently, there is a great deal of apprehension that the liberal contract has been broken: preoccupation with individual rights has pushed civic participation to the background. Also, intolerance prevails. A robust liberalism, "liberalism with spine" (Macedo 2000, 5) is proposed to combat intolerance and to generate a healthy civic life. Enter service learning: it is a pedagogy with promise to educate for tolerance and civic participation.

Difference is rendered invisible in this stance. Individual liberties should not be abridged by ascribed identities, and moral principles of fairness should be color-blind. Difference also is relegated to the private sphere. Cultural difference is treated like religion, as a matter of meaning and value, best left at home. As part of public discourse, diversity is feared as a politics of identity—potentially divisive and corruptive of common, shared purpose. Diversity should be "kept in its place" (Macedo 2000, 3) and valued to the extent that it enriches healthy civic life. These arguments misunderstand that cultural/social minority groups want to share power, to help shape shared values and define healthy civic life in ways that affirm diversity and pluralism.

Varlotta (1997) poses further that, in service learning discourse, a liberal view often is entangled with a communitarian stance. Civic responsibility is defined as collective action toward the common good. Benjamin Barber (1992; 1998) is a prominent proponent of this amalgamated view. According to Barber, service learning helps student-citizens understand that their rights depend upon their responsibilities to be civically active. Additionally, service learning develops dispositions and skills for collaborative, deliberative civic participation. According to Barber, the "service learner's ultimate goal is not to serve others, but to learn to be free, which entails being responsible to others" (1992, 251).

Morton (1995) proposes project as another paradigm for service learning. Community organizations devise and implement programs that address immediate local needs. Organizational leaders "get something done" to, for example, help children achieve in school, or make youth employable. Tutoring, building character, or practicing job skills reflect this perspective. Leaders of places like community centers struggle to create greater opportunities for their clientele with scarce resources. There is little sense that social institutions might be fundamentally flawed.

The project stance reasonably fits within the civic education paradigm. Projects are the result of civic responsibility to those in need. Often, projects aim to develop more productive citizens. Projects which promote equal access to scarce resources, like English language instruction for immigrant families or after school tutoring for low-income youth, clearly invoke liberal contract theory. Service learners act to equal the playing field and, thus, secure freedom for themselves and for those they serve. When preservice teachers observe parent or board meetings, in which projects are planned and monitored, they see liberal/communitarian imperatives at work. Citizens work together to equalize opportunities for the least advantaged.

Tutoring programs usually are a thin form of civic education. Homework is often of the remedial, skills/drills variety. Support for future citizens is at a low, functional level. Programmatic interventions, which involve local citizens as planners, respond to specific local needs, and foster youth's capacities, exemplify thick civic education.

What type of democratic education do preservice teachers receive from service learning underwritten by civic education aims? Service is considered an integral aspect of citizenship, rather than a charitable aside to it. Democracy is discussed mainly in terms of equal rights and opportunities. As a result, service learning is perceived as helping citizens take advantage of opportunities and become more autonomous and productive. Service learning is considered an action in the public interest, which serves one's enlightened self-interest. Justice is perceived as an even distribution of rights and opportunities. Equality and justice are color-blind: people are all alike; all students should have an equal opportunity to learn and no child should be left behind. Social change occurs one person at a time, as some individuals strive to develop their talents and as others give their time to civic projects.

The Paradigm of Community-building

A third paradigm joins two positions that might be considered unlikely bedfellows: communitarian and critical or social justice views. Arguably, an impetus toward community building, among neighborhood residents and across cultural, social, and economic borders, provides the core for both. For communitarians, community-building focuses on development of joint aims and action toward common ends. For social change adherents, appreciation for cultural diversity, equality, and equity marks development and pursuit of common goods. I imagine these perspectives as diverse outlooks within a single paradigm. I sketch each view separately and then suggest their intersection.

Communitarian Views. Communitarians aim to cultivate public community through conjoint endeavors. The work of John Dewey roots this stance. Community-building involves the coming together of individuals to join forces, develop mutual aims, and take responsive actions. According to Dewey, deliberation is central to the development of mutual purpose. Members of collectives mull over ideas, and possibly change their positions in the process. Deliberation can be transformative: it can exercise intelligence and contest narrow views (Dewey1916/1966). Dewey claims that virtues of tolerance, open-mindedness, and imaginative sympathy foster willingness to entertain others' positions (Festenstein 1997, 88). Ideally, individuals mesh their interests with those of their larger community, and interests of separate groups harmonize.

I take a communitarian stance in my multicultural education course and in its service learning addendum. I think of my actions as building a sense of community, an "esprit d'corps." Preservice teachers work as teams, they participate in service learning as a group and complete a final project together. They attend brown bag lunches in which decisions about the course and the service learning are made. Together, we construct mutual purpose and achieve common cause.

I also cultivate a collective sense of endeavor with my community service learning partners. Service learning principles call for reciprocal, mutually beneficial relations with community representatives. In my case, partnership signifies balanced, collaborative aims and actions. I think of my efforts as kindling connections, sharing control, and facilitating a community of teachers. My partners and I plan service learning as a collective, from the syllabus to the final project. We serve as co-educators, supervising and assisting preservice teachers in the classroom and in the field.

These acts of building community are necessary but insufficient for multicultural education. Team building efforts can overlook issues of diversity and equality. Goals for commonality, for example identification of a singular, consensual common good, can obscure diverse perspectives and needs (Varlotta 1997). In order to respond to these limitations, communitarian efforts should ensure diverse representation, sponsor inclusiveness, attend to equality, and seek multiple points of view. In so doing, communitarian and social change impulses intersect and undergird multicultural education.

Social Change Views. A number of scholars propose a paradigm of social critique and change (Chesler 1995; Chesler and Scalera 2000; Harper 1999; Kahne and Westheimer 1996; Morton 1995; Rhoads 1997; Rosenberger 2000; Varlotta 1997). This stance is identified with multiple terms such as: systemic justice, social change, and critical community service. For this position, attention to power, difference, and culture is central. Consensual understanding of the common good is questioned. Instead, the "good" is thought to be fluid and constructed, particular to local communities served. It is important to search for root causes of injustice and to build a sense of collective power. Individuals shift from being clients to participants in the reconstruction of more humane, just communities. Oppressed people are thought to have assets and skills to act on their own behalf (Sleeter 2000; Woodson 1998). This position takes a long view of social betterment and discounts short term, temporary solutions. Partnerships, between local communities and outside resource groups, are promoted, but paternalistic relations are avoided.

Like their communitarian counterparts, advocates for social change call for a "spirit of true connectedness" (LeSourd 1997, 158) to foster community-building. Empathy *with* people different from oneself is a primary impulse for social change. Rhoads (1997, 90) positions an ethic of care at "center stage" for critical service learning. However, social, systemic critique often claims the center for this stance. Reasonably a spirit of true connectedness taps into an emotive force for social change that should not be disregarded.

Chesler (1995) points out three confusing aspects of service learning for social change. First, the promotion of individual learning, like attitudinal change, does not necessarily lead to social change. Second, "fitting in" to prescribed roles in community organizations usually does not prompt critique of them. Third, service learning can foster thoughts of change, but clear, realistic notions of social change-making are needed. Opportunities to participate in genuine, social advocacy or institutional change are rare for service learning. However, service learning as part of multicultural education can help prepare future teachers to be change-makers in schools. It can debunk their stereotypes, reduce their bias, and heighten their regard for the communities from whence many students come.

Working with community partners as co-teachers is pivotal to service learning for social change. Issues related to culture, race, racism, and poverty often arise during service learning. When community partners mentor in the field, participate in reflective discussions, and give feedback on reflective writings, their outlooks on these issues are shared. Their input diversifies what preservice teachers can learn. Their presence gives a sense of reality and urgency to multicultural change-making in schools.

I have found that Black churches (i.e., African-American in leadership, style, and congregation) often bring a social change perspective to life (Boyle-Baise, in press). African-American identity is affirmed and celebrated. Social equality is addressed in sermons and in casual conversations. Self-help programs support personal responsibility-taking. Many European-American preservice teachers experience this affirmative posture for the first time. For some preservice teachers of color, service to these churches is an occasion to "give something back" to people from their racial group (Boyle-Baise and Efiom 2000). In such churches, future teachers can experience a thick sense of change making.

What type of democratic education do preservice teachers receive from service learning adopted according to this stance? At the crossroads of community-building as a communitarian and a social change impulse, preservice teachers learn to cultivate a sense of connectedness, but in so doing, to carefully attend to diversity and equality. They learn to be civically engaged with people from pluralistic groups. They grapple with meanings of equity, as defined among people impacted directly by unfairness. They practice working in alliance with people different from themselves. They confront multiplicity and conflict, as inevitable aspects of cultural diversity and pluralism. Finally, preservice teachers prepare to advocate for equality and justice within their roles as public school teachers.

Democratic Teacher Education through Multicultural Service Learning

I return to the caveats set by Battistoni (2000) and consider their implications for democratic teacher education through multicultural service learning. First, I describe multicultural service learning as an alternative interpretation of the service learning/civic education agenda. Second, I revisit other paradigmatic stances and search for signs of complementarity with multicultural service learning. Third, I describe multicultural service learning in action.

Multicultural Service Learning. Multicultural service learning is short-hand for service learning as a dimension of multicultural education. Meanings for multicultural education can be confusing. It is an umbrella term that shelters a range of approaches which affirm cultural diversity, cultural pluralism, equality, and equity. My interpretation of multicultural education is grounded in a seven-part framework delineated by Sonia Nieto (2000). Nieto defines a "broadly conceptualized" multicultural education as: antiracist education, basic education, important for all students, pervasive, education for social justice, a process, and critical pedagogy (2000, 304). A broadly conceptualized multicultural education does not skirt racism or other forms of prejudice and discrimination. It is an education targeted toward humane, just, equal, excellent education for all students. It is a continual process of educational transformation guided by critical evaluation of the status quo.

A correspondent multicultural service learning should be inclusive, anti-racist, critical, and socially just. It is a service learning suited for the community-building paradigm, situated at the cross-roads of communitarian and social change impetuses. Multicultural service learning should offer chances to build community and to question inequality. In a spirit of true connectedness, it should offer occasions for the ups, or the powerful, to associate with the downs, or the disenfranchised (Sleeter 1996). The ups can listen to what the downs have to say, especially about educational equality and quality for their children. Additionally, multicultural service learning should afford opportunities for racial mixing and for learning from youth and adults. It should take time to interrogate stereotypes, debunk bias, and question assumptions. It should provide space to probe real, daily events for roots of inequality. These explorations should serve as springboards for the consideration of change-making in schools, especially as pertinent to a broadly conceptualized multicultural education.

Multicultural service learning is not just a perspective and pedagogy for preservice teachers. It is an opportunity to work with community liaisons as equal partners. The counsel of a diverse coalition of community people, as co-teachers, should be central to multicultural service learning. Local leaders can address issues of race or poverty in ways that a university instructor can not. Multicultural service learning should cultivate a community of teachers and learners; preservice teachers can learn from community partners and from each other. Community-building as interconnections across divisions of race, culture, class, neighborhood, and social position should characterize multicultural service learning.

What kind of democratic education do preservice teachers receive from multicultural service learning? I visited this question earlier, when I considered educative dimensions of a cris-cross between communitarian and social change views. Allow a bit of amplification here. Preservice teachers wrestle with core democratic values—respect for human dignity, appreciation for cultural diversity, support for equality, and regard for social equity—as prompted by engagement in real life situations. They question their own racism, biases, and assumptions, usually upset by personal interactions across race, culture, and class. They reexamine presumptions of second-class citizenship for culturally diverse and/or low-income youth and adults. They begin to contemplate broader views of community, of who we are as a people. They build bonds across cultural and social divides that can serve as foundations for future interchange with similar communities. With assistance, preservice teachers utilize real events to spur an interrogation of systemic injustice. Through multicultural service learning, they prepare to become change-makers in schools: teachers who champion excellent and fair education for all youth. This advocacy is their special opportunity for civic activism. If democracy is an associated way of living and a call for participation in civic life, then multicultural service learning lays the groundwork for associations that are pluralistic and for civic engagements that affirm difference and share power.

Links to Multicultural Service Learning. As I have contemplated and practiced multicultural service learning, I have confronted many roadblocks. A primary problem is the reality of multiple, conflictive views. Preservice teachers hold diverse perspectives, agencies advance their own missions, and community partners impart their own values and beliefs. As a position of respect for diverse viewpoints and as a teaching tool, I have found it helpful to consider the match or mismatch of different positions with multicultural service learning, to cultivate possible juxtapositions, and to point out dissonance.

Morton's (1995) reflections on his practice of service learning pointed the direction for me. Morton calls upon service learning practitioners to support their students' development of thicker (deeper) interpretations of their current paradigms and to expose students to dissonance among several orientations to service learning. In the following paragraphs, I probe perceptions which might be deepened and others which should be questioned in conjunction with multicultural service learning.

I have witnessed the power of spiritual beliefs to motivate deep examination of biases and stereotypes, particularly for White prospective teachers (Boyle-Baise and Efiom 2000). A deep sense of charity does not conflict with multicultural service learning. Caring deeply about another human being usually denies denigration and sponsors respectful assistance. Belief in unconditional love for all humans can be directed to affirm cultural difference and challenge injustice, or it can serve as a stepping stone from charity to social change views.

I have found placement in charitable, social service agencies troublesome for multicultural service learning. Programs for youth often assume a compensatory, deficit mentality. Preservice teachers tend to discuss youth in terms of labels: "that learning disabled child," or "that child from a terrible home." A compensatory posture could stimulate critical analysis (e.g., What is valued as proficient and why? What makes you think a child is from a terrible home?). However, I try to avoid such placements. They foster a second-class status at odds with democratic education.

The civic education stance can assist aims of multicultural education. Individuals are considered equal in terms of rights and opportunities. If democratic ideals, rights, and opportunities embrace a range of cultural and social groups, aims for equality and fairness are supported. Also, the development of youth capacities addresses some forms of disadvantage. Because these aims are worthwhile, I find it hard to root out their limitations. It is especially vexing to critique community projects, developed in relation to this paradigm. Programs usually are capacity driven and locally derived. For example, a program of character building seems ultimately reasonable; there is nothing wrong with respectful, responsible future citizens. Yet, from a multicultural perspective, skills of critique or social action should be included as aspects of good citizenship. These skills can assist youth in understanding and challenging inequities in their lives. Most preservice teachers find it hard to question respected aims for equal opportunities. Moreover, it is tough to criticize worthy programs as band-aids, as moments of reprieve which do little to alter adverse life conditions.

Community-building can be a powerful force for multicultural service learning. It is taxing to construct a sense of community. It requires actions which forge mutual regard, build trust, and develop common cause. Yet, especially if groups are culturally diverse, honest dialogue that crosses borders of race, ethnicity, and/or poverty can begin. Participants can "hear" where others "are coming from," perhaps for the first time. Frank conversation about realities, dreams, and concerns can spark ties that bind. We-they barriers can decline.

A social change view of community-building underscores multicultural service learning. However, regard for issues of culture, difference, and power must permeate service learning, from placements, to projects, and to partnerships. Making connections with diverse social and cultural groups is requisite. Value for multiple cultural frames of reference is essential. Community assets must be sought and demonstrated. While moments of authentic social change are rare, change-making, as a goal for one's future teaching must be stressed. In the last section, I describe two strategies that provide democratic teacher education through multicultural service learning.

Multicultural Service Learning in Action

Battistoni (2000) claims that many service initiatives are disconnected from civic learning. Service learning programs often fail to accentuate values and skills for democratic education. Battistoni's critique could benefit from a further probe: democratic education for what? Placements made, projects required, and reflections fostered ideally should complement and enact one's paradigmatic stance toward service learning.

Service-learning in-action can be distinguished according to a placement or project approach (Stanton, Giles, and Cruz, 116). For a placement approach, service learners go to a location and learn from the serendipity there. For a project approach, service learners do community development work or action research pertinent to their placement sites. Multicultural service learning is a little of both. Throughout the chapter, I mentioned placement sites but, given space limitations, I do not explore them fully. The reader is advised to read Boyle-Baise and Kilbane (2000) for a thorough consideration of placement locations. Also, this chapter draws from a book length project in which I describe field-based projects at length (Boyle-Baise, in press). Here, I sketch two major strategies which undergird my approach to multicultural service learning. I selected these techniques because of their centrality to my efforts; however, they are forms which could be altered to suit the civic education paradigm.

Task-based Contract. The tasks set for service learning count. If service learning is to connect with democratic education, then field activities must enhance democratic, classroom goals. I use a task-based contract to structure field activities for multicultural service learning. It is a tool that firmly links the classroom to the community. It sets parameters, yet allows for discretion on the part of community co-teachers and for variation among service learning sites. The task-based contract establishes a compact between a preservice teacher and his/her community instructor. Each promises to fulfill obligations to the other. Prospective teachers agree to complete five major tasks for service learning, the community instructor agrees to supervise them in return. Preservice teachers accomplish three of the four following tasks: assist as a tutor, mentor, or teacher's aide; attend a parent or board meeting; participate in a special site event; and/or interact with one family in-depth. They also conduct a limited field study and reflect on their learning via reflective essays and discussions.

Although common in structure, past contracts reveal a range of service learning activities. For example, for one category "assistance as a tutor or mentor," preservice teachers instituted a tutoring program, implemented a reading incentive program, or organized a safe alternative to Halloween. Events that fostered close acquaintance with youth and families included child care during parent meetings, participation in an overnight "lock-in," and help during a fall carnival. Field studies, or mini-inquiries, touched upon an assortment of family/community issues. Questions for mini-inquiries included: What makes a church that is culturally diverse work? Why are parents involved in Head Start? How does Boys and Girls Club impact the local community?

The tasks nudge preservice teachers beyond charitable, volunteer work toward positive and trustful relations with youth and families. For example, preservice teachers shadowed a family for a day to learn about their perspectives and concerns. Tasks showcase community people in leadership roles, as neighborhood resources. For example, preservice teachers attended Board meetings for community organizations; they observed parent involvement and self-government in action. The mini-inquiry is part of the contract. It helps preservice teachers learn how to learn about communities like those they will one day serve. Reflective invitations round out the contract. Preservice teachers write three reflective essays, in which they probe their learning about cultural diversity, racism, and poverty. They participate in three discussions, led by community co-teachers, and examine local concerns from insider views.

The contract is a blueprint for democratic education through multicultural service learning. It fosters civic engagement as service to and learning with people different from oneself. It structures opportunities to hear concerns of students and families, often marginalized or ill-served in public schools. It requires reflection upon issues of equality and equity. Further, it demonstrates a culturally diverse and pluralistic alliance among university/community partners, who uphold the contract.

Mini-Inquiry Project. The primary purpose of the mini-inquiry is to investigate questions that emerge from the field, related to ideas studied in the multicultural education course. The mini-inquiry is a bonafide research effort, with specified steps from proposal to data collection, to narrative, and to analysis. My community co-teachers and I assist preservice teachers in the development of their proposals, then approve the intended study. Community partners agree to invite in-group informants (insiders to the question studied) to participate in the study. Often, the community instructor serves as a key respondent. Preservice teachers work as site-based teams to collect data. They report their data via videotape or traditional paper, some do a mix of both. Based on their findings, preservice teachers consider changes that they, as future teachers, can sponsor in schools and communities.

As part of my advice during the proposal stage, I prod preservice teachers to "dig into" underlying causes for community concerns. However, projects of inquiry often are less critical than I envision. The mini-inquiries tend to describe, then applaud intervention programs. In service learning, the experience leads. If placed in organizations which emphasize programmatic resolutions to poverty, then meliorative approaches seem sound. As noted earlier, I find it difficult to critique worthy local programs, especially as they reflect upon community people who are my service learning partners. Several challenges remain. I need to provide opportunities for preservice teachers to practice social and institutional critique. Moreover, I need to find ways to foster critique without disrespect to community programs and partners.

Another aim of the mini-inquiry is to teach preservice teachers to conduct field research. Field study is a tool that can assist teachers in learning about students and their families. Preservice teachers practice ethnographic investigation, complete with in-group interviews, participant observations, and collection of documents (organizational pamphlets, etc.). Study of second-hand, library resources augments field research. As an analytical frame, teams compare their findings with concepts learned in class, and thus deepen their grasp of abstract ideas.

Civic participation depends upon skills of deliberation and collaboration. The mini-inquiry introduces skills of investigation, data analysis, and decision-making. It fosters teamwork. It probes problems and proposes solutions. The mini-inquiry rehearses the arts of civic participation.

One Case. Allow me to share one story drawn from my qualitative research (for more details see Boyle-Baise, in press). As part of the story, I trace and reconsider one service learning team's field experience. I ponder the extent to which their "real" corresponded to my "ideal" for multicultural service learning.

The team at Bethel African Methodist Episcopal (AME) church instituted a tutoring program as a service to their site. They created the program from scratch, with assistance from their community instructor. Parents requested tutoring for their children and specified its nature. Preservice teachers offered a range of help, from assistance with secondary level Spanish (one preservice teacher was bilingual) to reading storybooks. The project generated sustained interaction with youth and parents.

Additionally, the team assisted with plans for the implementation of a Hallelujah Party, a safe alternative to Halloween. Two team members, one an African American and the other a European American preservice teacher, invited their families to the event. A wonderful time was had by all, parents exchanged passages of scripture with the pastor, families shared stories about their college daughters, everyone joined in games, and enjoyed bountiful food. Afterward, the White preservice teacher's parents, previously dubious about her service learning placement, lauded the learning opportunity, and the future teacher declared it a significant life experience.

The team also attended an open house for the African American Culture Center, along with their community instructor. As in the church, preservice teachers interacted within a milieu shaped by African-American values and views. The team completed a mini-inquiry in which they questioned church elders about the role of religion in the education of their youth. They found the church to be a major influence in children's lives. As one example, they learned about attempts of the church to intervene in disproportionate suspensions of their Black youth.

Preservice teachers wrote three reflective essays. They received feedback from me and from their community instructor. For one team member, the essays spawned a critical dialogue with her community instructor about race, ethnicity, and racism. According to team members, the experience was a time of very hard work that generated meaningful new insights. According to the instructor, the experience validated her beliefs, legitimated her role as co-teacher, and spurred her own self-development.

This service learning engagement exemplifies community-building from a social change perspective. Community-building proceeded in multiple directions, as a kindling of connections across race, ethnic, age, and gender groups. Preservice teachers participated in grass-roots change in their establishment of a tutoring program. They gained understanding of school issues, as articulated by parents and youth of color. The community instructor was acknowledged as a co-teacher, a status which fostered respect for wisdom outside confines of the university. Preservice teachers heard multiple perspectives, about life and teaching, from their community instructor, from youth and parents, and from me.

These examples show multicultural service learning at work. Attention to cultural and social difference is at center stage for democratic teacher education. But, multicultural service learning does not emphasize identity politics or prod divisiveness. Instead, it enlarges one's sense of community and circle of citizens. It affords a hearing for what minorities and/or disenfranchised groups have to say. It prompts rethinking about education which genuinely serves a broad public of "we the people."

A Balance of Pluribus and Unum

R. Freeman Butts considers the balance between pluribus and unum a central dilemma for civic learning. "In a desirably pluralistic society, civic education must honor cultural pluribus, but it must also strengthen political unum" (1989, 44). Butts chooses civic learning over civic education to stand for a range of experiences by which one acquires values, commitments, and motivations for citizenship in a pluralist democracy. He maintains that students from all backgrounds benefit from civic learning. Schools, he says, "should be training grounds for acquiring the sense of community that will hold the political system together" (Butts 1989, 41-42).

It is important for preservice teachers to acquire a broad sense of community. They should think of their teaching as something that does not stop at the classroom door. Their educative concern should encompass students' lives outside, as well as inside, school. In order to assist students and families, preservice teachers must disrupt negative attitudes and stem misinformation about cultural diversity and poverty. They need to learn how to build bridges between schools and communities. These qualities should be considered part of a democratic teacher education.

Teaching is a form of public service. Teachers serve the public as guides and advocates for all children. Prospective teachers must learn to cast a wide net in their understanding of and commitment to diverse communities. Preservice teachers, unfortunately, tend to have limited direct contact with groups other than their own. Multicultural service learning can provide affirmative, cross-cultural engagements. Multicultural service learning can sponsor a sense of community among diverse constituents. Multicultural service learning can help future teachers feel comfortable working *with* a culturally and socially diverse public to provide equal, excellent education for all youth. Multicultural service learning can underpin aims for democratic teacher education.

References

Barber, Benjamin. *An Aristocracy of Everyone: The Politics of Education and the Future of America*. New York: Oxford University Press, 1992.

Barber, Benjamin. *A Passion for Democracy: American Essays*. Princeton, NJ: Princeton University Press, 1998.

Battistoni, Richard. "Service Learning and Civic Education." In *Education for Civic Engagement in Democracy*, Sheilah Mann and John Patrick, eds. Bloomington, IN: ERIC Clearinghouse for Social Studies/Social Science Education, 2000.

Boyle-Baise, Marilynne. In press. *A Journey Toward Shared Control: Community-based Service Learning for Multicultural Teacher Education*. Manuscript submitted for publication.

Boyle-Baise, Marilynne, and Patricia Efiom. "The Construction of Meaning: Learning from Service Learning." In *Integrating Service Learning and Multicultural Education in Colleges and Universities*, Carolyn O'Grady, ed. Mahwah, NJ: Erlbaum, 2000.

Boyle-Baise, Marilynne, and James Kilbane. "What Really Happens? A Look Inside Service-Learning for Multicultural Teacher Education." *Michigan Journal of Community Service Learning* 7 (Fall 2000): 54-64.

Butts, R. Freeman. *The Civic Mission in Educational Reform: Perspectives for the Public and the Profession*. Stanford, CA: Hoover Institution Press, 1989.

Chesler, Mark. "Service, Service-Learning, and Change-Making." *Praxis III: Voices in Dialogue*. In Joseph Galura, Jeffrey Howard, Dave Waterhouse, and Randy Ross, eds. Ann Arbor, MI: OCSL Press, 1995.

Chesler, Mark, and Carolyn Scalera. "Race and Gender Issues Related to Service-Learning Research." *Michigan Journal of Community Service Learning* (Fall 2000): 18-27.

Dewey, John. *Democracy and Education*. New York: Free Press, 1916/1966.

Ehrlich, Thomas. "Civic Learning: Democracy and Education Revisited." *Educational Record* (Summer 1997): 57-65.

Eyler, Janet, and Dwight Giles. *Where's the Learning in Service-Learning?* San Francisco: Jossey-Bass, 1999.

Festenstein, Matthew. *Pragmatism and Political Theory: From Dewey to Rorty*. Chicago: University of Chicago Press, 1997.

Gabelnick, Faith. "Educating a Committed Citizenry." *Change* 29 (January 1997): 30-35.

Harper, Niles. *Urban Churches, Vital Signs: Beyond Charity Toward Justice*. Grand Rapids, MI: William B. Eerdmans, 1999.

Kahne, Joseph, and Joel Westheimer. "In the Service of What? The Politics of Service Learning." *Phi Delta Kappan* 77 (May1996): 593-599.

LeSourd, Sandra. "Community Service in a Multicultural Nation." *Theory Into Practice* 36 (Summer 1997): 157-163.

Macedo, Stephen. *Diversity and Distrust: Civic Education in a Multicultural Democracy*. Cambridge, MA: Harvard University Press, 2000.

Morton, Keith. "The Irony of Service: Charity, Project and Social Change in Service-Learning." *Michigan Journal of Community Service Learning* (Fall 1995): 19-32.

Myers, Carol, and Terry Pickeral. "Service-Learning: An Essential Process for Preparing Teachers as Transformational Leaders in the Reform of Public Education." In *Learning with the Community: Concepts and Models for Service-Learning in Teacher Education*, Joseph Erickson and Jeffrey Anderson, eds. Washington, DC: American Association for Higher Education, 1997.

Nieto, Sonia. *Affirming Diversity: The Sociopolitical Context of Multicultural Education*, 3rd ed. New York: Longman, 2000.

Rawls, John. *A Theory of Justice*. Cambridge, MA: Harvard University Press, 1971.

Rhoads, Robert. *Community Service and Higher Learning: Explorations of the Caring Self*. Albany: State University of New York Press, 1997.

Rosenberger, Cynthia. "Beyond Empathy: Developing Critical Consciousness through Service Learning." In *Integrating Service Learning and Multicultural Education in Colleges and Universities*, Carolyn O'Grady, ed. Mahwah, NJ: Erlbaum, 2000.

Sleeter, Christine. *Multicultural Education as Social Movement*. Albany: State University of New York Press, 1996.

Sleeter, Christine. "Strengthening Multicultural Education with Community-based Service Learning." In *Integrating Service Learning and Multicultural Education in Colleges and Universities*, Carolyn O'Grady, ed. Mahwah, NJ: Erlbaum, 2000.

Stanton, Timothy, Dwight Giles, and Nadine Cruz. *Service-Learning: A Movement's Pioneers Reflect on Its Origins, Practice, and Future*. San Francisco: Jossey-Bass, 1999.

Vadeboncoeur, Jennifer, Irene Rahm, Dorothy Aguilera, and Margaret LeCompte. "Building Democratic Character through Community Experiences in Teacher Education." *Education and Urban Society* 28 (February 1996): 189-207.

Varlotta, Lori. "Confronting Consensus: Investigating the Philosophies that Have Informed Service Learning's Communities." *Educational Theory* 47 (Fall 1997): 453-476.

Wade, Rahima, ed. *Community Service-Learning: A Guide to Including Service in the Public School Curriculum*. Albany: State University of New York Press, 1997.

Woodson, Robert. *The Triumphs of Joseph: How Today's Community Healers are Reviving our Streets and Neighborhoods*. New York: Free Press, 1998.

10

Education for Citizenship in a Democracy through Teacher Education: Examples from Australia

Murray Print

The price of democracy is eternal vigilance.

We get the politicians we deserve.

The prognosis for democracy is poor, perhaps even critical in the longer term.

The ultimate determination of what students learn about democracy is vested with the teacher.

Democracy is not a perpetual motion machine. It is an idea about how to construct and sustain a just civil society and government, which depends upon constructive engagement of citizens. The quality of a democracy depends upon its citizens, who, in turn, are dependent upon their teachers for the knowledge, skills, and dispositions of citizenship in a democracy. So teachers as civic educators are the ultimate maintainers and reviewers of democracy.

Vigilance

Within most Western democracies there appears to be an overwhelming sense of malaise concerning the practice of government and democracy. A widespread despondency pervades, a sentiment which claims that politicians and political institutions have failed the populace and that the future looks worse. Research informs us that civic engagement is declining: voting has decreased, political parties are struggling for membership, everyday civility is disappearing, and many civil associations barely exist at all. Unsurprisingly, the gap between a growing rich and a growing poor is widening, crime is high, and the vitality of the local community, as a site

of democracy, is under threat of extinction. In particular the very fundamentals of our democratic way of life appear to be threatened, not from
what were traditionally seen as enemies, but from within.

Much has been made of this phenomenon and the related decline in
social capital, particularly in the United States of America, which sees itself
as the exemplar of freedom and democracy. In a piercing analysis of social
capital in American society over the past half century, Robert Putnam (2000)
has argued that, "In short, Americans have been dropping out in droves,
not merely from political life, but from organized community life more
generally." As young people in the United States demonstrate increasing
indifference towards even the minimal requirements of citizen participation, such as voting, jury duty and being informed on issues, so the future
of democracy comes under threat (Advisory Committee on Citizenship
1998; CEG 1994; Niemi and Junn 1998; Putnam 2000). Indeed Bennett (2000,
9) suggests that "If large slices of Generations X and Y are politically indif-
ferent and avoid the mass media, democracy's future dims considerably."
Given the rise of non-democratic global organizations, particularly powerful multinational companies with higher incomes than most national
budgets, the potential for the demise of democracy is exacerbated. The con-
solidation of globalism in the 21st century may well see a parallel decline
of democracy as we've come to know it. But that is another issue to be
addressed elsewhere.

Although declining confidence in established democracies by young
people and adults is well recorded, recent research suggests this is more
a lack of confidence with individuals and in representative institutions,
such as parliaments and political parties, than with the ideals of democracy itself (Norris 1999; Pharr, Putnam, and Dalton 2000; Putnam 2000).
Norris (1999) suggests that, despite this situation, commitment to democratic values and concepts is higher than ever. If this is the case, then this
phenomenon is all the more worrying for the future of democratic practice. If people support the idea of democracy, but avoid participating and
making an active commitment to sustain it, the very fabric of democracy
will slowly disintegrate from a lack of nurturing until it is replaced. Consequently modern Western democracies must redirect and intensify their
attention to the education of all young citizens about democratic principles, processes, and values.

Traditionally, fulfilling the democratic civic mission was the role of the
public school. Mass education served multiple functions, but as McDonnell (2000, 1) noted, its role in sustaining democracy was paramount: "The
original rationale for public schooling in the United States was the preparation of democratic citizens who could preserve individual freedom and
engage in responsible self-government."

The latter half of the twentieth century, however, saw excessive demands placed on public education many of which were incorporated within the school curriculum, often at the expense of democratic education. Meanwhile the first half of the century saw, in one form or another, the evolution of civics within the school curriculum as the primary vehicle for explicit democratic education. Yet by the 1960s, in countries like Australia, the strength of civic education was waning and for the past two decades purposeful civic education has been difficult to identify. In the United States, a similar phenomenon has been observed and decried. In an analysis of this decline McDonnell (2000) argued that civics has become a small and insignificant part of the school curriculum. The sidelining of democratic purposes of schooling has been, she contends, the result of four factors: the ascendancy of private over public, collective purposes of schooling, declining political and civic participation, weakened common civic identity (shared values are problematic in an increasingly diverse society), and finally values conflicts inherent within education and liberal democracy. These factors continue to exacerbate societal problems and as a consequence, she argues, American education needs to be refocused:

> The growing diversity of the population, our inability to reach consensus on key social and cultural values or even to deliberate about our differences, and the weakening of other societal institutions all suggest a stronger role for education in maintaining social comity. . . . With the exception of the family, education is the only major social institution in which all Americans participate over a sustained period and that also focuses on the values and skills necessary to maintain a civil society. (McDonnell 2000, 910)

To maintain free and democratic societies civic education should be one of the clearly identified cornerstones of modern schooling. That it is not is both a tragedy and an explanation for some of the major societal trends over the past three decades. Should civics not be reaffirmed in a central role, we will witness the demise of democracy as we know it. In its place would be a pale imitation of democratic society, wherein its democratic character is overshadowed by the power of multinationals, unelected officials, and the media, and where final decisions on most aspects of life are made by the courts.

Emergent Civics and Citizenship Education

The problems facing democracy have been identified and observed for some time though much of the reporting has been recent (Bennett, 2000; Dahl, 1998; McDonnell 2000; Patrick 1999; Putnam 2000). Similarly, for nearly a decade there has been a growing involvement in reconceptualizing and energizing efforts to engage students to become knowledgeable, active citizens. If young people become more engaged in civic life, the argument goes, the probability of sustaining democracy is that much greater. Within the established Western democracies these expressions of concern and attempts to actively engage young citizens have come through reviews, inquiries, and assessment reports. For example, the National Commission on Civic Renewal in the United States (1998) was instigated from mounting concern at the condition of civic engagement within its populace. The Commission's report warned that the United States was becoming a nation of spectators, evidenced by significant declines in both the quantity and quality of civic engagement. Education was seen as a logical vehicle for enhancing citizen participation. More boldly, Britain (Advisory Committee on Citizenship 1998) and Australia (Civics Expert Group 1994; Kemp 1997), have undertaken reviews which in turn have led to government policy on how democratic processes might be sustained through educational programs.

In the United States precise data on student understanding of democratic education have been collected which confirms the need for greater action within schools. In the NAEP Civics study in the United States, the "National Report Card" revealed that about three quarters of students achieved at a 'basic' level in civic knowledge across grades 4, 8 and 12 (Lutkus et al. 1999). Despite substantial teaching of civics in the school curriculum, only about a quarter of students were judged to perform at "proficient" (22%) or "advanced" (3%) levels (Lutkus et al. 1999). Significant differences between subgroups were found. Females outperformed males in grades 8 and 12, while White and Asian students had significantly higher scores than other groups. Non-public school students outperformed their public school counterparts. For public education the outcomes were problematic, particularly in the context of a belief that considerable curriculum input existed to sustain democratic principles, processes and dispositions through education.

Making a Difference

In light of the 1998 NAEP study findings, can civic education make a difference to student democratic understanding and participation? The most basic response appears that education generally, and civic education specifically, do make a difference and both could make a greater difference if taught better in schools. This gives us confidence to continue advocating civic education in schools, though perhaps a somewhat different civics than traditionally presented through the school curriculum.

At a fundamental level we know that students can learn to be more politically enlightened and engaged if they participate in schooling. The Citizen Participation Study showed clear positive correlations between level of education (years of schooling) and civic knowledge, civic engagement, and other attributes of democratic citizenship (Nie, Junn, and Stehlik-Barry 1996). The more years of schooling the more likely students were to be both politically enlightened and politically engaged (Nie, et al. 1996). These are comforting outcomes nurturing our belief that if schools teach democratic citizenship effectively, then students are more likely to become enlightened, participating democratic citizens. But what of civic education specifically?

The earlier 1988 NAEP study found, however, even after controlling for home and demographic factors, that the amount and recency of civic course work had a significantly positive effect on student civic knowledge (Niemi and Junn 1998). Levels of civic knowledge were also enhanced when teachers employed current affairs, a variety of topics in civics courses, and used more active pedagogies. Participating in civic education positively affected student attitudes towards and trust in government, though not as clearly. For Niemi and Junn the results were clear, particularly when juxtaposed with earlier literature that schools were failing students in their preparation for democratic citizenship.

> The most important message to come out of our study of the political knowledge of high school seniors is that the school civics curriculum does indeed enhance what and how much they know about American government and politics. Furthermore, these educational effects on civic knowledge persist even after accounting for other powerful predictors of knowledge.... [However] ... we should not overemphasize the impact of simply taking civics courses. Rather, the magnitude of this effect must be considered in the context of other factors—both inside and outside the educational setting—that also enhance student knowledge. (Niemi and Junn 1998, 147-148)

A decade after this study American students at grades 4, 8 and 12 were assessed on their civic knowledge and participation as part of the NAEP (National Assessment of Educational Progress) on-going reporting process. Clearly many students do possess considerable civic and political understanding, despite the apparently problematic results from the 1998 National Report Card in Civics (Lutkus, et al. 1999). Furthermore the NAEP assessments understate student performance in civics on two grounds. First, the level of difficulty to achieve the proficient and 'advanced' standards were set high, perhaps unnecessarily so, in terms of expectations of student performance generally. Where the "bar" is set for the proficient and advanced standards determines the percentage of students in each category. These are arbitrary decisions, though supported by expert consensus, when researchers and officials tackle the vexed balancing of normative

and criterion assessment. Levels do not have to be set at minimal competencies, but for this assessment the conceptual level for the three "standards" was too high with consequential results.

Second, national standardized measures in the United States experience
difficulties meeting the relative differences within and between state and
school-system curricula. This creates concerns over content validity of the
assessment. Is the assessment a true measure of what students have been
learning? Unlike centralized, national education systems, education in the
United States, due more to competing than complementary curricula control by 50 states and some 15,000 school districts, experiences extensive
variability. In the case of civics, the NAEP assessment drew heavily upon
the National Standards for Civics and Government (Lutkus, et al. 1999).
While these standards possess great merit as well as direction for the future,
they are neither national in application nor necessarily reflective of civics
curriculum as found in schools. In all, the NAEP results cast less of a shad-
ow than was initially the impression.

Research in Australia has provided a more optimistic view of the link
between schooling and learning about politics and democracy. Using participation in the 1996 federal elections as a base, McAllister (1998) found
generally low levels of voter and student political knowledge. However,
where civic education was taught, regardless of what form it took, the relationship between studying civics and political civic understanding was
positive. Expressing some concern, McAllister also found the effect of civic
education on political knowledge of high school students to be curvilin-
ear. His study showed Year 12 students, not surprisingly, had the most
knowledge, but Year 8 students know more than Year 10 students.

A recent review of secondary students in two Australian locations found
that civics instruction in schools was positively and significantly related
to political knowledge and knowledge-related behavior (Saha 2000). His
conclusions are supported by related Australian research although the
amount of civic knowledge acquired is highly problematic. Nevertheless,
as McAllister (1998) demonstrated, political knowledge can be taught and
more knowledgeable people are likely to be more participative democratic citizens.

Over the past few years a major international study of student civic
understanding has been conducted by the prestigious and rigorous International Association for the Evaluation of Educational Achievement (IEA)
(Torney-Purta et al. 1999; Torney-Purta et al. 2001). The IEA Civics Study
found that while students in most countries have a reasonable understanding of fundamental democratic values and institutions, they lack
depth of understanding (Torney-Purta et al. 2001). In both the United States
and Australia, students were considerably weaker in their civic knowledge

than their civic skills, the reverse of similarly performing countries like Poland, Greece, and Hong Kong. This suggests that students in different countries acquire civic content knowledge and interpretative skills differently. Furthermore, for Australia and the United States students performed relatively better because of transferred learning in skills from other learning. In terms of future directions for the study of civics in schools, the research also found that schools which model democratic practices are most effective in promoting civic knowledge and engagement. Researchers found evidence of a "new" civic culture amongst students which was characterized by less hierarchy, more individual decision making, and less traditional political allegiances, such as supporting political parties. Unfortunately the study found extensive differences between the vision of citizenship education (critical thinking, values development) for teachers and the reality of classrooms dominated by textbooks, teacher talk, and worksheets. Nevertheless, teachers recognize the importance of citizenship education for young people, and they want it pursued in schools.

Finally, the IEA study found that "In every country, the civic knowledge of 14-year-olds is a positive predictor of their expressed willingness to vote as adults." It is the most powerful predictor in many countries even when accounting for other factors (Torney-Purta et al. 2001, 46). Despite this positive outcome, the IEA report demonstrates overall that, despite the input of current educational programs, much is needed to help prepare active citizens for our future democracies. For teachers and schools to provide civic education more effectively, we need, at the very least, appropriately prepared teachers. This is one component of the equation that we have addressed in Australia. More recently we have targeted preservice teacher education specifically. But first we need to understand the context of education and civic education in Australia.

Education in Australia

In 1901 Australia was formed as a federation of six states (and subsequently two territories) with constitutional control over selected aspects of government vested in the new national government. Many important areas, however, such as education, remained in the control of the states. Each state has an autonomous educational system, with control over policy, curriculum, and assessment for primary, secondary, and tertiary education. In this way a balance was created between the states and the Commonwealth Government.

However, over the past half century two major changes have occurred to upset this constitutional balance. From the 1940s the Commonwealth (Federal) Government has gained increasing control of financial revenues until it now clearly dominates finances. Second, associated with this enhanced financial power, the Commonwealth has become increasingly interested in policy areas such as education. Over the past three decades, for example, the federal government has directly funded many "national" initiatives in schooling such as literacy, numeracy, disadvantaged students, science, Asian studies, technology, and recently, civics and citizenship education.

Nevertheless, the states guard their constitutional rights zealously, and as the Federal Government has no direct control over any Australian school, to implement policies it must seek the support and cooperation of the states. This is achieved through a combination of financial inducements and disincentives. Mostly consensus is sought, but where this cannot be achieved, particularly with inducements, then disincentives may be applied.

To achieve consensus the states and Commonwealth come together to formulate policy on a regular basis. The most significant of these groups, which have met in many forms over the years, is now called MCETYA— the Ministerial Council for Education, Training, and Youth Affairs. Recently MCETYA endorsed the *National Goals for Schooling in the Twenty-first Century*. This set of goal statements was designed to guide Australian education for the beginning of the new century. One of the important goals stated that students should: "Be active and informed citizens with an understanding and appreciation of Australia's government and civic life" (MCETYA 1999).

Policy is translated into educational guidelines, and then hopefully into practice, by systemic curriculum documents known as syllabuses and frameworks. In the more centralized states, such as New South Wales, subject syllabuses are very influential and teachers have more curricula autonomy but are still guided by systemic frameworks. Textbooks tend to be less influential in Australia than in many countries as curriculum documents provide clear guidance to teachers. Most recently these documents have incorporated educational outcomes that state what students should know and be able to do. Due to the significance of curricular documents, an innovation seeking successful implementation requires high curricular correspondence with the mandated syllabuses and frameworks. This is the situation facing the introduction of civics in Australian education in the late 1990s.

Civic Education and Discovering Democracy

The concerns facing the United States about declining social capital, disengaged youth, decreased civic participation, and reduced consensus on key social and cultural values are similar to those found in Australia. One response has been to examine what role the education system might play in addressing these issues. The developments that led to the Federal Government devising a specific policy in civic education have been addressed elsewhere (Erebus

Consulting Group 1999; Jimenez 2001; Print 1999). Suffice it to say that widespread agreement existed that Australia needed to tackle the "civics deficit" through a targeted program in primary and secondary schools.

Released in May 1997, the *Discovering Democracy* program was designed to engage students by advancing their understanding of political and legal systems and developing their capacities as informed, reflective, and active citizens (Kemp 1997). The program proposed that students should (1) gain knowledge and understanding of Australia's democratic processes, government, and judicial system and of the nation's place in the international community; (2) understand how participation and decision-making operate in contemporary Australia, and how the nation's civic life might change in the future; (3) develop personal character traits such as respecting individual worth and human dignity, empathy, respect for the law, being informed about public issues, critical mindedness, and willingness to express points of view, listen, negotiate and compromise; (4) understand how our system of government works in practice, and how it affects citizens; and (5) understand the rights and responsibilities of citizens, and the opportunities for exercising them at local, state, and federal levels (Curriculum Corporation 1998).

A key feature of the program is an explicit statement of democratic and civic values. Teachers are encouraged to employ these values in order to reflect and enhance the cohesive, pluralistic nature of Australian society. They include democratic processes and freedoms (such as speech, association, religion), civility, government accountability, tolerance and respect for others, the rule of law, social justice, and acceptance of cultural diversity. These were seen as essential to how young Australians would understand and practice their democracy. In launching the program, the Federal Minister argued: "Such values should be explicit and public within the program. Students should learn about the importance of principles such as popular sovereignty, the principle of government accountability, and the rule of law. The program will articulate values such as tolerance, respect for others, and freedom of speech, religion, and association" (Kemp 1997, 4).

To achieve these goals, a national program was devised, which consisted of multiple sets of civics and citizenship education curriculum materials delivered to all 10,000 Australian schools; extensive and on-going teacher professional development on *Discovering Democracy*; financial support for key players in civic education, such as parents, principals, academics, and subject associations; and the establishment of the Civics Education Group (CEG) to oversee all aspects of civic education associated with the Federal Government.

After some consideration the subject matter of *Discovering Democracy* was identified through four themes presented as eighteen units of study (see Figure 10-1 at the end of this chapter) over middle primary (Years 3-4), upper primary (Years 5-6/7), lower secondary (Years 7/8), and middle secondary grades (Years 9-10). In Australia primary school education includes Years K-6 for half the states and Years K-7 for the remainder. Consequently secondary education covers either Years 7 or 8-12. Four subject matter themes provide the construct for civics: (1) **Who Rules?**—How power has evolved and exercised within Australia's democratic system as well as the rights and responsibilities of citizens and the principles underlying Australian democracy; (2) **Law and Rights**—the rule of law, its origins in Australia and how laws are made including the role of constitutions, parliaments and courts; (3) the **Australian Nation**—the establishment of Australia's democratic institutions and how civic identity has changed over time in our nation; and (4) **Citizens and Public Life**—the ways people participate in Australia's civil society, particularly how people can effect change within our democracy.

Teaching Civics

With substantial consensus on subject matter and well-resourced curriculum materials available, the *Discovering Democracy* program focused its attention on support for teachers. Acknowledging that the active involvement of teachers was vital to the success of the program, the CEG allocated significant resources for a range of professional development activities. As the Federal Government, under the Australian Constitution, has no direct role to play in education, the CEG sought consensus among state education systems. State and territory professional development committees were formed to enable teachers to become familiar with the *Discovering Democracy* program. In the process these committees ensured that what was delivered was also consistent with state curriculum requirements.

Concern for the rate and nature of adoption of *Discovering Democracy* prompted two national studies of teacher use and implementation of the program (Print 2000; Print and Craven 1999). Over this period Australia also participated in the IEA Civics Study to ascertain student performance and teacher responses to civic education (Print, Kennedy, and Hughes 1999). The outcomes of these studies are reported elsewhere, but they served to stimulate greater attention to the implementation in schools of *Discovering Democracy* specifically and the teaching of civic education more generally. One outcome clearly identified was the need for an enhanced presence of civic education, through the application of *Discovering Democracy*, in teacher education programs (Erebus Consulting 1999).

The studies demonstrated that school reactions to the curriculum materials were positive, but application of the resources in classrooms, especially the eighteen units of work (see Figure10.1), was problematic. Many teachers have been critical of the program on the grounds that it is an intrusion into their subject domains (Erebus 1999; Jimenez 2001; Print 2000). As *Discovering Democracy* takes a somewhat narrow perception of civics, and emphasizes history as the principal curricular vehicle, it has not been fully adopted by the states and territories. Their curriculum documents and practice manifest a broader conception of civics and support multiple vehicles of implementation within schools. While state governments agreed to support *Discovering Democracy*, most have not changed school curricula to accommodate the programs' themes or resources. Consequently curricula in many states are not highly compatible with the federal initiative and teachers have been highly selective in what they have used from the program in their classrooms (Jimenez 2001; Print 2000).

Part of the problem arises from the classic dilemma of the overcrowded curriculum: to add more to the curriculum requires something to be removed. Yet civics is but one of many recent educational initiatives, all contending for a place in an overcrowded curriculum. This dilemma has been addressed within the states by the integration of civics within existing school subjects. In high schools these include Studies of Society, History, and Geography; while in primary schools these are forms of social studies. This decision, by state educational authorities, has not been without great pain. As curriculum developers and teachers tackle the integration process, it has become clear that both the traditional subjects and civics have suffered. Common problems include haphazard adoption, poor utilization of resources, inadequate knowledge base, and inappropriate pedagogy (Erebus 1999; Jimenez 2001; Print 2000). Given that for many teachers integrating the program is perceived as a burdensome task, many have avoided the problem by ignoring civics altogether. As there is little or no incentive or accountability to teach civics, and no specific assessment and reporting of civics, the situation remains problematic.

Teacher Education in Australia

Across the Australian states and territories, teacher education is conducted in faculties of education in much the same way as the United States. All but two of Australia's universities offer teacher education programs, and many are foundational faculties. Consequently the competition between universities is intense. Universities generally offer two forms of teacher education programs. Most common is a four-year pre-service, integrated program as preparation for primary and secondary teaching. However, many secondary teachers select an alternative mode—a post-degree qualification such as a specialist diploma, a second degree or a Master of Teaching to supplement their cognate degree.

Primary teachers are trained as generalists and as such must learn to teach the generic social studies usually known in Australia as SOSE (Studies of Society and the Environment). Given that primary teachers need to study 6-8 major subjects over their four year course in order to be generalists, their subject matter background within particular disciplines is usually not substantial. With the introduction of civics and citizenship education from the late 1990s, we found many primary teachers concerned about the adequacy of their knowledge and pedagogical preparation to teach civics (Erebus 1999; Print 2000; Print and Craven 1999).

Secondary teachers usually have a degree in arts or sciences or a subject major if they take the four year integrated model. However, majors are usually studied in specific disciplines and do not provide breadth of subject matter knowledge. Thus a history teacher may have an "Arts" degree with a major or even double major in history, but have studied little that assists directly with the teaching of civics. This was certainly the situation found in both national studies of teachers. In the first study we found that only 10% of responding teachers in the sample claimed to have undertaken courses in their preservice programs related to civics (Print and Craven 1999). Primary teachers were less likely to have taken either preservice courses or professional development courses in civic education. What was taught focused on social justice and community issues, especially related to media and the environment, with almost nothing on democracy, systems of government, civic rights and responsibilities, and political institutions. There was consensus across the national surveys and case studies in the research that, as a consequence of their training programs, teachers were not well prepared to teach civics (Erebus1999; Print and Craven 1999). In this Australia has much in common with most Western democracies.

Civics and Teacher Education

The principal reason few teachers claimed to have studied civics in their preservice education was the lack of opportunity existed to do so. Most courses offered little in the way of civic education and consequently it was mostly left to student initiative to identify appropriate learning through elective study. In turn this situation reflected the lack of status, or even overt omission, of civic education within systemic curricula or school curricula (Erebus Consulting 1999; Print and Craven 1999). This problem was quickly identified in the early stages of conceptualizing and developing *Discovering Democracy*. However, due to competing pressures on resources, only an insignificant part of the initial *Discovering Democracy* program addressed civics in teacher education. While the central role played by teachers in making the program work effectively was recognized, this was not transformed to subject matter within most preservice preparation programs. Nevertheless, beginning teachers were identified as being considerably more likely to be in the vanguard of change in schools. They were seen as possessing a fresh, enthusiastic, energetic approach to their teaching, one more likely to carry forth the torch of democratic education. But beginning teachers need more than inspiration and the availability of curriculum materials in schools in order to succeed. Like the very students they teach in schools, neophyte teachers require an opportunity to learn civics before they teach it.

Discovering Democracy included funding for three small components to support civics within teacher education programs. As a starting point to stimulate civics, all teacher education programs were provided with complete sets of the program's curriculum materials. This tended to be one set of materials for each campus on which teacher education was located. Second, *Discovering Democracy* financially supported a number of small projects for key players. One such group was the Academics Consortium, which was formed to provide support for *Discovering Democracy* through research, advice to education systems and schools, publications, university teaching, and disseminating information. The Consortium has conducted numerous minor projects to encourage schools and universities to apply the materials as a means of enhancing civic education. These include teacher professional development sessions, producing publications on civic education, developing resources such as videos on teaching civics, operating a civics website, and devising courses at undergraduate and graduate levels within universities. The Consortium has also conducted two national studies on the teaching of civic education and *Discovering Democracy* (Print 2000; Print and Craven 1999). Third, towards the end of the initial *Discovering Democracy* program, the Federal Government funded a small awareness-raising project in teacher education. Conducted in 2000 by education academics at the University of Queensland, this small project sought to stimulate interest in *Discovering Democracy* by visiting all state capital cities and demonstrating how the program was progressing through teacher professional development, as well as how it might be integrated within teacher education programs.

The formative evaluation of *Discovering Democracy* in late 1999 identified a need for a higher profile for the program within preservice preparation and recommended direct support for civics within teacher education programs (Erebus 1999). The Federal Government accepted the review's recommendations and agreed to continue support for the *Discovering Democracy* program into 2004. As part of this, it was agreed to fund a minor but national project to stimulate the enhancement of the program within teacher education.

Program development for the project was conceptualized in late 2000 and applied in 2001. This consists of a small team of teacher educators visiting 24 sites across the country for a focused day of seminars, workshops, and group problem-solving discussions. The project is designed to assist teacher educators with the adoption and implementation of civic education, particularly the use of the *Discovering Democracy* program, in their courses for teacher preparation. It is especially concerned to identify and overcome any obstacles to civics being learned by student teachers. Many issues have been identified through interaction with teacher educators participating in these projects.

Issues for Teacher Education

Over the period of renewed interest in civic education and particularly the application of the *Discovering Democracy* program since 1997, several issues have been identified as significant to the development of civics within teacher education. In this analysis informal evidence is drawn from the two projects directed specifically towards enhancing *Discovering Democracy* within teacher education programs.

Considerable variability existed in the adoption of civic education in teacher education programs, ranging from almost nothing to substantial components within SOSE areas. There was evidence of thoughtful, proactive components of civics, but these were rare. The core of supportive, active teacher educators is relatively small, if growing. More common was limited evidence of civics depending on the perceived curricular imperative from schools. In all cases these situations reflected the influence of individual SOSE teacher educators rather than programmatic responses to need.

The best approaches have concentrated on active engagement of student teachers in various ways, ranging from inquiry and simulations to real world experiences. The integrated program at Monash University in Victoria, for example, employs a combination of class-based problem solving exercises in democracy using small groups, videotaped exercises of teaching civics in schools, case studies on civic literacy, group discussions on topical issues, simulations of class parliaments, and fieldwork, such as visiting Parliament House.

We found civics was likely to be addressed only in SOSE courses, even within primary teacher education. There was negligible evidence of cross-curricular applications of civics. Secondary programs including civics taught either an integrated SOSE for lower secondary or separate academic subjects such as history and geography. Again, the amount of civic education addressed reflected the interest of individual academics.

This situation reflected the lack of a perceived need for civics and its relatively low status within teacher education and school curricula. This is a problematic situation, for although it was common to hear that "yes, civics is needed," many teacher educators added: "but others are needed more so." In all, civic education faces a dilemma within universities. While it is difficult to identify any group or individual who opposes civic education being taught, there is clearly a lack of support for programmatic implementation by high level administrators within teacher education programs and education faculties.

Resistance to the implementation of civic education was quite commonly found across campuses in three forms. A low level of resistance was argued on the grounds of competing elements within teacher education, such as technology, literacy, special education, and child protection. These are very real issues to be grappled with by teacher educators, as they are both new and mandatory for prospective teachers. Without the inclusion of this preparation, student teachers won't find jobs in teaching. These demands are exacerbated by the general demise of humanities and social sciences within teacher education over the past decade or so and the presence of rather unexciting pedagogy within SOSE teacher education.

Second, and more significant in its level of opposition to civic education, is the concerted resistance from history teacher educators. Most programs train history teachers and in some states history is the chosen vehicle for the inclusion of civic education within the school curriculum. In the more conservative universities with more traditional programs, it is difficult to establish a presence for civics.

A small number of teacher educators argued that they required more resources to teach civics, but *Discovering Democracy* has provided an abundance of materials about which, more than likely, they are unaware. More disconcerting is that the presence of few graduate students in programs reflects employment prospects and perceived status of civic education for the future.

Conclusion

The need for civic education in teacher education programs has been well demonstrated in terms of the growing need for appropriate civics within the school curriculum. Given that many consider the prognosis for democracy to be poor, perhaps even critical in the longer term, much needs to be achieved in the near future. Public education has served an important role in the past but, currently being challenged by powerful forces, it appears unable to sustain its educative role for democracy. Civic education, particularly a revised form which emphasizes active engagement of students, offers a promising prospect. However, a reflection of the current malaise is that civic education in schools is currently ignored, limited in its presence, or taught poorly. Teacher education programs largely reflect the scene in schools. This reciprocal relationship needs to be challenged if civic education is to be consolidated within schools and our democracy preserved.

Within Australian education systems considerable support exists for the implementation of new programs in civics and citizenship education. The Federal Government both leads and supports the states in this initiative. Remarkably high consensus exists as to what should be taught in schools through civic education which sees an emphasis upon democracy, government, the rule of law, civic engagement, citizen rights and responsibilities, and the value base upon which democracy is dependent. In large measure, ensuing programs and curricula are being adopted and implemented in schools, though with varied responses. After nearly four years of the federally funded *Discovering Democracy* program, about half of schools across the country are employing the materials.

However despite positive developments in policy, curricula, curriculum materials, and teacher professional development, considerable resistance exists within teacher education. Mostly this reflects the low status of civics in Australian schools, the lack of perceived need for civics within teacher education, fierce reaction by history teacher educators, and the competition for space in overcrowded curricula. Despite these limiting factors, a genuine groundswell of support for civic education in teacher education programs is forming, if slowly. The challenge ahead will be to consolidate that support within teacher education and from there to the schools. In this way, the future of our democracy will be more positive.

Figure 10.1

Discovering Democracy Unit Matrix

Theme	Middle Primary	Upper Primary
Who Rules?	Stories of the People and Rulers • Types of governance: absolute monarchy, direct and representative democracies • Citizenship and citizens' rights *Contexts: Ancient Egypt, Ancient Greece, contemporary Australia*	Parliament versus Monarch • From absolute to constitutional monarchy • Parliamentary power and the development of the Westminster system *Contexts: the Magna Carta, King Charles I, contemporary Australia*
Law and Rights	Rules and Laws • Rules and laws: definition and comparison; purposes and functions • The qualities of good rules and laws • Types of law: customary and parliamentary *Contexts: school and game rules, road law, Ancient Roman law, Aboriginal law, parliamentary law*	The Law Rules • The qualities of good judicial process: elements of a fair trial, judicial independence and equality before the law *Contexts: Historical and contemporary judicial procedure, operation of the law in early colonial and contemporary Australia, the Myall Creek massacre (case study)*
The Australian Nation	We Remember • Symbols of state and nation • National celebrations, commemorations of significant lives and events over time *Contexts: historical and contemporary Australia*	The People Make a Nation • Federation in Australia, arguments for and against • Structure and functions of federal government today *Contexts: pre-federation and contemporary Australia*
Citizens and Public Life	Joining In • The nature, purpose, structures and procedures of community groups • Project planning and evaluation *Contexts: school and community groups, Clean Up Australia Campaign, local government services*	People Power • Citizen action • Strategies for achieving change *Contexts: the Australian Freedom Rides, the Eight-hour Day movement, the campaign for equal pay and equal opportunities for women*

Theme	Lower Secondary	Middle Secondary
Who Rules?	Should the People Rule? • Types of governance: monarchy, aristocracy, tyranny, democracy • Features of Australia's system of representative democracy *Contexts: Ancient Athens and Sparta, contemporary Australia*	Parties Control Parliament • Political parties in Australia: origins, purposes, objectives, ideologies, constituencies, operations • Impact of the party system on parliament, pre-Federation to contemporary Australia *Contexts: the 1949 and 1972 Australian federal elections (case studies)* A Democracy Destroyed • Features of a democracy • Threats to a democracy • Safeguards to democracy *Contexts: Nazi Germany, contemporary Australia*
Law and Rights	Law • Origins of our law and its development • Types of law: common, statue, customary, criminal, and civil • The Australian Constitution and the role of the High Court • Elements of a fair trial *Contexts: Ancient law, Saxon law, Aboriginal customary law (case study), club and national constitutions, court operation*	A Democracy Destroyed • Use of the justice system for undemocratic purposes Human Rights • The nature and definition of human rights and responsibilities • Historic development of the concept of human rights • Protection of human rights in Australia • Human rights of Australia's Indigenous people over time *Contexts: The Declaration of Independence (USA), the Declaration of the Rights of Man and Citizen (France), the Bill of Rights (USA), UN Declaration of Human Rights, Australian Constitution, civil rights organizations, Indigenous peoples' human rights in the 20th century*

The Australian Nation	Democratic Struggles • Key elements of democracy • Objectives and strategies of struggles to establish these elements in Britain and Australia • The establishment of franchise for Australian women and Indigenous people *Contexts: Chartism in mid-19th century Britain, the Eureka rebellion, the Australian Constitution, the 1938 day of Mourning, and the 1967 referendum*	Making a Nation • Processes of federation: rebellion and peaceful change • Constitutions as a basis for national government: the balance of power between state and federal governments • The dissolution of federations • The republic debate in Australia *Contexts: The American War of Independence, federation of the colonies in Australia, the American and Australian constitutions, the American Civil War, the secession movement in Western Australia, the republic debate* What Sort of Nation? • The meaning and relevance of images of a nation • The demography of Australia: immigration policies and practices • Economic policies: work and the marketplace • Social policies: historical and contemporary debates about welfare *Contexts: images of Australia, Australia's population over time, changes in the nature of employment and working conditions, the impact of globalism on trade policies, systems of welfare and their limits*
Citizens and Public Life	Men and Women in Political Life • The nature of political activity • Parliamentary lives • Activist political lives outside parliament *Contexts: lives of Chifley, Menzies, Goldstein, Cowan, Spence, Street, Gibbs, Nicholls*	Getting Things done • Processes of influencing the views and actions of others • The evolution of a community political debate • Party political policies and practices • The role of the media • Resolution of disputes between state and federal governments *Contexts: The Franklin River Dam dispute (case study)*

References

Advisory Group on Citizenship. *Education for Citizenship and the Teaching of Democracy in Schools*. London: Qualifications and Curriculum Authority, 1998.

Bennett, Stephen. "Political Apathy and Avoidance of News Media Among Generations X and Y: America's Continuing Problem." In *Education for Civic Engagement in Democracy*, Sheilah Mann and John J. Patrick, eds. Bloomington, IN: ERIC Clearinghouse for Social Studies/Social Science Education, 2000.

Boyte, Harry, and Nancy Kari. *Building America: The Democratic Promise of Public Work*. Philadelphia: Temple University Press, 1996.

Center for Civic Education. *National Standards for Civics and Government*. Calabasas, CA: Center for Civic Education, 1994.

Civics Expert Group (CEG), S. MacIntyre, chair. *Whereas The People... Civics and Citizenship Education*. Canberra: Australian Government Printing Service, 1994.

Curriculum Corporation. *Discovering Democracy Schools Material Project*. Melbourne: Curriculum Corporation, 1998.

Dahl, Robert. *On Democracy*. New Haven, CT: Yale University Press, 1998.

Erebus Consulting Group. *Evaluation of the Discovering Democracy Program*. Canberra: Department of Education, Training and Youth Affairs, 1999.

Jimenez, S. *The Impact of Benchmarks on Teaching Civics and Citizenship Education: Case Studies of Three Secondary School History Teachers*. PhD Thesis, Sydney: University of Sydney, 2001.

Kemp, D. *Discovering Democracy: Civics and Citizenship Education*. Ministerial Statement. Canberra: Minister for Schools, Vocational Education and Training, 1997.

Lutkus, Anthony, et al. *NAEP 1998 Civics Report Card for the Nation*. Washington, DC: U.S. Department of Education, 1999.

McDonnell, Lorraine M. "Defining Democratic Purposes." In Lorraine McDonnell, P. Michael Timpane, and Roger Benjamin, eds. *Rediscovering the Democratic Purposes of Education*. Lawrence: University Press of Kansas, 2000.

Ministerial Council for Employment, Education, Training and Youth Affairs (MCETYA). *National Goals for Schooling in the Twenty-first Century*. Adelaide: MCETYA, 1999.

National Commission on Civic Renewal. *A Nation of Spectators: How Civic Disengagement Weakens America and What We Can Do About It*. College Park: Institute of Philosophy and Public Policy at the University of Maryland, 1998.

Nie, Norman, Jane Junn, and Kenneth Stehlik-Barry. *Education and Democratic Citizenship in America*. Chicago: University of Chicago Press, 1996.

Niemi, Richard, and Jane Junn. *Civic Education: What Makes Students Learn*. New Haven, CT: Yale University Press, 1998.

Norris, P. *Critical Citizens: Global Support for Democratic Government*. Oxford: Oxford University Press, 1999.

Pharr, Susan J., Robert D. Putnam, and Russell J. Dalton. "A Quarter-Century of Declining Confidence." *Journal of Democracy* 11 (April 2000): 5-25.

Patrick, John J. "Education for Constructive Engagement of Citizens in Democratic Civil Society and Government." In *Principles and Practices of Education for Democratic Citizenship*. Charles F. Bahmueller and John J. Patrick, eds. Bloomington, IN: ERIC Clearinghouse for Social Studies/Social Science Education, 1999, 41-60.

Print, Murray,. "Building Democracy for the Twenty-first Century: Rediscovering Civics and Citizenship Education in Australia." In *Principles and Practices of Education for Democratic Citizenship*. Charles F. Bahmueller and John J. Patrick, eds. Bloomington IN: ERIC Clearinghouse for Social Studies/Social Science Education, 1999.

Print, Murray. *Discovering Democracy in Practice in Australian Schools*. Report to the Department of Education, Training and Youth Affairs: Canberra, 2000.

Print, Murray, and R. Craven. *Civics and Citizenship Education Practice in Australian Schools.* Report to the Department of Education, Training and Youth Affairs: Canberra, 1999.

Putnam, Robert. *Bowling Alone: The Collapse and Revival of American Community.* New York: Simon and Schuster, 2000.

Torney-Purta, Judith, John Schwille, and Jo-Ann Amadeo, eds. *Civic Education Across Countries: Twenty-four Case Studies from the IEA Civic Education Project.* Amsterdam: International Association for the Evaluation of Educational Achievement (IEA), 1999.

Torney-Purta, Judith, Rainer Lehman, Hans Oswald, and Wolfram Schulz. *Citizenship and Education in Twenty-eight Countries: Civic Knowledge and Engagement at Age Fourteen.* Amsterdam: International Association for the Evaluation of Educational Achievement, 2001.

11

Education for Citizenship in a Democracy through Teacher Education: The Case of an American-Russian Partnership

Stephen L. Schechter and Charles S. White

This is the story of a work in progress. The work is educational reform in the Samara Oblast (Region)—one of the eighty-nine constituent units of the Russian Federation. The immediate goal of this reform initiative is the development of a certificate-granting, preservice teacher education program in civic education for university students seeking accreditation as teachers of pre-school, elementary, and secondary education. The larger goal of this initiative is to show by example that teacher education at the university level can indeed be reformed by a concerted partnership effort involving inside university players and outside players from the local inservice community and from the United States. We will henceforth refer to this effort as the University Reform Initiative (URI).

URI relies on a partnership model of program and curriculum development. It serves as a reminder that preservice educational reform—for democracy education or any other worthwhile end—involves a collaborative effort among partners who come together from different vantage points. At minimum, those vantage points will represent the three corners of many social studies education programs today—a school or department of education, the school of liberal arts, and the participating elementary or secondary schools where student teaching occurs. However, those vantage points might also represent profound intercultural differences across the racial boundaries within one country or international borders between countries.

Here, we report a complex and truly multi-cultural partnership bringing together Russian and American educators from the liberal arts, from

227

schools of education, from inservice training centers, and from elementary/secondary schools. With this variety of vantage points, a major element of partnership formation and maintenance has been an ongoing process of discovery and mutual adjustment. Wherever appropriate, we fold these discoveries into our narrative; however, the focus of this chapter is primarily on the process of building a bilateral partnership for civic education and less on the substantive lessons learned for comparative civic education.

URI is now completing its first of three years of implementation. Following completion of its preservice program, there will be several years of shake-out and dissemination. Before the first implementation year, there were five years of discovery, planning, and development. So, we are now approximately midway through a ten-year effort that we hope will result in a durable preservice civic education program that has been adopted by at least one region and is ready for adoption in other regions throughout Russia.

Hence, the nature of this chapter is historically descriptive. First, we provide the setting, and what a majestic setting it is: the Volga River Valley, embracing 17 regions of Russia and 20 percent of the population of Russia. Given the great variety of players involved in this story, the telling is easiest to begin with the cast of characters. We will then proceed to the plot in its first two acts: (1) The Plan as it unfolded from discovery to design to funding; and (2) Implementation as that has unfolded during the first of three years. The third act, Adoption, is yet too far in the future to write.

The Setting

The Volga and Don River Valleys constitute the industrial heartland of European Russia in much the same way as the extended Mississippi and Ohio River Valley function in the Northeastern United States. There are 17 regions along the Volga River Valley (see Figure 11.1). Some of these regions are oblasts; others, republics. In Soviet times, this distinction had real meaning, though a centralized party and government system tightly hemmed the actual powers of both. Today, the distinctions between oblasts and republics are insignificant, while their powers have grown to full partnership with the federal government in post-Communist Russia.

Samara is an oblast located in the Middle Volga region, with a population of nearly 3.3 million people. Samara has a strong self-perception, shared by many other Volga regions and outside investors, as a regional leader of development and reform in the areas of market reform, economic development, political stability, educational reform in general, and civic education reform in particular. It is certainly one of the most industrially developed regions in Russia with 400 large firms and 20,000 small and medium size

Figure 11.1
Greater Volga Association of Education Ministers

Name of Region	Population as of 1989
Astrakhan Oblast	998,000
Chuvashia Republic	1,336,000
Ivanovo Oblast	1,317,000
Kalmykia Oblast	322,000
Kirov Oblast	1,694,000
Kostroma Oblast	809,000
Mari Republic	750,000
Mordovia Republic	964,000
Nizhny Novgorod Oblast	3,713,000
Penza Oblast	1,502,000
Samara Oblast	3,266,000
Saratov Oblast	2,690,000
Tatarstan Republic	3,640,000
Ulyansk Oblast	1,400,000
Vladimir Oblast	1,654,000
Volgogrod Oblast	2,593,000
Yaroslavl Oblast	1,471,000
Total Population and as % of Russia's Pop.	30,119,000 (20.4%)
Education Statistics for Greater Volga	
Estimated Number of Students	8,000,000
Estimated Number of Education Employees	1,000,000
Estimated Number of Teachers	500,000
Estimated Number of Social Studies Teachers	50,000—100,000
Estimated Number of Civics Teachers	10,000—20,000
Estimated Number of K-16 Schools	30,000

firms generating a combined industrial output amounting to 4 percent of Russia's overall production.[1] Like Nizhny Novgorod, Samara has embarked upon a much-watched program of educational reform including a new civic education curriculum. Samara's current civics curriculum is based on the theme of "self-identification and self-improvement." It is a product of earlier collaboration with Yacov Sokolov, President of *Grazhdanin* (see below). However, like all successful curricula, it is a living document and a work in progress. Therefore, we expect it to grow and change as a result of the new ideas gained from this partnership. The political culture of Samara, like Nizhny Novgorod, sustains a value of "active citizenship," which has supported both general reforms and a program of educational reform in which civic education has played a critical role.

Preservice Teacher Education in Russia: Who Are the Players?

Introducing a civic education curriculum for preservice teachers across the grade levels requires an understanding of the system of teacher education as it is currently organized in Russia.[2] The following description of that system is applicable throughout Russia, although recent reform efforts have produced some small variations in the basic structure.

There are three basic routes to becoming a teacher in Russia, depending on the grade level one wishes to teach. (See Figure 11.2.) A pedagogical college is the usual path for individuals planning to teach in the primary grades. Students enter the pedagogical college after completing the nine-years of basic education required under the 1992 Law of Education. The program is typically a three-year course (sometimes four years) culminating in a "secondary-specialized education qualification," as distinct from a diploma. Pedagogical colleges are not considered part of higher education, so no diploma is awarded. However, graduates of these colleges may be admitted to the third year of study in a pedagogical university to complete work for a diploma.

Teacher preparation for the secondary grades is carried out by two diploma-granting higher-education institutions. Pedagogical universities (formerly referred to as pedagogical institutes) were established specifically to prepare teachers for the secondary grades; 90 percent of Russian secondary teachers completed studies at pedagogical universities. The remaining 10 percent took diplomas at state universities (we might refer to these as the "classical" universities to distinguish them from "pedagogical" universities; there are also very few private universities in Russia.) The universities themselves draw their faculty from university graduates.

Plans to design and implement preservice teacher education programs across the grade levels, then, require work in at least three types of institutions. And, of course, since teacher education involves not only academics but also school-based practica and experience with new curricula, the URI project must include other institutions and organizations in the partnership, bringing together a substantial number of players.

The Cast of Characters

URI is a product of three partnerships: Civitas@Russia (a partnership in civic education of organizations in the United States of America and

Figure 11.2
Russian Pre-Service Teacher Education System

Age at entry	Year		Institution		
21	16		University	Pedagogical University ("Pedagogical Institute")	
20	15		University	Pedagogical University ("Pedagogical Institute")	
19	14		University	Pedagogical University ("Pedagogical Institute")	
18	13		University	Pedagogical University ("Pedagogical Institute")	
17	12		University	Pedagogical University ("Pedagogical Institute")	Pedagogical College*
16	11		Complete (General) Secondary** including Lycée & Gymnasia		("Specialized Secondary School")
15	10		Complete (General) Secondary** including Lycée & Gymnasia		("Specialized Secondary School")
14	9		Basic Secondary***		
13	8		Basic Secondary***		
12	7		Basic Secondary***		
11	6		Basic Secondary***		
10	5		Basic Secondary***		
9	4	3	Primary****		
8	3	2	Primary****		
7	2	1	Primary****		
6	1		Primary****		

*The Pedagogical College lasts four years for those who were admitted after the 9th grade and three years for 11th grade graduates.

**Students in Complete (or General) Secondary, including Lycée and Gymnasia, can take pedagogical classes (pre-professional preparation) as part of the obligatory preliminary vocational education.

***Primary + Basic (Secondary) Education constitute the nine years of basic schooling required under the 1992 Law of Education.

****Primary (elementary) education typically lasts 3 years, grades 1 through 3. The reform of 1984 introduced an 11-year school, with the 1st grade beginning at the age of 6. The earlier start required a longer primary education, so 6-year-old first-graders attended a 4-year primary school. Currently, those children who enter school at age 6 study for four years and go to grade 5 after grade 4. Those who enter school at age 7 (the vast majority) go to grade 5 after grade 3.

Russia; the Samara Consortium for Civic Education; and the Greater Volga Association of Education Ministers—an association of ministers in seventeen regions and republics along the Volga River. American and Russian partners have worked together very closely since 1995 on Russia-wide projects and, since 1997, on projects in Samara. Our cooperation has been guided by an approach toward international education in which partners work together as colleagues to assess local needs and develop shared responses, which reflect the best possible combination of cultural contexts, best practices, and available resources.

The Civitas Network. Civitas@Russia is a member of the Civitas International Civic Education Exchange. The Civitas Exchange is composed of sites in the United States working with international sites in EEN/NIS countries. The Exchange is administered by the Center for Civic Education in California with the support of the United States Departments of Education and State (formerly USIA). The Civitas@Russia partnership includes: the American Federation of Teachers Educational Foundation (AFTEF), the Council for Citizenship Education at The Sage Colleges, the Boston University School of Education, the Greater Philadelphia School District, the *Grazhdanin* Citizen Training Center, the *Uchitelskaya Gazeta* (Teacher's Newspaper) of Russia, and the Russian Association for Civic Education (ACE) which is housed at the *Uchitelskaya Gazeta* (Teacher's Newspaper).

Civitas@Russia was established in 1995 and has become a successful force for civic education throughout Russia. Today, it has active programs in over 25 percent of Russia's 89 regions. It has concentrated primarily on in-service teacher education workshops and curriculum development. Its workshops and curriculum development initiatives have concentrated primarily on in-service teacher education, in large part because teacher training reform in Russia has moved forward more quickly through in-service teacher training institutes. One of Civitas@Russia's programs, "I am a Citizen," designed in Samara, was recently adopted for national field test by the Federal Ministry of Education.

Civitas@Russia provides the benefits of multi-year funding as well as an international support network including the opportunity to share experiences with colleagues in NIS countries. At the same time, it provides the flexibility and autonomy to work with our Russian partners in the development of Russian programs and material designed to work in Russian contexts.

On the American side, the primary URI partners in Civitas@Russia are the Council for Citizenship Education at The Sage Colleges in Troy, New York (hereinafter, the Sage Council) directed by Stephen Schechter who is also a professor of political science; and the School of Education, Boston University, represented by Charles White, who is a professor of social studies education.

The Sage Council serves as the administrative agency of URI. It was founded in 1990 by Stephen L. Schechter to undertake programs and publications, which advance the civic understandings and skills of individuals of all ages. Since its creation, the Sage Council has organized a variety of international civic education programs. The Sage Council has over ten years' experience as a higher education institution in the organization of multi-year, multi-partner relationships in civic education in the United States, Russia, and other NIS countries. Sage and Samara have collaborated on civic education projects since November of 1997.

The Samara Consortium. The Samara Consortium for Civic Education is composed of the Samara Oblast's state university, pedagogical university, pedagogical college, and teacher training center. This arrangement of higher education institutions is quite typical of other regions throughout Russia. Each institution, and the distinctions among them, is briefly described below.

Samara State University is the region's state or classical university. Like other regional classical universities it is much like the main campus of an American state university with a liberal arts school at its center surrounded by such professional schools as required. (However, the teachers' university is rarely if at all included in the classical university system.)

Samara State University was founded in 1969. Today, enrollment totals approximately 7,000 students. Approximately 20 percent of that enrollment consists of students of non-Russian origin, of which the largest groups are Tatar and Chuvash. Samara State University has a strong history department, and most history majors become teachers. There is no political science department, since in Soviet times that was the center of the party intelligentsia. Approximately 250 students will be eligible for our certificate program during the current implementation period (fifty each year).

Samara State University brings four strengths to the Consortium: (1) its history department has a strong major with an increasing recognition of the importance of teaching as a profession for its graduates; (2) its graduates are becoming a larger and larger share of teachers who are entering the teaching profession in Samara (up now to one-third and rising); (3) its faculty is highly professional and ready for a partnership like this; and (4) it has an administration which supports this initiative and is supported by Samara Education Minister Efim Kogan who will play a key role.

Samara Pedagogical University, like other regional pedagogical universities in Russia, is separated from the classical university and responsible for the preparation of future elementary and secondary school teachers. We hesitate to use the American parlance, elementary and secondary school teachers, since most Russian students attend unitary ten-year schools. Many of the schools are held to 700-900 students in the belief, shared by many

American school administrators, that this is the optimum size range. Unlike American education, it is common in Russia for students to move as a whole class from one grade to the next in the name of socialization.

Samara Pedagogical University has a social studies and history faculty, and much as in the United States, there is a distinction between content and methods faculty, even though the former are expected to be more "hands-on" than their counterparts in the classical university. By contrast, the history department in the classical university, like most in Russia, and unlike their American counterparts, has a small education methods faculty in recognition of the high numbers of Samara history majors who eventually become secondary level and university teachers.

Samara Pedagogical University was founded in 1929. Its current enrollment is 15,000 with a 30 percent non-Russian student population including Tatar, Chuvash, Mordva, Ukrainian, Byelorussian, and Jewish students. The university has thirteen departments in Samara City and seven in Tolliatti. Its social studies departments include history and economics, but, like the state university, there is no political science department. Each year, seventy to eighty students will be eligible for our program.

Samara Pedagogical University is an essential complement to the state university. In addition: (1) 90 percent of its graduates teach in Samara schools; (2) it has many students from rural areas who need a broader range of specializations when they return to teach in small, understaffed, rural schools; (3) it offers a strong pedagogical education; and (4) it has a long record of preservice education.

A third preservice institution in the partnership is *Samara Pedagogical College*, which prepares students for teaching at the kindergarten and elementary levels. Founded in 1939, the college currently enrolls 1,500 students who have completed nine years of schooling. Sixty percent of the student body comes from rural areas. Each year, sixty to eighty students will be eligible for our project. Samara's new civic education curriculum begins with kindergarten, and its teachers must be prepared to teach it. Also, most college students are from rural areas and small cities, and they need the opportunity for specialization.

Samara Center for Civic Education was created in June 1998 by the oblast education department as a direct result of work with the Sage Council through Civitas@Russia. The center has ten qualified staff members coming from other research and education institutions. Though an independent entity, the center has strong ties to the Samara Teacher Training Institute, and the center director, Vladimir Pakhomov, is vice president and director of the institute's department of history and civic education. In December 1998, the center sponsored its inaugural event, a major conference on "Civic Education: Theory, Practice, and Perspectives," hosting seventy educators, co-sponsored with the Federal Ministry of Education and the Council of Europe.

The Samara Center serves as the coordinator of the Samara Consortium for several reasons. It has (1) the institutional capacity, the staff expertise, and the political connections within the Samara education establishment; (2) the respect of the national civics network; and (3) the strong personal and professional relations with the American partners to provide the partnership with the kind of strong coordinative organization needed to achieve the goals of the program. Created with the blessing of the Greater Volga Association of Education Ministers and the support of Civitas@Russia, the center also has an openness to learn from international exchange and a strong commitment to dissemination within the Greater Volga region while retaining a well-respected position within the oblast and the oblast-based educational community.

In oblasts like Samara along the Volga River, regional inservice teacher training institutes (like the one to which the Samara Center for Civic Education is linked) are doing double duty in fields like civic education. On one hand, they are performing their official duty by providing inservice training to practicing teachers on the basis of need and as part of the recertification process required of teachers every five years. At the same time, these institutes are often functioning as the first point in the teacher training system where young and veteran teachers alike are exposed to new civics teaching methods and new content.

The *Grazhdanin* ["Citizenship"] Training Center is a nongovernmental organization founded by Yacov Sokolov in August 1991 immediately following the fall of the Communist regime. *Grazhdanin* publishes textbooks and conducts inservice training workshops for civics courses in grades five through nine. *Grazhdanin* has published textbooks covering a range of topics including an introduction to human rights, free market economics, and principles of democratic governance.

Grazhdanin is the largest publisher of middle-school civics textbooks in Russia. Its texts have received the official endorsement of the Federal Ministry of Education, and they have been adopted in sixty regions including Samara, where they form the foundation for the oblast's new civics curriculum. Its leader, Yacov Sokolov involves his best trainers and administrators in Samara and elsewhere in our international exchanges. He understands that international partnerships bring new experiences and ideas, and he also understands that new ideas bring change and the potential for improvement.

Greater Volga Association of Education Ministers. The Association brings together the education ministers representing seventeen oblasts and republics along the Volga River. The Association seeks to identify common concerns and coordinate policy responses for member regions in areas such as licensing of teachers, accreditation of educational institutions, and certification of programs. It also seeks to advance the educational interests of this extensive region that contains 20 percent of the population of the Russian Federation and 17 of the member units of that federation. Hence, the Association is a powerful ally and dissemination vehicle.

Act I: The Dream

The partners have been working toward a university reform initiative for four years. In March-April 1997, Civitas@Russia held its second Spring Institute on Civic Education in the United States for a group of Russian educators sponsored by ACE and *Grazhdanin*. Many institute participants (including Samara Center director, Vladimir Pakhomov) were from Volga regions and shared a common connection to the river. We dreamed of a civic education workshop cruising down the Volga on a river boat, which would gather teachers at ports along the way.

In June 1997, Schechter and White presented a session at the Annual Grazhdanin Conference at Gelendzhik on the Black Sea. Civitas@Russia partners hosted a special night for Volga participants to discuss possible areas of cooperation. Of 150 Russia-wide conference participants, 35 were from Volga regions; all attended this event. We all agreed there were strong reasons for cooperation both among Volga regions and between those regions and American partners. We also agreed that the best forum for further discussions of interregional and international cooperation would be at the next meeting of the Greater Volga Association of Education Ministers in September.

In September, a Civitas@Russia delegation (including Schechter and Sokolov) made a formal presentation at the fall meeting of the Greater Volga Association held at Astrahkan. We proposed that Civitas@Russia and the Greater Volga Association sponsor a working conference of civic education specialists from the Volga regions and the United States to identify possible priorities of international cooperation. The proposal was strongly supported by then-Association Chair (Minister Barmin of Nizhny Novgorod), and the motion endorsing it was approved. Association members selected Samara as the conference site, largely because it was generally accepted as the "second region" behind Nizhny and entitled to some of the international recognition that Nizhny had been the first to acquire.

The Samara conference was held in November 1997, hosted by Education Minister Kogan, who was an active participant throughout the proceedings. Specialists attended from two-thirds of the member regions. Schechter, White, and Sokolov were among the conference planners and participants; and Evgeny Belyakov worked closely with Samara and Association sponsors in organizing the conference. Conference participants identified preservice teacher education at the university level as the greatest need facing their regions and the highest priority for international cooperation. It was decided that Samara and Nizhny Novgorod regions should work with Civitas@Russia partners to build a university partnership in order to develop a model preservice program that other regions could replicate. Representatives from the Nizhny and Samara regions were invited to Boston, Massachusetts and Albany, New York to observe preservice programs and to craft a university partnership proposal.

In February 1998, project co-directors from Samara and Nizhny came to the United States for an observational tour. The tour was held in Boston, where the participants had an opportunity to visit with teacher education faculty and observe classes at Boston University's School of Education. They also had an opportunity to study various models of preservice and inservice teacher education.

Later that February, the partners met at the offices of the Sage Council in Troy, New York, where we spent a week devoted to planning for a university partnership in general. We reached agreement on partnership goals and objectives, tangible outcomes, a schedule of activities, a management plan, an evaluation procedure, a dissemination and outreach plan, and a plan for program continuation.

We applied for but did not receive a University Partnership grant, then administered by USIA, partly because of our broad focus on Samara and Nizhny Novgorod. We decided that we would narrow our focus to Samara, and that we would shift our attention to other priorities set at the November 1997 conference in case we decided to reapply for the preservice university priority in 1999.

One of those priorities was the establishment of the Samara Center for Civic Education. This center was established in June 1998 with the strong support of the oblast education minister and Civitas partners. The purpose of this center is to coordinate civic education programs in Samara and between Samara and other partners in the U.S. and the Greater Volga region. During its first eighteen months, the Samara center held an inaugural conference for 70 educators followed by two seminars totaling 51 educators. The center developed both an extra-curricular drug prevention program and an inquiry-based policy issue project that involved 1,000 students in twelve schools. They have produced a video program and teacher's guide for this issues project for use in future teachers workshops in Samara and elsewhere. One of these workshops was held outside Moscow in October 1999 for trainers of the Russian Association of Civic Education; the second, in Ulyanovsk in January of 2000 for other Volga regions. A conference for thousands of Samara students participating in the policy issues project was also held in January 2000. The Samara center has been building a track record of effective administration, meaningful results, and international cooperation with the Sage Council and other Civitas partners.

In February 1999, we applied a second time for a University Partnership grant, again unsuccessfully. Continuing to work on our general partnership and our university partnership throughout 1999, we applied a third time in February 2000, and the University Partnership grant was funded. In August of 2000, Charles White and Stephen Schechter traveled to Samara to initiate Act II of URI.

Act II: Reality

URI Goals and Objectives. As funded, URI is based on the idea that we can extend civic education as an applied field of study and as an engine of educational reform to the higher education level in Samara and from there to other regions along the Volga River by pursuing a strategy of three complementary sets of objectives: (1) to develop a certificate-based preservice program of study in civic education in Samara; (2) to organize a center for civic education which will work with its American and Russian partners to develop and sustain that program; and (3) to implement a dissemination and outreach plan in which the Samara center and its American and Russian partners extend the results of their work within Samara region and beyond to other regions along the Volga.

Objective 1 of URI is to develop a certificate-based preservice teacher education program of study in civic education for pre-school, elementary, and secondary levels at Samara State University, Samara Pedagogical University, and Samara Pedagogical College.

The program of study at those three institutions will consist of four components providing students with a total of 1,000 hours of coursework. The four components are (1) a five-semester sequence of content courses in civics; (2) a two-semester sequence of methods courses; (3) practicum experiences which parallel practice in other fields; and (4) assessment requirements similar to other fields. (One hundred hours is equivalent to a seventeen-week semester-long course that meets six hours per week.) At the pedagogical college, the requirements will be 250 hours total. To meet this objective of the project, we must carry out the following six tasks.

Objective 1.1: Develop a scope and sequence for the program of study setting forth all content, methods, and practicum courses with an outline of teaching units and projected readings for each one. This will include civics in the program of study.

Objective 1.2: Establish civics as a discipline-based area of study with a five-semester sequence of new content courses totaling 560 hours (120 hours at the college level) on subjects such as constitutional government, civil society, and the public policy process with a core textbook and reader for those courses so that future teachers have the basic knowledge needed to teach civics for a democratic society.

Objective 1.3: Design a teaching methods component that acquaints the student with traditional and nontraditional methods of instruction and assessment through a two-semester sequence of methods courses totaling 200 hours (50 hours at the college level) and an accompanying methods book designed for use in those courses.

Objective 1.4: Construct a practicum sequence of 240 hours (80 hours at the college level) of practical experiences for students that place them in classrooms where they can practice and observe civic education with experienced teachers who have received special training in supervisory techniques.

Objective 1.5: Develop a summative assessment of the student's mastery of the understandings and skills needed for successful completion of the program.

Objective 1.6: Obtain approval from the Samara Oblast Department of Education to grant certificates to students who successfully complete all program requirements. After a trial period, seek the approval of the Federal Ministry of Education to enter the program on the student's diploma.

Objective 2 of URI is to work with and support the Samara Center for Civic Education. The establishment and accomplishments of the Samara center have been described earlier. Beyond its good work in other areas of civic education to date, the center will play an especially important role in the URI project.

Objective 2.1: The regional center, working with other Russian and U.S. partners, will coordinate the development of the program of study at the primary university/college partners named above.

Objective 2.2: The regional center, working with other Russian and American partners, will coordinate the replication of the program by other higher education institutions in Samara.

Objective 2.3: The regional center, working with other Russian and American partners, will coordinate the dissemination and outreach of URI accomplishments to other regions as described below.

Objective 2.4: The regional center, working with other Russian and American partners, will coordinate the follow-up plan to sustain the work of the partners after completion of the grant.

Objective 3 of URI is to disseminate program accomplishments to sixteen other oblasts and republics which are members of the Greater Volga Association of Education Ministers. As described earlier, the Association has served as the locus in Russia for the groundwork developed thus far by the primary partners.

The Association approved the selection of Samara on the understanding that it will share what it has accomplished with other members.

Objective 3.1: The regional center will keep its education minister informed of the progress of URI, and the minister will report findings to other Association members.

Objective 3.2: The regional center, working with other Russian and American partners, will coordinate ongoing dissemination and outreach activities within Samara as well as outreach and the summative dissemination of program accomplishments to other regions during the third year of the grant.

Objective 3.3: The regional center, working with other Russian and American partners, will provide its expertise to other Association members seeking to replicate URI and its program of study.

What May URI Accomplish? The benefits of URI need to be understood in context. Samara Oblast has taken an essential first step in educational reform by designing its own civics curriculum in the schools with the technical assistance of *Grazhdanin*. But it is only a first step. URI will seek to broaden the knowledge base of those early efforts, increase the sophistication of its teachers, and foster discussion among university scholars and practitioners. In this, we envision several important benefits of URI.

Paramount among the anticipated benefits of URI is *strengthening* civic education reforms in Samara by forming lasting effective partnerships between lower and higher education levels. Second, we believe that the project will *institutionalize* civic education reform at the higher education level in Samara by developing a model program of study that can be replicated at other institutions in that region. Third, the project will *raise* the professional competencies of college and university graduates in civic education who will begin their teaching career better prepared to enrich their teaching and their contributions to their schools and their students. Fourth is the *outreach* that will occur by sharing accomplishments with other regions under the umbrella of the Greater Volga Association of Education Ministers. Finally, we think there may well be *return knowledge* and *experience* gained by The Sage Colleges in the improvement of its own course offerings in civic education, especially within a new M.A.T. program currently being developed.

Tasks to Meet the Goals

To accomplish the objectives we have laid out for ourselves, the partners have developed a plan composed of a mix of collaborative projects and exchanges. This plan rests on the belief that the exchange process is an instrument—not an end in itself. At the same time, we also realize that the exchange process can be a powerful and protean instrument for change because it can enable the participants to do things together that they could not do alone for a variety of reasons: the learning curve which comes when participants see new ways of doing things for the first time; the complementarity of skills and perspectives that international partners in education can bring to the task; and the careful ways in which insiders can rely on outsiders to help bring about change.

Year I: Start Up and Design. Program start up commenced on August 15, 2000. Shortly thereafter, the project director (S. Schechter) and associate director (C. White) went to Samara to join Samaran and other Russian colleagues in preparing a rough draft of a scope and sequence for elementary and secondary levels. This blueprint for the program serves as a guide for developing a sequence of courses, outlining their component units, and designing accompanying textbook and resource material. The first part of the Samara visit included meetings with colleagues and class observations to gain a better understanding of the current state of preservice education.

By the end of September, the partners had (1) established, organized, and begun to equip both university partners and strengthen the regional center for civic education in Samara; (2) organized a working team coordinated by the Samara center composed of representatives from each of the institutional partners; and (3) built a working American team composed of Schechter, White, and participating Sage faculty and Sage Council Associates. We also had in place a communication system to allow reliable and routine daily email and fax exchanges, which has been essential to the effective working relations among the partners. During the fall 2000 semester, Russian partners worked in consultation with American colleagues to complete a draft scope and sequence.

In January/February 2001, the American partners hosted a month-long institute involving Russian authors who had been selected to prepare textbook material for the content and methods courses. Schechter (a political scientist) worked with the content team; Charles White worked with the methods team. Both teams met together for the first half of the program at The Sage Colleges where they reviewed the scope and sequence, fleshed out the courses to be developed, observed Sage classes, and met with American liberal arts and education faculty.

White then took the methods team to Boston University for meetings with its education specialists on teaching methods and supervision. During this time, Schechter worked more intensively with the content team, joined by Sage faculty and Council Associates. On their return to Samara, Russian team members shared their institute experience with colleagues in the ongoing seminar series in their region and with other Volga regions in a conference in Kirov in April. They began preparing course syllabi for the scope and sequence and commenced preparation of a two-volume documentary collection or resource book for the content-based courses (one volume elementary; the other, secondary).

In May 2001, McDermott spent one month in Samara to follow up with colleagues who participated in the January institutes. At the time of this writing, he plans to lecture, observe classes, and work with elementary as well as secondary education faculty at both the pedagogical university and college. Meanwhile, program administrators will be organizing a series of week-long summer institutes on university faculty development.

In Summer 2001, the remainder of Year I will find Russian authors working to complete a first draft of the content book while program administrators are putting the finishing touches on the summer institutes. The first institute will be held at the Annual *Grazhdanin* Conference in Civic Education on the Black Sea. This will provide an excellent opportunity for university faculty, advanced graduate students, and administrators to interact with elementary and civics teachers and inservice trainers. Participants will review the content book and receive special training in its use. The second institute will be held back in Samara. Schechter and White will be part of the American team participating in that institute, and White will stay on for the entire fall semester in Samara.

Year II: Program Development. In the Fall 2001 semester, program faculty will pilot the core content course, begin preparation of the resource book and initiate plans for follow-on content courses, drawing on course experiences and student feedback. At the same time, program faculty will begin work on the methods courses (to be piloted the next semester) and the methods book with the assistance of C. White. During this semester, the final draft of the content book will be reviewed, revised, and prepared for publication. While in Samara, White will observe pilot courses and provide faculty with feedback, meet with authors and advise on their work, offer presentations at the ongoing seminar series, and be available for consultations with program administrators on developing student practica and other matters.

The Winter/Spring 2002 semester will begin with a month-long writers' workshop and retreat in January at Russell Sage College for six Russian authors and American partners. Content authors will spend one week with Schechter and Sage faculty on campus; methods authors will spend one week with White and McDermott at Sage. Schechter and White will then accompany both groups to the Center for Civic Education in Los Angeles County where the authors will have an opportunity to work on their book drafts in a retreat-like setting and consult as the team deems appropriate with Center staff. In May, McDermott will return to Samara to follow up with colleagues on the January exchange and to assist colleagues in developing the field practice for students. By the end of this second year, partners will have produced a video program on teaching methods at the studios of the Samara Teacher Training Institute.

Year III: Completion, Dissemination, and Outreach. The third year, August 15, 2002 to August 14, 2003, will focus on completing the work begun and disseminating its results. It has been our experience that the final year of a complex multi-year project like this needs to be dedicated to completing initiatives begun earlier and not starting new ones. The exchange component will take the form of constant electronic communication to assist in bringing this phase to completion. During this phase, the partners will also meet in Samara. In particular, we will need to complete and assess: the program sequence, the content and methods courses themselves, the student practica, all of the accompanying textbooks and related material, and the institutionalization of programs at their respective universities and of regional centers at their respective oblast teacher training institutes. We will conclude this year with a major dissemination/outreach conference for the other sixteen oblasts and republics in the Greater Volga Association.

Evaluation Program

The three sets of program objectives—developing a program of study, assisting a regional center, and undertaking dissemination and outreach—require careful formative and summative evaluation along each of these dimensions.

Curriculum Development. Each phase of curriculum development (scope and sequence, course development, practica development) will follow a pattern of draft, review, and revision prior to implementation. Each review will be guided by a set of criteria appropriate to the task (see Figure 11.3). Much of the evaluation and revision of courses and their material will be guided by (1) their applicability to civics principles and the Russian context; (2) their consistency with the scope and sequence; (3) their relationship with one another; and (4) their likelihood of successful implementation. In each phase, reviews will include three to four U.S. and Russian peers with recognized expertise in the domain being reviewed.

Exchanges in the first year are crucial for initial design and development of courses and material. The specific content of later exchanges will be adjusted on the basis of survey results and formative evaluation of courses and materials as implemented.

Implementation. During the implementation phase, formative evaluation is essential in order to identify the need for mid-course correction. In fact, one of the primary functions of the exchanges will be to evaluate and refine work underway. The results of formative evaluation will be summarized in annual project reports. Summative implementation evaluation

---

Figure 11.3: Program Evaluation
Evaluation Criteria

Scope and Sequence Review Criteria

A. Scope component
1. Does the document address fundamental content in civics for democracy that preservice teachers must know? To wit:

- principles of democracy and democratic government?
- the role of citizens in a democracy?
- intellectual skills necessary for effective and responsible citizenship?
- participatory skills necessary for effective and responsible citizenship?
- civic virtues and commitments necessary for effective and responsible citizenship?

For each of the above, provide recommended additions, deletions, or alterations, if any.

2. Does the document address an appropriate range of active pedagogical methods that support the education of young citizens? To wit:

- critical reading and thinking
- discussion and decision-making skills
- cooperative learning and participation skills
- observation and inquiry skills

Provide recommended additions, deletions, or alterations, if any.

3. Does the document describe an appropriate range of practica requirements and tasks that support effective teaching for democracy, fostering skillful use of active pedagogical methods and thoughtful transmission of civic knowledge, skills, and attitudes to children? If not, what should be added or altered?

B. Sequence Component

1. Does the proposed sequence of civics content course represent a logical progression of knowledge development for preservice teachers?

2. Does the proposed sequence of pedagogical methods course(s) represent a logical progression of knowledge and skill development for preservice teachers?

3. Do the content and methods courses provide an adequate foundation for each of the required practica experiences?

will inform program revisions prior to dissemination within and beyond the regions and will be included in the final project report. Evaluation will focus on the quality of courses as well as the implementation performance of the regional centers.

For course reviews, we will rely on fairly typical data: student assessments; student and faculty surveys and interviews; observation and assessment instruments of student practica; mid-practica meetings between students, university supervisors, and cooperating teachers; and end-of-practica questionnaires. To assess in-country coordination and implementation work, review of the regional center will require development of a system of document collection (including course materials, evaluation summaries, correspondence, etc.) as a basis for formative evaluation in order to identify key decision points and to track outcomes as the preservice program of study is implemented and as the project is disseminated to the regions.

Assisting in program monitoring and evaluation is an advisory board for the regional center. Board members will meet to review the progress of the program at times when American partners are scheduled to be in Russia. Non-Samara board members will include: E. Belyakov, S. Schechter, Y. Sokolov, and C. White. Annual reports will summarize formative evaluation results, corrective measures implemented, and outcomes from those measures. This will sharpen the focus of the following year's work plan. Reports will be distributed to all project partners including the oblast education minister.

Dissemination and Outreach. At the beginning of each year, the Samara center will identify opportunities to disseminate information about project accomplishments and will invite participation by other higher education institutions in replication efforts. These opportunities will include local, regional, and national teacher conferences, meetings of the Greater Volga Association of Education Ministers, regional and national news and professional publications, and other appropriate venues. The annual review and reporting process will collect and assess supporting documentation including descriptions of events (number of participants, target audience), conference proceedings, meeting agendas, and outlines of presentations. The dissemination conference in May 2003 will provide an excellent outside assessment of the value of project results for other regions.

Program Continuation and Follow-on Activities

Our planning for program continuation has included three essential ingredients: (1) the buy-in of regional gatekeepers (e.g., the Greater Volga Association of Education Ministers and the Samara Ministry of Education) and the higher education community without losing the support of civics teachers and their schools; (2) an institutional capacity and vested interest in ongoing and effective administration; and (3) a clear agreement among the partners as to program goals and outcomes.

The next steps to secure program continuation flow from the political-administration foundation. Long-term institutionalization of preservice teacher education in civics will require formal recognition of our program of study from the oblast education minister, enabling this program to grant certificates to its graduates. This step is designed to ensure that the program becomes an ongoing part of the curriculum and faculty teaching load of participating colleges and universities. Since a significant element of any program is its texts and materials, we must obtain agreement with the oblast department of education to recognize program publications and support their distribution through oblast teacher training institutions. We will also work with all oblast partners to secure continued support for the regional center of civic education so it can continue to monitor and update the programs in its region and disseminate results to other regions. Finally, we need to obtain the oblast minister's support in requesting diploma status from the Federal Ministry of Education. This will provide the foundation for implementation beyond the oblast.

We are under no illusions about the challenges this project faces. As university academics, the authors know first-hand the difficulty of instituting change in American colleges and universities, even under the best of circumstances. In this respect at least, we and our Russian partners share a common experience. But preservice teacher education is the next logical step, given the development of civic education in Samara to date. It is the next significant milestone to be sought and an essential milestone to reach if durable teacher education for democracy is to be achieved.[2]

Notes

1. IEWS Russian Regional Report, "Samara Oblast: Political and Economic Overview" (New York City, September 1997). Also see: "Samara Emerges as an Important Regional Hub," in *Russia: A Review* (January 27, 1997): 28-29; "Samara—Port in the Middle of the Volga," in *Russian Commerce News* (1997): 21-22; and "Samara Region," excerpts from G. V. Alexushin, Samara Goverenes (Samara House of Press, 1996), distributed in 1997 by Samara-Internet.

2. This work draws upon two main sources, Stephen L. Webber, *School, Reform and Society in the New Russia* (New York: St. Martin's Press, 2000); Brian Holmes, Gerald H. Read, Natalya Voskresenskaya, *Russian Education: Tradition and Transition*, (New York: Garland Publishing, 1995). The authors are indebted also to Anatoli Rapaport and Natalya Voskresenskaya for their assistance in clarifying some of the finer points. They are not responsible for any lingering inaccuracies.

Conclusion: Recommendations and Reactions

John J. Patrick and Robert S. Leming

Participants in the meeting of May 18-22, 2001 in Indianapolis—"Education in Democracy for Social Studies Teachers: An Institute for Teacher Educators"—met daily in four focus groups to discuss the papers that became the chapters of this book. In this conclusion to the book, we summarize recommendations of the focus groups about improvement of civic education in programs of teacher education for prospective social studies teachers.

The four focus groups generally endorsed the need to renew and revitalize education for democracy in the preparation of social studies teachers. The rationale for civic learning in teacher education, expressed by R. Freeman Butts in Chapter 1, was endorsed by the focus groups.

Core content, anchored in the academic disciplines of history and the social sciences, was recognized as an essential part of the civic foundations of teacher education. One of the focus groups, for example, recommended that social studies teacher education programs should cultivate or nurture among prospective teachers the following characteristics and capacities:

1) The disposition of a scholar. Preservice teachers should be committed to scholarship, to inquiry after knowledge or truth, tempered by skepticism and a healthy respect for democratic principles. They should understand that good teachers are constantly learning themselves and that professional growth depends upon their ability to find and critically examine new ideas and perspectives in content as well as pedagogy.

2) A depth of knowledge. Preservice teachers must know their content well. By content knowledge, we mean more than the ability to recite facts, dates, concepts. Rather, we mean an understanding of what has been called the structure of the disciplines, an understanding of the major issues, questions, or conceptual themes that organize an academic discipline as well as the methods of inquiry a scholar in the discipline uses to generate new knowledge.

Another focus group emphatically expressed the importance of teaching prospective teachers ways of thinking or processes of inquiry associated with core subjects of the social studies, such as history, geography, economics, and political science/government. The group concluded, "We believe that teachers must understand 'habits of the mind' such as identifying public issues, analyzing the issues, evaluating alternative responses, and exchanging ideas with others through democratic deliberation." This focus group recommended that university-based courses in methods of teaching and in core subjects of history and the social sciences should emphasize cognitive processes. Thus, the prospective teachers might develop competence to teach these "habits of the mind" to students in elementary and secondary schools.

There was support for the conjoining of core content and processes in teaching prospective social studies teachers how to teach. Teaching prospective teachers the skills of conducting deliberative discussions was recommended. These deliberative discussions would pertain to public issues anchored in primary documents and core content in the academic disciplines of history and the social sciences. These uses of deliberative discussions in civic education were discussed in Chapter 5, 6, and 7 of this book and were addressed by focus group participants. One focus group recommended that prospective teachers should have, "Experience in the translation of content." The "deliberative discussion" was emphasized in another focus group report:

> Deliberative discussion should serve as the primary means by which students translate historical and social science knowledge into civic understanding. Deliberative discussions share characteristics that are consistent with democratic theory and practice: students are engaged in the analysis of powerful texts that examine content ideas and issues of American society and government; students examine their ideas and the ideas of their colleagues; and students engage in the very core of the democratic process, the understanding of texts and public issues throughout the co-investigation of those texts, their contexts, and issues with other students.

The four focus groups stressed that the task of educating prospective social studies teachers requires close collaboration between schools or colleges of education and historians and social scientists in colleges of arts and sciences. They recommended that core content from academic disciplines should be conjoined with exemplary methods of teaching in pedagogy courses and in history and social science courses.

Participants in the focus groups discussed different conceptions of democracy and education for democratic citizenship. Some participants favored a liberal democracy model. Others advocated a multicultural democracy model. One focus group concluded, "We are more likely to advance the goals of multicultural education if we embrace a view of multiculturalism that is supportive of core democratic values."

Participants in the focus groups generally agreed about the need to emphasize democracy and education for democratic citizenship in the curricula of elementary and secondary schools and in programs of teacher education. And they tended to agree on the value of ongoing debates about alternative conceptions of democracy and civic education. Further, participants agreed that these debates about different models of democracy and various conceptions of education for democracy should be part of teacher education programs. They recommended that prospective teachers should be engaged in debates about the meaning of democracy and how to practice it.

In conclusion, focus group participants strongly endorsed the five-day meeting in May 2001, which yielded the contents of this book. They recommended that a second meeting on "Education in Democracy for Social Studies Teachers: An Institute for Teacher Educators" should be convened in 2002. Steps have been taken to carry out this concluding recommendation. Thus, the discussions on civic education in teacher education, started in May 2001, will continue.

Appendix A

Reactions to a Keynote Address
by R. Freeman Butts

Professor R. Freeman Butts was the keynote speaker at the opening session of "Education in Democracy for Social Studies Teachers: An Institute for Teacher Educators." His presentation—"Why Should Civic Learning Be at the Core of Social Studies Teacher Education in the United States?—is included in this volume as Chapter 1.

Two Indiana University Professors of Education, B. Edward McClellan and Donald Warren, were the designated reactors to Professor Butts' keynote address. Their reaction papers are presented in Appendix A.

A-1: Civic Education: A Time for Challenge and Hope
  B. Edward McClellan
A-2: Civic Education in Untroubled Times
  Donald Warren

Appendix A-1

Civic Education: A Time of Challenge and Hope

B. Edward McClellan

It is a great honor for me to appear on this program with R. Freeman Butts and with my colleague Don Warren. When I first learned of the work of Professor Butts, I was a history graduate student with an emerging interest in the history of education. I knew Professor Butts then as a historian with an unusual ability to understand the connections between American education and the political and cultural contexts in which it operated. But in the 1980s, I came to know his work in a different way. He had become a powerful voice for civic education, and I had developed an interest in the history of moral education. Neither was a particularly mainstream preoccupation at the time.

In fact, the context was not at all a friendly one. Americans had become rather suddenly conscious of a vigorous global competition, and they had responded by proposing dramatic reforms in our schools. Some of the reforms were overdue. Schools of the seventies had become so eager to placate alienated students that they had abandoned many of their most important academic responsibilities. Yet, the proposed reforms had problems of their own. Although they contained a heartening endorsement of traditional academic subjects, they had a hard-edged economic emphasis to them. As schools made preparation for global competition their overriding concern, civic education lost its once-honored position in the curriculum of both the public school and schools of education. Educators gave less and less attention to what it meant to be good men and women, and what it took to create a good society. It was at this point that Professor Butts raised a stern warning in what was then a frighteningly lonely voice.

In many ways, the alarm still resonates. The challenges have not just continued, they have deepened, and I think we need to take a sobering moment to consider them.

We had only a vague understanding of the meaning of an emerging global economy in the 1980s, and even now we are just beginning to explore its implications. We know this much, however, that its sheer immensity and complexity challenge traditional political institutions and civic commitments. The problem is not simply that multinational corporations render national institutions less able to control events; it is that people have come to feel helpless in the face of what appear to be inexorable forces. The effects have operated with special impunity on those segments of our society who benefit least from globalization. It is after all their jobs that can at one stroke be moved to a far corner of the world. The global economy has created a vast class who have lost faith in political institutions to give them a measure of control in their lives.

In a different way, technological change and global economics have affected the civic commitments of more privileged classes as well. As Robert B. Reich has pointed out in his recent book, *The Future of Success*, middle-class workers find themselves on career tracks that offer increasingly less predictable earnings and less professional stability. Unable to imagine a secure future and fearful that technological change will render their skills obsolete, they simply throw themselves into work, focusing with incredible intensity on making money and having little time for civic activities of any sort.[1] The degree to which this spirit has penetrated the culture of our young is graphically illustrated in a recent article in *Atlantic Monthly* by David Brooks. Describing conversations with students at Princeton University, Brooks said that he felt as if he were attending a meeting of the Future Workaholics of America. And even though this was at the height of the presidential campaign, he saw not a single Bush or Gore poster on the entire Princeton campus.[2]

But the global economy and the new attitudes that go with it are only one part of our challenge. We face as well discouragement from within. At about the time that Professor Butts was calling for a new civics, Robert Bellah and his colleagues at Berkeley were raising similar alarms about "the habits of our hearts." In a word, Bellah found what he termed a cancerous individualism in America and a growing tendency to retreat from public responsibilities into private pleasures. Individualism had always been sacred to Americans, but it had traditionally existed hand-in-hand with a rich civic life. Now it threatened to overwhelm public life and weaken forever the hope for freedom, democracy, and community.[3] More recently, Robert Putnam's *Bowling Alone* has added impressive documentation to Bellah's fears, finding a frightening decline in what he calls social capital, represented most notably in the weakening of voluntary organizations, which astute political theorists since Alexis de Tocqueville have seen as essential to the maintenance of a sense of community. Putnam has a variety of explanations for this retreat from public responsibility—including the nature of modern work, residential patterns, our tendencies toward mobility, and the effects of modern media—but the primary point for us is that powerful forces, many within our ability to control, have raised new challenges for those concerned to create a vibrant democracy and a good society.[4]

What these critics show is the extraordinary challenges of creating good citizenship in our time. The low rate of political participation is simply the top of a very large iceberg. Surely this creates enormous difficulties for the brave souls who enter our classrooms to teach history, government, political science, and other subjects that constitute a civics curriculum. It creates equally difficult problems for those of us who labor in teacher education. The young, even more sensitively then their elders, understand the pulls of the private life. They understand the nature of modern work and the pleasures of modern consumption, and they are assaulted daily by a national media that defines human triumph as the production of a single winner, not as the labor of a community working together for the good of all.

I think we must continue to have a tough-minded appreciation of the obstacles we face as we try to renew the place of the civics curriculum in the school and in our teacher education programs. And, yet I think there is a glimmer of hope in our history. When American civic educators in the first forty to fifty years of the twentieth century faced a social change as vast as the one we now face, they made the transformation itself the central subject of their civics. In turn they found a way to make the civics curriculum central to the nation's course of study and to the preparation of teachers. Indeed, in some respects the 1930s and 1940s were golden years for the belief that every teacher should have a thorough civic education. Professor Butts himself was no small player in the development of foundations programs that helped to create a generation of teachers who understood their society and who felt strong civic commitments.

Subsequent generations of critics have found some things not to like about civic education of that era, but there is much to appreciate in its legacy. A few years ago, I did an extensive survey of the textbooks of these years, both school texts and pedagogical texts. I was astonished to find an extraordinarily frank and full discussion of the transformation of the American economy and society, even including exploration of radical possibilities for reform. Clearly, civic educators had been compelled by the startling changes of their time to abandon the formalism of nineteenth-century courses in history and government and to create a fresh and probing way of looking at the institutions of civic life and at the sentiments that sustained a good society. This was far from a simple-minded civic boosterism, and it bore little resemblance to what Diane Ravitch has derisively called "tot sociology." There were problems to be sure with this progressive civics, yet there was in it a hope that vast social transformations, even ones that create large, impersonal institutions, can also stimulate new forms of civic commitment and, what is most pertinent to us, the will to study them.

Although the challenges are enormous, we do not face an entirely unreceptive public. Americans have expressed in many ways, including initiatives and referendums, a growing desire to influence public life. Figures ranging from Amy Gutmann to William Bennett have given a growing public voice to many concerns raised so powerfully in the 1980s by Professor Butts. And, if the students at Princeton do not yet involve themselves in presidential elections, they do at least find time for some forms of community service and express yearnings that might still be transformed into civic commitment. My hope is that as civic educators we can build on these impulses by taking a fresh look at the hard world around us, by using our disciplines to understand the vast transformations of our time, and by beginning the quest for a civics appropriate to a world far different from anything we have even known before. If we do that, we will have answered at last the bold summons of R. Freeman Butts.

Notes

1. Robert B. Reich, *The Future of Success* (New York: Alfred A. Knopf, 2001).

2. David Brooks, "The Organization Kid," *Atlantic Monthly* 287 (April 2001): 41-54.

3. Robert N. Bellah, Richard Madsen, William M. Sullivan, Ann Swidler, and Steven M. Tipton, *Habits of the Heart: Individualism and Commitment in American Life* (Berkeley: University of California Press, 1985).

4. Robert D. Putnam, *Bowling Alone: The Collapse and Revival of American Community* (New York: Simon & Schuster, 2000.)

About the Author: B. Edward McClellan is a professor of the history of education at Indiana University's School of Education.

Appendix A-2

Civic Education in Untroubled Times

Donald Warren

The question posed for Professor Butts was: Why should civic learning be at the core of social studies teacher education in the United States? The answer that I shall try to explain and justify is that civic learning is (not ought to be) at the core of social studies teacher education, as it is at the center of all education. Uncertain is whether it is the civic learning wanted and needed. Other questions follow immediately: Wanted by whom? Needed by whom? For what purposes in the short and long term? And how will success be measured? In his unique way Professor Butts has raised such queries for our consideration.

As he has indicated, he and I have discussed this institute's topic and related issues many times. Given these exchanges, I could easily perform my assignment as respondent to his lecture by simply saying "amen" and sitting down. But that would be an inadequate response. For one reason, with all of our private discussion of civic education, we have never explored the topic together in public. So far as I can recall, this will be the first time, and the opportunity should be used. Second, the issues he has examined are too important to be treated with even the appearance of dismissiveness. They and he warrant analytical responses. Third, there is this disagreement he and I have, more of a nuance, actually, but a large one, that might be aired profitably. On other occasions, with the grace, insight, and learnedness of a superb historian, he has placed American public education, including its original institutional form, the common school, at the intellectual and moral heart of civic and cultural development in the United States. To which I respond, to put it succinctly and provocatively, that American public education is such a good idea we ought to try it sometime.

My point is not the usual one made with regard to ideals, namely that they always exceed our reach and thus pull us into renewed effort. This is an important emphasis to make, but my aim, deduced from history, is to encourage inquiry and action based, first, on the reasons the idea of public education has remained fragile and contentious over the centuries; second, on the cycles of reforms that have come to little or naught; and third, on the implications of the repeated, and hence now predictable, failures to actualize, nuances and all, the idea of American public education in law, policies, and educational practice and achievement. To keep the discussion focused, I will survey this landscape only briefly.

The dominant mode of educational reform in the United States has been enforcement, despite the absence of the kind of national ministry of education found in most other countries. Cascading from the top down, although typically without much evidence to support the proposals, recipes for improvement have come from state and federal law makers, policy analysts, career reformers, and others operating in or seeking the public eye. The entrepreneurial spirit of business organizations and consultants has spiced the cyclical dynamic. Rona Wilensky, an economist and school principal in Colorado, pronounces the approach "wrong, wrong, wrong."[1] The alliteration is hers not mine, and she draws it from an analysis of the school reform and economic results that have accrued in the years following publication of the much cited 1983 report, "A Nation at Risk." If she, a Yale Ph.D., or any of us here, thinks that effort to impose national measurable standards began a new strategy, she and we are mistaken. If we believe the push toward uniform testing and accountability structures, inspired by comparisons with student achievement scores in other countries and propelled by measurement experts, has such recent origins, we are misinformed. Plans to enact measured student learning and teacher effectiveness through externally imposed and uniform requirements are as old as the nation, as Professor Butts has observed. The under-explored issues are not whether the United States should have a national system of education, founded through constitutional amendment and law, as Thomas Jefferson judged would be necessary, or by informal policy and practice, or even whether we the people want to advance student and teacher learning, including preparation for citizenship. These topics have been debated off and on over the years with few signs of durable consensus emerging. The deeper and relatively unaddressed questions, as Richard Rothstein proposed in the *New York Times*, have to do with the kinds of learning we want to advance, the kinds of behaviors and values we expect as consequences, and the kinds of policies and pedagogies that can promote and sustain the desired results.[2] Note: Wilensky and Rothstein both comment wryly on the educational reform directions displayed currently in the United States and Japan, which has a centralized educational system. Each country seems inclined to fashion a school governance structure like the other.

If we are failing to promote the civic learning we want and need, the exploration of such anomalies and paradoxes may help us understand why and devise other strategies than the ones that have dominated our history. It may be the case that the United States educates its citizens, including teachers, in generally acceptable ways and to generally acceptable levels. In short, there may be no existential concern about civic learning and thus no troubling questions to drive inquiry, curriculum planning, and reform.

As for the nuance mentioned earlier, hints of it have crept in, so let me address it specifically. In Butts' analysis, civic education occurs on two related but distinct fronts. Let's examine them. First, there is the public school itself. Its very existence teaches citizenship in a democratic society, and this function attaches to all its components. The entire curriculum, ranging across courses, clubs, and activities; pedagogy in these formal and informal settings; assessments of students and teachers; school architecture and decor; school-based counseling; enacted policy and informal practice—all the institutional elements, cultures, habits, and auras deliver messages about what citizenship means practically in American society, about children's realistic hopes and opportunities for belonging to it, and about their prospects for confident aspirations. Covering assortments of agencies and influences, not schools alone, an enormous and still growing research literature in history and the social sciences tracks the footprints of these formative civics lessons.[3]

Listen to Rona Wilensky's connection of the school and social policy environment to civic learning: "Like other reformers, I want schools where every kid is valued, where high expectations are set for everyone, where graduates have the skills to shape their lives according to their values and talents, and where preparation for citizenship is a robust undertaking." She continues: "As Thomas Jefferson taught us, schools are rightfully the training ground for democracy. The issues of citizenship, of the relationships among racial and ethnic groups, of the desire for equality among men and women—these are just a few of the proper subjects that our schools are turning away from in the race to catch the Japanese geometry scores."

"Schools," she concludes, "are our collective effort in human development. What sort of people do we want to be? How shall we live? What is the nature of responsibility, of caring, of initiative, of integrity? Schools are about all those characteristics that make individuals good and bad. Schools can and should deal overtly with all the values that once were grouped under the quaint name 'virtue.'"[4] The questions echo those being posed in the research literature.

In addition to the lessons in citizenship taught by and learned within the education policy environment, there is specifically relevant academic content offered in civics, history, and philosophy courses. Here we find the classical, founding literature of the nation and the political structures that have evolved from it. The temptation is to emphasize this portion of civic learning, to require courses, set national curriculum standards for teaching it, and test students to see if they have learned it at least temporarily. My nuance comes down to a question: assuming that all master the academic content, will students, including prospective teachers, thereby come willingly to vote, serve on juries, stand for elective office, treasure each other equally as citizens, insist on their fair wages, and defend their rights, responsibilities, and liberties? This is not an either/or choice, but we will do well to remember that it is the realities of the latter practices, more than any acquired academic content, from which the lived future of our democratic republic emerges.

To ensure that schools are indeed the cradles of democracy that Horace Mann and Indiana's own Nebraska Cropsey, among others, envisioned, we necessarily attend to the structures, programs, policies, and cultures that shape and permeate the schools themselves and prepare teachers equipped to notice and care about the lessons in citizenship these nuances teach with such great power. Giving this depth of attention is an endless task—and often a lonely and unpopular me. Certainly, no paragon from the past, Thomas Jefferson included, can do it for us, although there is help and inspiration from such sources. Recall that his educational plan for Virginia was never enacted, and if it had been, the beneficiaries would not have been all of Virginia's children, not even all the white ones. And if Jefferson had been required to translate his broad and edifying educational and political ideals into measurable standards for student achievement, what timely compromises would he have felt predisposed to make?

Fortunately, we do not have an answer to that question. He left for later generations to decide about public education for girls, Roman Catholic children, non-English-speaking immigrants, and the children of former slaves and of poverty. We here constitute one of those subsequent generations and the decisions have come down to us. Our troubled and troubling history advises us to practice what we preach. Much is at stake, and it cannot be safeguarded in civics and other social studies courses alone, elegant and poignant through they may be. They are only the tip of the proverbial iceberg. Remember too Jefferson's warning about slavery as the nation's firebell in the night. Voiced in the early nineteenth century, his was an urgent appeal to advance democratic citizenship democratically, a goal still pertinent to the Republic's well being. But that was then. What alarm sounds in our night?

Notes

1. Rona Wilensky, "Wrong, Wrong, Wrong." *Education Week*, May 9, 2001, 48, 32.

2. Richard Rothstein, "Weighing Students' Skills and Attitudes," *New York Times*, May 16, 2001, A25.

3. See, e.g., Nancy Beadie, "The Limits of Standardization and the Importance of Constituencies: Historical Tensions in the Relationship Between State Authority and Local Control," in Neil D. Theobald and Betty Malen (eds.), *Balancing Local Control and State Responsibility for K-12 Education*, 2000 Yearbook of the American Education Finance Association, Larchmont, NY: Eye on Education, Inc., 2000, 47-91; Barry Bull, "Political Philosophy and the Balance Between Central and Local Control of Schools," in Neil D. Theobald and Betty Malen (eds.), *Balancing Local Control and State Responsibility for K-12 Education*, 2000 Yearbook of the American Education Finance Association, Larchmont, NY: Eye on Education, Inc., 2000, 21-46; Caroline Gipps, "Social-cultural Aspects of Assessment," *Review of Research in Education*, Vol. 24 (1999): 355-392; Patricia Albjerg Graham, *S.O.S.: Sustain Our Schools*, New York: Hill and Wang, 1992; Ellen Condliffe Lagemann and Lee S. Shulman (eds.), *Issues in Education Research: Problems and Possibilities*, San Francisco: Jossey-Bass, 1999; Patrick J. McEwan, "The Potential Impact of Large-Scale Voucher Programs," *Review of Educational Research*, Vol. 70, No. 2 (Summer 2000): 103-149; Jeffrey Mirel, *The Rise and Fall of an Urban School System: Detroit, 1907-81*, Second Edition, Ann Arbor: University of Michigan Press, 1999; Wayne J. Urban, *More than the Facts: The Research Division of the National Education Association, 1922-1997*, Lanham, MD: University Press of America, 1998. Also see almost any publication by Barry Bull or Amy Guttman and the *New York Times* series on student testing in schools, beginning on Sunday, May 19, 2001.

4. Wilensky, 32.

About the Author: Donald Warren teaches the history of education at Indiana University, where he was the University Dean of the School of Education from 1990-2000.

Appendix B

Participants in "Education in Democracy for Social Studies Teachers: An Institute for Teacher Educators"

The individuals listed below were participants in "Education in Democracy for Social Studies Teachers: An Institute for Teacher Educators," which met in Indianapolis, Indiana from May 18-22, 2001. This meeting was co-sponsored by the Center for Civic Education in Calabasas, California and the Social Studies Development Center of Indiana University, Bloomington.

Patricia Avery
College of Education
University of Minnesota
Minneapolis, Minnesota

Marilynn Boyle-Baise
School of Education
Indiana University
Bloomington, Indiana

Margaret Stimmann Branson
Center for Civic Education
Calabasas, California

R. Freeman Butts
Professor Emeritus
Teachers College
Columbia University

Roger Desrosiers
Millbury High School
Millbury, Massachusetts

Paulette Patterson Dilworth
School of Education
Indiana University
Bloomington, Indiana

Frederick D. Drake
Department of History
Illinois State University
Normal, Illinois

Sarah E. Drake
Social Studies Development Center
School of Education
Indiana University
Bloomington, Indiana

Letitia Hochstrasser Fickel
School of Education
University of Alaska
Anchorage, Alaska

Gerardo Gonzalez
Dean, School of Education
Indiana University
Bloomington, Indiana

Anita Griffin
Peifer Elementary School
Schererville, Indiana

Robert Green
Educational Foundations
Clemson University
Clemson, South Carolina

Mary E. Haas
Department of Educational
    Theory and Practice
West Virginia University
Morgantown, West Virginia

Nancy Haas
College of Education
Arizona State University
Phoenix, Arizona

Gregory Hamot
College of Education
University of Iowa
Iowa City, Iowa

Diana Hess
School of Education
University of Wisconsin
Madison, Wisconsin

John D. Hoge
School of Education
University of Georgia
Athens, Georgia

Marlene LaCounte
School of Education
Montana State University
Billings, Montana

Glenn Lauzon
Social Studies Development Center
School of Education
Indiana University
Bloomington, Indiana

Robert S. Leming
Center for Civic Education
Calabasas, California

Terrence C. Mason
School of Education
Indiana University
Bloomington, Indiana

Denee Mattioli
College of Education
East Tennessee State University
Johnson City, Tennessee

B. Edward McClellan
School of Education
Indiana University
Bloomington, Indiana

Steven Miller
College of Education
The Ohio State University
Columbus, Ohio

Lynn R. Nelson
School of Education
Purdue University
West Lafayette, Indiana

Kathryn M. Obenchain
School of Education
University of Nevada
Reno, Nevada

Walter C. Parker
College of Education
University of Washington
Seattle, Washington

John J. Patrick
Social Studies Development
   Center
School of Education
Indiana University
Bloomington, Indiana

Murray Print
Centre for Research and Teaching
   in Civics
University of Sydney
Sydney, New South Wales,
   Australia

Beth Ratway
Wauwatosa East High School
Wauwatosa, Wisconsin

David Richmond
Centennial High School
Bakersfield, California

Stephen L. Schechter
Department of Political Science
Russell Sage College
Troy, New York

Diane Yendol Silva
College of Education
University of Florida
Gainesville, Florida

Philip VanFossen
School of Education
Purdue University
West Lafayette, Indiana

Thomas S. Vontz
Social Studies Development
   Center
School of Education
Indiana University
Bloomington, Indiana

Lynnette Wallace
Canterbury School
Fort Wayne, Indiana

Donald Warren
School of Education
Indiana University
Bloomington, Indiana

Charles S. White
School of Education
Boston University
Boston, Massachusetts

Michelle Zachlod
School of Education
California State University
Bakersfield, California